Anthony Minghella: Interviews

Conversations with Filmmakers Series

Gerald Peary, General Editor

Anthony Minghella
INTERVIEWS

Edited by Mario Falsetto

University Press of Mississippi / Jackson

www.upress.state.ms.us

The University Press of Mississippi is a member
of the Association of American University Presses.

Copyright © 2013 by University Press of Mississippi
All rights reserved
Manufactured in the United States of America

First printing 2013
∞

Library of Congress Cataloging-in-Publication Data

Minghella, Anthony.
 Anthony Minghella : interviews / edited by Mario Falsetto.
   pages cm. — (Conversations with filmmakers series)
 Includes bibliographical references and index.
 Includes filmography.
 ISBN 978-1-61703-820-4 (cloth : alk. paper) — ISBN 978-1-61703-821-1 (ebook)
 ISBN 978-1-4968-5800-9 (paperback)
 1. Minghella, Anthony—Interviews. 2. Motion picture producers and directors
—Great Britain—Interviews. I. Falsetto, Mario. II. Title.

 PN1998.3.M526A3 2013
 791.4302'33092—dc23   2012050642

British Library Cataloging-in-Publication Data available

Contents

Introduction

About a decade ago, I was preparing a book of original conversations with film directors, and I was very keen to interview Anthony Minghella. I pursued the filmmaker for about a year, but because of Minghella's complicated work schedule, and the fact that he was in the midst of shooting *Cold Mountain* (2003) in Romania when I first corresponded with him, it took some time before we finally met. Our first meeting took place following the *Cold Mountain* shoot in the summer of 2003 at his offices, a converted chapel near Hampstead Heath in London. Minghella was in the midst of editing *Cold Mountain* when we met for the first of our conversations. After this first three-hour conversation, we agreed to meet again later in the week, but as sometimes happens when you plan interviews with film directors, this was not to be. Eventually, it was decided that we would meet again later in the year in North America. We aimed for December 2003 when Minghella was due to come over to the U.S. and Canada for the launch of *Cold Mountain*. Once again, that meeting was delayed until the following summer when we met again in London for another lengthy conversation.

Most of those two conversations found their way into a volume entitled *The Making of Alternative Cinema, Volume One: Dialogues with Independent Filmmakers*, first published in 2008. I have taken this interview and reprinted it here, mostly intact, but segmented into two halves, as both a way to introduce Minghella, and to cover all of his major films up to and including *Cold Mountain*. The segments are placed strategically in the present volume, and although they slightly break the chronological ordering of the rest of the material in the book, they add a necessary, structural coherence.

Of the dozens of film directors I have interviewed over the past twenty years in what are mostly career-spanning conversations, Minghella was amongst the most generous, erudite, and illuminating artists I have had the pleasure to meet. In retrospect, this only made the news of his untimely death in 2008 more shocking. Anthony Minghella and I barely knew each other, and yet I felt that I had lost a good friend when the news broke in March of that year that Minghella had died of a hemorrhage following surgery.

In a strange way, *Cold Mountain* formed a pivot to our two conversations. Even though we did not discuss the film during our first talk, *Cold Mountain* was clearly not far from Minghella's thoughts. He had come off the grueling shoot a few months before, and he had been meeting daily for several months with his editor, the legendary Walter Murch, in the editing facilities he had set up at his offices. The post-production process would not end until the fall of 2003, not long before the December launch of the film. When we finally met for the second time in the summer of 2004, we discussed *Cold Mountain*. The disappointment of the film's reception was still apparent even though *Cold Mountain* had done good business and was well enough received by most critics. It also garnered seven Oscar nominations, mostly in secondary categories—a respectable showing but nothing like the rapture that greeted *The English Patient* a few years before when Minghella's film won five Academy Awards, including the coveted best director nod for Minghella himself. *Cold Mountain* felt like a failure even though it clearly was not.

The difficult physical challenge of making *Cold Mountain*, and its disappointing reception, marked something of a turning point for the director. When we spoke for the last time, Minghella was writing an original screenplay that would eventually become *Breaking and Entering*, his final theatrical film as a director. In his final years, Minghella would also go on to direct a television film for HBO, an opera, and handle a number of producing chores for Mirage Enterprises, a company he owned with the late American filmmaker Sydney Pollack. On top of what already seemed like a punishing work schedule, Minghella also took on the daunting challenge of Chairing the Board of Governors of the British Film Institute, a position many thought he was mad to take on. It is generally regarded as a political headache with few tangible rewards. After the punishing experience of making *Cold Mountain*, the third of three large-scale films in a row, Minghella felt a creative shake-up was needed in his way of doing things. His process of working with his creative team was turning into a set procedure, and Minghella was not entirely happy about it. As he said to me in our conversation:

> I felt that this process of how to make a film, which started with *The English Patient* and developed in *Ripley*, came to some kind of culmination in *Cold Mountain*. As I was doing it, I was thinking, "I shouldn't do this again.

I shouldn't make a film in this way again because I don't want it to become a procedure." It felt to me like it was becoming institutionalized with my group of people, the way I go about making the movie, the way I go about the adaptation, the way I go about bringing the image to the screen. It felt to me like it was hardening into a procedure as I was doing it. I wanted it to be the best one done this way, but I want it to be the last one. I don't want to repeat the shaping of process. Even though I felt every part of it was a better expression of that process than I'd managed before: the research was more detailed; the collection of the research was more structured; the design process was the most rigorous.

Despite Minghella's feeling that his procedures needed to be re-thought, the films he had made using these particular methods were thoughtful and meticulously crafted movies that clearly and powerfully articulated his creative vision. Yet, he felt the need to take a step back to see if there was not a more direct, perhaps less mediated way of do-ing things. In retrospect, it is clear that the work he produced after *Cold Mountain* is in no way superior to the three large-scale films that form the greater part of his legacy. That Minghella wanted to recapture the feelings and methods that surrounded the making of his first film, the intimate and small-scale *Truly, Madly, Deeply*, is entirely understandable and in keeping with an analytical self-criticism that characterized the artist from his earliest endeavors. Beyond this, Minghella needed to re-connect with the writer of original material that characterized his work in the 1980s as a playwright and when he made his first film. In speak-ing to Tom Charity, Minghella said: "Even before I started to make *Cold Mountain*, I wanted to make a smaller film at home. . . . I thought, if I don't write an original film now, it will never happen. Everybody else has already forgotten I was a playwright and I will too. I'll get too fright-ened."

We will never know exactly how the filmmaker felt about this return to an earlier working method, or how it would have played out in his other films, since there is so little work upon which to base a judgment. But Minghella was no longer the inexperienced, neophyte filmmaker who had directed *Truly, Madly, Deeply*. He had evolved into the maker of intense, character-driven films that perfectly melded sound and image with the power and sweep of the best cinema.

Born in 1954 of Italian immigrant parents on the Isle of Wight, Antho-ny Minghella graduated from the University of Hull (England) in the mid-1970s and spent five years as a university lecturer before leaving academia to devote himself to writing. Over the next decade, he managed to carve out an impressive career as a promising playwright (*Made in Bangkok; Cigarettes and Chocolates*) and successful television writer (*Inspector Morse; Jim Henson's The Storyteller*). He won several important awards from the London Theater Critics, including "Most Promising Playwright" in 1984, and "Best Play" in 1986 for *Made in Bangkok*. By the end of the 1980s it seemed as if Minghella had settled into a well-regarded and thriving career as a writer. But as the decade closed, the opportunity to direct a film for the British Broadcasting Corporation presented itself, and the shift to film directing became irreversible.

The period teaching and writing for theater and television was obviously a crucial time for Minghella, and he learned important lessons about writing: "If nothing else, I learnt in that period of being a teacher and playwright that my job was not about putting words into people's mouths. It was about creating action, creating *mise-en-scène*. That continues to obtain for me and my interest in writing has not been to write dialogue but to write circumstance" (Falsetto). This is an important observation since most of us think of writing movies primarily in terms of dialogue. But as Minghella says in the Tomm Carroll interview: "In fact, as a writer I always thought that dialogue is the least interesting part of the job. It's often in the lapses between language, in the distance between what people want to say and what they do say, between the emotion and the stated position [that I find most interesting]." This early experience was also important in terms of solidifying Minghella's belief in the importance of the actor: "A great deal of what I've learned in the theatre is very valuable to me as a filmmaker. Not least is a real celebration of what actors can bring to both media and how significant performances are" (Carroll).

Minghella's first film as a director, the intimate, chamber piece *Truly, Madly, Deeply*, is the moving story of Nina, beautifully played by Juliet Stevenson, whose life is shattered by her lover's unexpected death. Jamie, her partner played by Alan Rickman, returns in ghost form with several of his music-playing ghost friends to complicate Nina's life. Eventually, he helps Nina move on and heal. What makes this first directorial effort so remarkable, apart from its blunt simplicity and humanistic belief in the healing power of the individual, is its almost artless, aesthetic directness. There is very little embellishment. Minghella claims that the film, which features many long takes utilizing big close-ups of an actor's face, was done this way because he did not know any other way of doing things. He claims not to have known what "coverage" was, with almost every shot of the film the result of one or two takes. It never seems to have occurred to this most sophisticated artist that sequences could be shot with many different angles utilizing variegated shot sizes and then organized with complicated editing patterns. "There was virtually no editing in *Truly, Madly, Deeply*—there was just assembly" (Falsetto), claims the director.

This simplicity of style, however, works well with the direct emotional subject matter of the film. The film does not need an overly elaborate style to achieve its ambitions. Such over-complication might in fact have worked against it. This tells us something important about what Minghella valued as a director even at this early point in his career. Although *Truly, Madly, Deeply* gives little indication that Minghella would go on to direct three of the most ravishingly beautiful and intricately constructed films of the contemporary era, it does indicate the high value he placed on the art of acting, as well as the importance of writing to his art. This first film is the perfect illustration of the director's notion that "ultimately I'd rather watch an actor against a wall opening up to the inner life, than to look at any ravishing vista" (Carroll). The focus on language and performance to the exclusion of much stylistic bravado seems entirely appropriate to a film with a sincere humanity at its core.

Truly, Madly, Deeply benefits greatly from Juliet Stevenson's vivid performance. The unabashedly emotional naturalism of its love story melds uneasily at times with the fantastic ghost story, but the film soon settles into its rhythms. There is an awkwardness about the film at times, the result both of directorial inexperience and the meshing of disparate genres. But for the most part, *Truly, Madly, Deeply* is a remarkable film debut. What was also remarkable, in terms of the film's reception, was the sheer intensity of divergent responses to the film. Many people admired the intimate character study while others strongly resisted its appeal to the emotions. As Minghella says, "It has been the best received film I've made and the worst received" (Falsetto). If Minghella had not gone on to direct more elaborate and complex films with precisely the "ravishing vistas" that he said held little interest for him as an artist, then perhaps this first effort would seem less remarkable than it does. But set against the later films, *Truly, Madly, Deeply* raises as many questions as it answers about Minghella's film aesthetic. The three large-scale epics that form the center of his cinematic achievement, *The English Patient, The Talented Mr. Ripley,* and *Cold Mountain*—all adapted from significant works of contemporary fiction—would seem to argue against the notion of simplicity and character-centered filmmaking that Minghella claimed were of interest to him. How then do we reconcile these seemingly opposite approaches to filmmaking? To some extent it is a question of inexperience. As Minghella gained more experience as a film artist, his work became more complex. But even as the films gain in complexity there is never any sense that he has abandoned the human element. Despite their visual sweep, attention to detail, and complex organizational patterns, the films always remain character-centered. Perhaps they are not so opposite in approach as they may first appear.

The success of *Truly, Madly, Deeply* inevitably opened doors for Minghella in Hollywood that resulted in the disappointing *Mr. Wonderful*, starring Matt Dillon, Annabella Sciorra, and William Hurt. Working with another writer's screenplay, the film is set in the Italian-American working-class milieu of New York City. What attracted Minghella to the film, apart from its evocation of the ethnic milieu, was the story of the central character's aspirations to broaden her experiences beyond the restrictive confines of her immediate world. Unfortunately, what interested Minghella in the story held little interest for the studio financing the film, although Minghella learned some key lessons about himself as a filmmaker. As he says in the Tomm Carroll interview: "I'm not . . . good at making studio films, and . . . there's something to be said for nursing my own passions, wrong-headed or otherwise, and reconciling myself to my own voice."

Mr. Wonderful was a painful experience for the director. The film was released to poor box-office and lukewarm reviews. But Minghella turned the experience into a pivotal event in his creative life, and it proved vitally important in his decision to pursue a career as writer-director of his own films on his terms. As he says in our interview, "That film made me a filmmaker, irrespective of its content and its result." Ultimately, the experience of making *Mr. Wonderful* proved to be Minghella's education into everything that was wrong with the film industry, at least as it operated in Hollywood. "I went into it with such absurd innocence about Hollywood and what it meant to be a film director. I never thought of myself as a director at all, then suddenly I was seen as a director and went through the motions of directing a film" (Falsetto).

Even if Minghella was to go on to make three large-scale "international" epics over the next decade, he was to remain firmly rooted to his British-Italian identity and to the British soil. He would also retain a fierce independence free from interference, although it would not necessarily be smooth sailing. He had his difficulties with production companies, especially Miramax. It would take another three years before he finally achieved a vision that truly represented the scope of his cinematic ambitions. Adapting Michael Ondaatje's poetic novel *The English Patient* and getting it to the screen proved a major challenge for someone with little directing experience. The film represented a huge creative leap for the director on a logistical level, partly because of its scale and also because Ondaatje's novel operates more as poetic meditation than as linear narrative. The film was a huge undertaking, but it benefited enormously from its remarkable cast of actors including Ralph Fiennes, Juliette Binoche, Colin Firth, Naveen Andrews, and Kristin Scott Thomas. *The English Patient*'s epic sweep still manages to deliver an intimate, moving love story. The film was released to great critical and box-office acclaim winning many awards including the Oscar for Best Picture and a Best Director award for Minghella.

For his next film, Minghella once again found himself adapting a well-regarded novel, this time from Patricia Highsmith's "Ripley" series. With *The Talented Mr. Ripley*, Minghella illustrated that he could temper the high romanticism and epic sweep of *The English Patient* with a more distanced, removed aesthetic. The film features Matt Damon as the title character Tom Ripley, Jude Law as the object of Tom's sadistic affection Dickie Greenleaf, and Gwyneth Paltrow as Dickie's lover Marge Sherwood. *The Talented Mr. Ripley* performed well at the box office and received mainly strong reviews. Although Minghella's take on the Ripley character is in many respects quite different than Highsmith's, his Ripley is a fascinating cinematic creation made all the more intriguing by Damon's riveting performance. The amoral, almost asexual character of the novel has been replaced by Damon's more psychological, sympathetic Ripley who seems to have some semblance of a conscience about his horrific act of extinguishing the lives of both Dickie Greenleaf and a male lover later in the film. As he mentions in one of the two interviews with David Gritten, "I suppose I wanted to emphasize what's familiar and human about Tom Ripley. . . . That way you can gauge the extent to which extreme action is linked to lying and other small sins of omission. For me that's more interesting than to judge him as a sociopath and watch him behaving badly."

Making *Ripley* became something of a personal exploration for Minghella of his working-class, immigrant roots. In many aspects of its style, the film also reverberates with Minghella's love of the great Italian cinema of the 1950s and 1960s. In telling Ripley's story, set in the 1950s Italy of Minghella's imagination, and drawn from the look and feel of the great Italian cinema of that era, the director was also telling his own story. He was telling the story of the outsider who longs to partake at the table of the rich, privileged universe of people like Dickie Greenleaf. In his interview with me, Minghella tells a charming story of how he picked up a couple of rich kids, not unlike Marge and Dickie, when he worked for his father on the Isle of Wight selling ice cream from a truck. The couple tell Minghella that they did not actually have any destination in mind when they decided to hitchhike, they just wanted to know what it felt like to mix with the locals. For Minghella, this incident, and growing up working class on the Isle of Wight, illustrates just how personal his adaptation of Highsmith's novel is. As he says in our interview:

> If you took off all of the blubber and skin of *Ripley*, and just peeled off all of its flesh, what you would end up with is the Isle of Wight. You wouldn't end up with Italy, you wouldn't end up with Americans, it really is as personal as that to me. All the rest of it is just "stuff." I remember when Ripley and Dickie go off on the boat on which Dickie eventually gets killed, and thinking, "That's San Remo 1959, I was there on that beach. I could be on that beach right now." My parents took me there when I was five. I looked around this beach hoping to find myself. For some reason, those were the things that I was thinking about: my own feelings about being in Italy, my own relationship to Fellini and Italian cinema. What I was delivering in that film was something almost solipsistic. That's the fact of it, and the rest of it is just blubber. It's just stuff.

After *Ripley*, and just before he filmed the Civil War love story *Cold Mountain*, Minghella directed a short film as part of the ambitious "Beckett on Film" project, produced by Alan Moloney and Michael Colgan with money mostly from Ireland's National Service broadcaster, RTE (Raidió Teilifís Éireann), and Britain's Channel 4. The aim of this project was to film all nineteen stage plays written by Samuel Becket, and it included a number of international directors, such as Neil Jordan, Atom Egoyan, and David Mamet. It is the only time Minghella has translated a play to the cinematic medium. *Play* is a strange, modernist exercise but was an interesting choice for Minghella to take on. It is one of Beckett's more abstract pieces, and since Beckett held a life-long fascination for the director, it is no surprise that Minghella was involved in the project. What may have been more surprising was his approach, which reveals a modernist streak not always apparent in the director's other films. As he says to Ted Sheehy, "I studied Beckett, I tried to do a doctorate on Beckett's work, *Play* was the first play I ever directed—it was a very particular reason to go into the world of short films and I'm not sure that anyone else would have got me into that arena." Minghella has taken a play and reimagined it for cinema, something that not only required delicate negotiations with the Beckett estate, but which perhaps aligns him with Samuel Beckett in a unique way: "When he [Beckett] goes into theatre he's like someone who's never been in a theatre before, he reimagines what the theatre could be about, how it might work. I feel that it forces you to, as Neil [Jordan] was saying when you go into the arena of cinema, to reconsider the fact that you've got a camera, you've got an actor, and you're making sound. Everything somehow is refreshed through his eyes" (Sheehy).

Play contains astonishing performances by Juliet Stevenson, Alan Rickman, and Kristin Scott Thomas. The speed and screeching of line delivery, the grating repetitions, the sight of dozens of giant urns on a strange, "de Chirico–like" landscape, and the overall abstract nature of the piece offered a unique set of challenges to Minghella and his actors. Most challenging of all perhaps is that this bizarre, abstract material must somehow still be about real human beings. It cannot remain a formalist exercise. In the resulting film, Minghella's actors pierce through the thicket of Beckett's unfamiliar language, and the stylized, theatrical presentation and make us see that these characters actually represent us. As strange as it may seem, we are those characters. Or at least we could be those people. No matter how formally audacious and abstract Minghella's Beckett film seems, it is not alienated from human feeling. As Minghella says in the Stayton interview, "Dramatic fiction has always intrigued me because it gives us all manner of different perspectives. But if the perspective is one that so alienates us that we can't join with it, then it's not very interesting to me. I want to *feel* in film."

Although the actors are central to the success of *Play*, the film also relies on the formal structures and abstractions of set, camera work, and dynamic editing for its effectiveness. The result is that *Play* is one of the strongest adaptations of Beckett in the entire project, and one of the most surprising. Surprising in its bold originality, and also because it puts to rest the notion that Minghella was only capable of creating cinema of high emotional impact, containing strong, empathetic, and conventionally realistic characters. Although it is convenient for many critics to categorize Minghella in such simplistic, largely inaccurate terms, the Beckett film, and a similarly abstract radio monologue on Verdi performed by Nicole Kidman around the time that I interviewed the director, are proof that such descriptions do not accurately describe the director's sensibilities. *Play* is as icy and distanced as *Last Year at Marienbad*. It is also as horrifying a vision of hell as we are likely to get in a medium that has so often been crammed with more conventionally horrifying images of destruction, violence, and apocalypse. Beckett's play, and Minghella's film version of it, ramps up its horrifying power with a single, final stage direction that the author brilliantly added at the end of the piece when his characters are instructed to "Repeat." Although only sixteen minutes long, *Play* is a singular achievement and one of Minghella's most fully realized films.

Minghella's next film was *Cold Mountain*, his film version of Charles Frazier's best-selling variation on Homer's *Odyssey* set during the American Civil War. Although on the surface an epic film, once again at its center is a love story. Ada (Nicole Kidman) and Inman (Jude Law) are lovers who spend most of the film separated from each other. *Cold Mountain*'s huge ambitions can at times feel weighed down with a degree of heaviness, but elements such as Renée Zellweger's vivid performance as the high-spirited, emotionally damaged Ruby go a long way in countering some of this weightiness. The exploration of its ultimately tragic themes is also counterbalanced by an exuberant, vivid cinematic style, as well as the outstanding level of performance that characterizes all of Minghella's films.

By the time Minghella directed *Cold Mountain*, he had accepted the fact that he was the maker of large-scale films, if not by choice then at least by circumstance. It turned out that he was more comfortable in this environment than he thought he would be. The small, intimate scale of *Truly, Madly, Deeply* was well and truly gone. The large scale of *The English Patient* and *Ripley* were no flukes. *Cold Mountain* only confirmed that Minghella's huge imagination often needed a large canvas to operate. In the interview with Andrew Pulver, Minghella says that he "came into film as a writer, dependent on language and actors—and gradually I found that the thing I like to do best is to open up the canvas. I feel more at home with this scale of filmmaking than I ever expected."

Cold Mountain is a meticulously researched and wonderfully crafted film, but it did not find favor with all audiences and critics. Although many reviewers appreciated the film, as did much of its large audience, others did not respond positively. "They were not in love with it" is Minghella's assessment. The somewhat reserved response was felt in the film's lack of major awards at the 2004 Academy Awards ceremony. Despite the film's seven nominations, it felt like a personal snub to someone who, just a few years before, had been basking in the glory of the Academy.

As in his previous two films, making *Cold Mountain* was a grueling experience for the director. As he said when I spoke to him in 2004, "There's nearly twice as much labor in *Cold Mountain* as anything I've done. *Cold Mountain* is five years of my life. . . . There is a banal element to making films in that it requires an enormous amount of energy to physically realize a film. I shot for five-and-a-half months in Romania and I probably had five-and-a-half minutes to myself. At the end of it, I could barely stand up in terms of what was required of me on a physical level. So I think there is the endurance element in directing a film."

Additionally, the film is a good illustration of the often unbridgeable gap between viewing a film and the complexities of its creation. We look at films, and we are either intrigued by them, and appreciate their many qualities, or we do not. We then move on to the next film. Some we treasure—and they may potentially have a huge impact on us—others we never think of again. This is the nature of film viewing. The modern landscape is filled with an endless stream of cultural objects that we devour with an insatiable appetite. But for those making the film, it is an entirely different proposition. Minghella makes this point in our conversation when he says:

> I realize that when you say *Cold Mountain*, you mean two hours and thirty-two minutes, and when I say *Cold Mountain* I mean five years, and those were a great five years of my life, a fantastic period of struggle and determination and experience and discovery, fantastic. You could give me nothing to replace that experience. Where I went and what I did and what I saw and what I asked of myself was an amazing thing. I wouldn't give you any of it back for anything. So I'm quite clear about that in my mind, that process has to be honorable, process has to be good, process has to be rigorous. The way that I work with people has to be rewarding to me.

In the period following the release of *Cold Mountain*, Minghella completed one additional theatrical film, *Breaking and Entering* (2006). Although he had wanted to make a smaller film for some time, it was not enthusiastically received. Minghella also produced a number of films by such directors as Richard Eyre, Tom Tykwer, and Todd Field. He wrote and directed the feature-length HBO pilot film to the series *The No. 1 Ladies' Detective Agency*. Additionally, Minghella's love of spectacle and the sensuous found a new outlet in opera, when he directed a highly regarded production of Puccini's *Madama Butterfly* for the English National Opera in London and the Metropolitan Opera Company in New York. On top of this seemingly full work agenda, Minghella also took on the position at the British Film Institute. The cultural importance of the BFI was something Minghella believed in strongly. In the few short years that he was at its helm, he made a significant impact on its operations, especially in broadening its reach beyond London to the rest of the UK.

As one reads the interviews in this book, the reader will see that Minghella's skillful use of language extends beyond his abilities as a playwright and screenwriter. He is a hugely articulate interview subject. But what exactly did Minghella care about as a film artist? What were the issues he wanted to examine and how precisely did he go about doing it? Was he a classical, romantic filmmaker as several critics claim or are there more modernist aspects to his oeuvre that question such simplistic categorizations? One of the main ambitions of the present anthology is to offer answers to these (and many other) questions. The main purpose of this collection is to present Anthony Minghella's voice as a film artist, to present his thoughts on the films he made and the film medium in general. The interviews are wide-ranging and cover many of Minghella's ideas about the filmmaking process. They tend to focus on key issues including his writing process, his thoughts on acting, the importance of music, and his overall theories of cinema.

In any discussion of Anthony Minghella, a key issue that must be examined is his relationship to writing. The importance of writing to Minghella's identity is clearly at the center of who he was as an artist, and is explored in a number of the interviews here. Minghella was always fond of saying that he was a writer first and a director second. He repeated this mantra in several interviews over the years, as he does in the Argent interview in this collection: "When anybody asks me what I do, I always say that I'm a writer. I think of myself as a writer. Because if tomorrow you said, I have to give everything up except one thing, I would have to keep writing. Because filmmaking is a luxury and a privilege, and writing is a necessity." Thus, writing was something Minghella felt he could do anywhere without the scaffolding of enormous resources necessary to direct movies. There is no question that writing played a central role in Minghella's life, but since writing and directing were so inextricably linked in his creative process, I suspect that the relationship eventually was weighted fairly equally.

When asked by Tomm Carroll whether there is an advantage to directing his own material, Minghella's responds that the "advantage I have when I walk on a set with my own writing is that I know every beat and impulse and nuance of it because it's come directly through me, and so there's nothing I don't know about the screenplay. It means I'm free to let go of it completely." Most of Minghella's films have been literary adaptations from generally highly regarded novels, although the poetic nature of Michael Ondaadge's *The English Patient* did not lend itself particularly well to the cinematic medium. "*The English Patient* is a poem disguised as a novel. It's not really a novel in the conventional sense, it's very much a product of a deconstructive, postmodern commentary on the novel rather than being a novel" (Falsetto). The unconventional nature of Minghella's writing process makes his adaptation process fairly unique. For Minghella, the one book he did not take with him when he holed up at a friend's farm in Hampshire to write his screenplays was the book he was adapting for the screen. What he did take was many other books that would allow him to research his subject in a way that the original author might also have done. It was the kind of deep research Minghella relished, given his academic background and unending curiosity. Of course, he was quite familiar with the novel he was adapting before he began the actual screenplay writing process. As he says in one of the interviews with David Gritten, "Part of adaptation is that you're trying to write your way back to the book, to those things that arrested you in the first place. You have to find your way through the thicket of writing to what's essential about the story. It's just like when you retell a joke—you emphasize those elements that move or excite or amuse you." The conventional notion of appropriating a book and trying to be as faithful to the original material as possible is not an idea that seems to fit our understanding of what Minghella did when he adapted a novel for the screen. In speaking of *The English Patient*, he says in the Stayton interview: "My job was not to appropriate the book and put the dialogue in quotes. It was to reimagine the book as a film."

The issue of dialogue is always crucial in any discussion of screenwriting, and for Minghella, as with a number of other directors, dialogue did not necessarily take prominence in the adaptation process. Some people probably imagine that a screenwriter's most important task is to get the dialogue right, to put the right words in the characters' mouths, and construct each scene as if all it contained was characters speaking to each other, engaged in a certain amount of action that propels the narrative forward. In simple terms, screenwriting equals dialogue and action. In other words, there is a story to tell, and the job of the screenwriter is to make the situations and the characters believable, to move the story along with hopefully enough truthfulness or insight into human behavior to make the viewer feel that they are fully engaged in the story, and can empathize with the characters. We should feel that we have taken some kind of emotional journey with them. There is nothing wrong with this description, and certainly characters and situations need to be compelling and interesting enough to hold the viewer's attention. But for Minghella, screenwriting was a very particular act that did not correspond to writing for the theater or fiction writing. It was a very unique form with its own set of rules. Minghella believed that imagining his movie at the writing stage went far beyond writing dialogue. He needed to imagine the situations as fully as possible. As he says in the Stayton interview, "good writers are making or writing films. They're not writing dialogue. They're writing situations; they're writing scenes that may have only visual information in them. . . . Most writers are not infatuated with dialogue. They're infatuated with how to construct a moment in a film." Minghella's ideas about screenwriting may sound surprising coming from someone whose life revolved around words, but I think he is genuine when he says that we are "overinfatuated with language, with dialogue, as if meaning is carried in dialogue, whereas meaning is nearly always carried in context."

When Minghella speaks in these terms, he is also getting at the nuances and subtleties of what we generally call subtext, as well as the complexities of how both language and the film medium itself can communicate. As any good filmmaker or sharp film viewer knows, film can just as easily communicate through a close-up or a reaction shot or the twitch of an actor's facial muscle as it can through dialogue. Films are always speaking through many elements of a scene or shot construction, from the *mise-en-scène* to complex editing patterns, from shot size or duration to dialogue or performance or music. The job of the screenwriter is to create the context with enough details to bring to life the situation at hand. Then, on the set, other aspects that were perhaps not even planned are inserted into the mix, and later in the postproduction phase editing, music, overdubbing, and all the other tools of the medium add more layers of textural meaning and form. The final form of any scene or completed film will always contain elements that may have only been hinted at in the screenplay or original novel because film always takes on its own life at every stage of its production. The screenplay is a crucial element in this creative process, of course, and a very specific one, but as Robert Altman was fond of saying, "A screenplay is just a blue print."

I think Minghella is of the same opinion, and although his screenplays contain many details, even there he has said that the situation changed over the years: "As a screenwriter, increasingly as I know I'm directing my own films, I put less and less information in the screenplay because I don't feel it's required. I feel like I'm designing a building when I write a screenplay. I'm just imagining a movie instead of a building. The obligation of the architect is to work in a space, and work within the constraints of planning. When I write, I imagine a movie in the same way that an architect imagines a functioning building" (Falsetto).

It must also be said that Minghella saw himself as a writer in the "auteurist" sense when he states that "the writer in film is the director. The writer has to be the director because the vision is articulated over the course of the film. The ink becomes the camera becomes the editing room. If you want to write film, you have to direct film" (Falsetto). Despite the hugely collaborative nature of the filmmaking enterprise, it is clear that Minghella believed in, and saw himself, as an auteur filmmaker in a long tradition of writer–film directors.

If there is one constant in every Minghella film, it is unquestionably the high level of performance to be found in his work. Perhaps above all other elements, Minghella valued the contributions of his actors to bring his material to life. He was clearly an actor's director. And he valued it in other films as much as his own: "When I think about the moments in movies that I have loved, it's always about an actor revealing himself or herself. I'm absolutely secure about that. I know that, finally, that is the thing that's always astonished me"(Bricknell). To some extent, Minghella's love of acting is a result of his early experience in the theater. As he says in the Carroll interview, "A great deal of what I've learned in the theatre is very valuable to me as a filmmaker. Not least is a real celebration of what actors can bring to both media and how significant performances are."

When Minghella came to direct his first film, it was no surprise that Juliet Stevenson's astonishing performance as Nina holds center stage. And can one imagine a more sympathetic rendering of a serial killer than Matt Damon's Ripley, as he gorges on Dickie Greenleaf's world of privilege? Of course, many cinematic elements do their part in creating Tom Ripley's universe, but without his troupe of actors, with all their primal, youthful energies on display, *Ripley* would remain a pretty backdrop of lush images and sounds. The same holds for all the key actors in *Cold Mountain* and *The English Patient*. No matter how intricate the narrative structures, or the visual sweep on display, it is the strength of the storytelling and the contributions of his actors that hold our attention. As a man of the theater, and mostly a certain kind of realist-based theater, it is to be expected that Minghella's films would valorize the art of acting and the complexities of text.

Minghella claimed not to have any theories of acting when he dealt with his actors although he discusses the importance of relaxation and giving his actors the space they need to create their best work. I have no doubt that Minghella's modesty underestimates his contributions to this process. In his interview with me, he expands on the idea of relaxation as an actor's tool:

> I think most things to do with film have to do with relaxation. One of the only jobs a director has is to still the noise of the clock so that there is no clock, and no reason to feel threatened, no reason to do anything other than to relax into this work. That's easily said when there is only you and me here talking, but it is an incredibly hard thing to pull off on a set. "There's nobody else, it's just us. We can do what we want, it's all fine." There's this quiet work that has to happen and the set must be very still and quiet. That's what I've managed to do in the last few films, to make actors feel that they can't be wrong and that they're fine.

The idea of creating a space for actors is a real thing for Minghella. As he says in the Bricknell conversations, "The only theory that I have about acting is that there's a space to work in, and the more of that space I occupy, the less space there is for the actor. And so one of the things I try to do is reduce the amount of space that I take up when I'm working with them, so that they feel that they can move into it." Of course, the relationship between a director and an actor extends far beyond the film set. It continues into postproduction when the actor may be asked to contribute another line or turn of phrase for the umpteenth time, something Minghella has accused himself of doing, knowing that there are an infinite number of ways to turn a phrase or say a line. Why should the acting stop just because the shoot is over? The creative act does not end until picture and sound are locked, and the film is released into the world. Minghella better than anyone knows how crucial editing and overdubbing are to a film. He makes this point in the Bricknell interviews when he states:

> The actor gives you a performance, and the filmmaker's job is to respect its intention. Beyond that are all the realities of the editing room, where

the performance has to be worked into the fabric of the film and where the performance can also be refined. It's rare that a director is trying to damage an actor's work in the cutting room. However, it's understandable if an actor feels aggrieved if what he or she perceived as a vital moment has been attenuated or cut or repositioned. There is a constant tension between the truth of the work and the fiction of it. You're making everything up and you're manipulating it.

Music has also been an integral part of every film that Minghella has directed. It is woven into the fabric of each film in sometimes surprising but always meaningful ways. Music is as much at the emotional center of a scene as the performances and dialogue. Music was Minghella's first love even before he discovered the theater and cinema. Growing up on the Isle of Wight it was popular music of the era that was his touchstone, especially after the island's famous music festival began in the 1960s. From his love of music evolved a love of language. And when he began to write plays and screenplays, he even wrote to music, as explained in the Nick Taylor interview: "It was Leonard Cohen's lyrics that first awoke a passion for words in a teenage Minghella. Ever since, he admits, music has remained a major influence on all his work. 'Every other serious writer I know works in silence. But I can't. When I write, I lock myself in a room and put on very, very loud music. If the music's right, I can work for eighteen hours straight. I only stop to change the CD.'"

Apart from a medium-length, fiction film ostensibly about his grandmother that he made in the late 1970s, *Truly, Madly, Deeply* is Minghella's first genuine film as a director. It has been described as a "chamber piece" by many critics, not merely because of its intimacy, and the fact that two central characters are at its center, but in the ways it incorporates musical structures that are absolutely essential to its construction. The music is not merely a backdrop or an accompaniment or music the two protagonists play in several scenes together. The weaving of Bach into the film's organization and emotional core goes far deeper. The film's screenplay did not evolve until Minghella settled on the specific music the characters were engaged in playing: "All I had was the idea of two people meeting once a week to play classical music. Then I found what they were playing—a collection of Bach's sonatas—and the story came from there. Everything grew out of the music" (Taylor).

If we examine each Minghella film carefully, we can see that source music and the orchestral score are as central as any other elements of the film's construction. This is reflected in Minghella's unique collaborative relationship with Gabriel Yared, his favored composer. Yared is to the music as Walter Murch was to Minghella's editing process. The relationship with Yared was never a conventional director-composer one. Yared was involved with each film early in the production process, sometimes even at the script stage. By contrast, many film composers are handed the film when the picture has been locked and are then asked to compose a score, sometimes under huge time constraints. As Minghella says, "Directors will get almost to the end of the process of making the movie and then a composer is asked to come in, under enormous time pressure, and decorate the film. Often directors are bewildered by the sounds that subsequently appear over their scenes. It's like adding a new character into the story at the last minute" (Taylor).

Minghella and Yared began sketching out ideas for the score early in the production process—sometimes at the same time Minghella was writing the first drafts of the script. "On *Cold Mountain*, Gabriel wrote some of the principal themes in my writing room—he was working on one side of the room writing the music and I was on the other writing the script. It's a very codependent relationship. It feels like we're making the movie together. In the same way that I'll write ten or twenty drafts of the script, I expect Gabriel to keep changing and redrafting the score" (Taylor).

Minghella says that "music is at the center of every film that I've made in some shape or form. I also think editing is musically oriented, rhythmically oriented. One of the things that interests me is the idea of visual rhythm. I realize what the power of those visual rhymes is. I've always felt that music and architecture are the twin reservoirs to me of how film is made" (Taylor). Minghella's thoughts on the importance of music in his work, and in his life, revealed a man who loved music, made music, and believed that music touched the inner core in ways that nothing else could.

Minghella claimed not to have any overarching theories of cinema other than to make films like the ones that inspired him or that he loved to watch. "Obviously, all you can do as a filmmaker is make the kind of movies which you've been excited by as an audience member. What you want is to be part of that process of making pieces that work, which repay analysis and revisiting, and which have their own poetry" (Bricknell). He is even simpler and more direct to Daniel Argent when he says, "In the end you make the films that you want to see yourself." In the Bricknell conversations, he reduces things to their essence when he says, "Crudely, film is about editing and marketing. It's about what we do with what we shot and what the company does with what we deliver. Those are the only two unequivocal things: how the film is assembled and then how the film is presented to an audience."

In terms of process, Minghella did a tremendous amount of pre-planning and thinking before he began his film shoots, but he was not locked in to his ideas when he arrived on set. In fact, it seems just the opposite. In one of the two pieces by David Gritten, he describes a procedure that he inherited from an artist friend: "A choreographer once told me that he began each day in the studio by writing down everything in his head and tossing the results into the bin, a kind of mental spring-cleaning. I try to observe the same exercise when arriving on set, abandoning the meticulous planning that preproduction has until that moment demanded, and telling myself that any obstacle is useful, every curse contains a blessing."

Once on set, of course, his attention turned to the actors, though not exclusively. Every director I have spoken to will say that one of the hardest parts of being a director is the constant barrage of questions you are asked every day and the notion that you must somehow always have answers to every question you are asked. This can obviously be overwhelming, especially since directors often attend to the needs of hundreds of technicians and artists on a film set. Amidst all this activity, the space and atmosphere for the actors to do their best work must somehow be made.

Obviously, Minghella had a certain aesthetic sensibility and ideas about the world that can be found everywhere in his work. In simple terms, he would say that it was in the image-sound relationship where the essence of cinema was to be found: "The greatest weapon film has is the relationship between an image and sound. That is the thing that most preoccupies me when I'm making a film." But such generalizations do not tell us what exactly interested Minghella as a film artist, or the kinds of films he made or might have gone on to make if he had lived longer. Clearly, Minghella was liberal and humanist in his politics and world view. He believed passionately in the notion that a better world can only happen if more points of view are expressed. Like many other artists, Minghella never tired of asking himself why he did what he did. Why did the world need more films or artworks? "The thing that I cling to is that the nature of dramatic fiction—and it's the most simple thing to say about it, but finally it's the most fundamental and powerful thing to say . . . it shifts perspective. It allows a multiplicity of perspectives. If you get to the truth of that then the world is a better place" (Falsetto).

Minghella's strong sense of morality is also ever present in his work, whether he was writing and directing films, writing plays or television, producing other films, or even in his position as head of the BFI. In the Jason Davis interview, he makes the argument that we are all flawed, and the function of fiction is mainly to show us flawed individuals and their attempts at being decent. He sees the world "as comprised of people who make mistakes and, largely, are all aspiring to be decent and failing to be. If a fiction could achieve one thing, which is to make us an ounce more compassionate, that would be a good result." Minghella's work has a strong moral center, but he never judges his characters. He was a moral filmmaker, a moralist certainly, but he was not a moralizer. He had strong opinions about the world but he never forced you to adopt those opinions. He never told the viewer what to think or feel. As he says in the Carroll interview, "I've tried not to judge the behavior in the work that I do. If a writer or director judges behavior, it gives nothing for the audience to do. It closes the moral circle of the film, and presents and demonstrates feeling and emotions, rather than asking you to participate in the struggle that people have."

Minghella had strong ideas about the function of storytelling and fiction in general. He says to Carroll, "Stories exist in order to do two things: to enlarge experience and also to force us into perspectives that we're not otherwise afforded." Beyond these multiple perspectives, the director believed that cinema offered a kind of universality if handled properly. As he states in the Bricknell interviews: "It is clear to me that if there is a very focused intention in a shot, if there's purpose in a shot, it is absolutely catholic. Everybody will understand it. When you achieve that transparency of purpose, it's the most marvelous thing. It absolutely transcends boundaries of language or creed or ideology. People just know what it's about. They know to be moved. They know to laugh."

This kind of democratic purpose was important to Minghella's humanist values. It helped shape his aesthetic sensibilities and his taste as a filmmaker. He was clearly attracted to films that had an emotional center and could be viewed by different kinds of audiences from different backgrounds and cultural formation. For Minghella, cinema also contained an important vicarious thrill. Film allows people to experience things they would otherwise never experience. As such, it is an art form that appealed to his ideas about enlarging experience through dramatic fiction:

> There's something about the camera as a window into other people's souls and other people's experiences. As an audience we want to watch oth-

er people engage in activities that we do ourselves and in activities we are afraid or unable to do ourselves. Why do societies all over the world make up stories of people doing things we do ourselves in one form or another? Why is it that we need to reenact those things? At some level, it's a requirement for us to be able to experience without danger. We need to be able to stare at violence and stare at fear—without a safety belt on." (Bricknell)

In several interviews, my own included, Minghella often speaks about the physical stamina needed to make films, how physically and emotionally exhausting they are to make: "In the end, directing movies is entirely about stamina. It's got nothing to do with anything else. It's about making sure that you can stand up at the end of every day. One of the main things going through my mind on set is, how can I sneak off and lie down for five minutes? That, to me, is the only activity going on. Directing is survival and stamina, because, I believe, once you're on set, your creative work should mostly be done" (Bricknell).

Beyond the physical energy needed to make films, Minghella had the tenacity and stubbornness necessary to succeed in the business of making movies. Many otherwise talented individuals lack this fierceness, and sadly, never achieve what their talent would otherwise allow them to achieve. Despite a gentle demeanor, Minghella knew that the business of making movies was as tough or tougher than any other business, and it needed a steeliness that many observers were unaware he possessed. He says to Gritten: "I've had visions of films that have seemed overambitious or difficult to achieve. . . . I've often been advised they would never be realized. So many people in my career have put an arm around me and said: 'Please give up on this, it can't be done.'. . . All this has trained me to believe films are willed into being, often in unlikely circumstances. . . . So I'm used to fighting hard for what I believe in."

Like some other directors, Minghella also claimed not to see his films after he had made them. They were part of his creative life in ways that made it impossible for him to be a mere viewer of his work. He lived his films over the several years he spent with each of them. At every stage of production, he was engaged in an all-consuming process of discovery. His great curiosity about the world allowed him to use each film as a personal journey into the fascinating landscape of human behavior. But once they were made, his journey was over: "I have never seen my movies again since delivering them. I have no interest. I have no interest whatsoever. I think that in purgatory we'll be required to watch our films repeatedly. I'm happy to wait until then" (Bricknell).

It is important to remember that Anthony Minghella, despite all the awards and accolades he received over the years, especially for *The English Patient*, has never been a critic's darling. There has always been a begrudging quality to much of the praise that his films have received, not to mention a downright hostility by some critics. For example, in Nick James's generally positive article about *The Talented Mr. Ripley*, James cannot help but criticize Minghella when he speaks about *The English Patient*: "Yet though well written and superbly put together, the film rarely lets you forget its glossy package of international stars and exotic locations. You're always aware you're watching a prestige work designed to dazzle." Even while praising the film, James seems to be critical of it. For some critics, "a prestige film designed to dazzle" would be a high compliment. But when James applies the judgment to Minghella's film, it feels somehow like a deficiency that the film manages to overcome through its superb craftsmanship and the excellent work of its actors.

There is a view that when an artist dies, one tragedy is that now the world will be deprived of new creative work from that individual. A famous instance of this is a snatch of dialogue between William Wyler and Billy Wilder supposedly overheard at Ernst Lubitsch's funeral: "Isn't it awful. No more Ernst Lubitsch." "Worse than that. No more Lubitsch pictures." It is true that now there will be no more Anthony Minghella films. We will not have another new work from a man who, at the time of his death, was at his creative peak and able to access great resources to make films. This is indeed tragic.

As revealing as the interviews in this collection are about Minghella's creative process, he has never received the kind of critical analysis and attention that many other directors have. The books that explore and carefully examine his films in precise detail have yet to be written. It is my hope that the present anthology encourages more film scholarship about one the most significant filmmakers of the contemporary era.

Anthony Minghella was an artist of uncommon taste and sophistication who created an impressive body of work in a number of areas of creative endeavor. There is little doubt that his legacy—both human and artistic—will live on. This anthology is my contribution in helping to keep that legacy alive.

• • •

This project owes a great debt to the considerable efforts of two remarkable research assistants. Matthew Reed conducted crucial research at the British Film Institute in London at an early stage of the project. Adam

Bagatavicius was involved at virtually every stage of this project, and his exceptional efforts proved invaluable time and again. I offer both of these individuals my heartfelt thanks. At Concordia University (Montreal), I want to acknowledge the financial support of the Aid to Research Related Events, Publication, Exhibition and Dissemination Activities (ARRE) Program and the Dean of Fine Arts, Catherine Wild. This project would not exist in the form that it does without this support. Of course, Anthony Minghella generously granted me the original interviews in 2003 and 2004 that provided the material for my conversations with him, and which I have included in this anthology. Finally, I thank Carole Zucker for her unwavering support and encouragement.

MF

Chronology

1954   Born January 6 in Ryde, the Isle of Wight. Parents are Gloria (née Arcari) and Edward Minghella, who run an ice cream company. Early years attends Sandown Grammar School on the Isle of Wight and St. John's College in Portsmouth. He also plays music in several bands around the Isle of Wight as a teenager until he leaves for university.

1972–80   Attends University in Hull (Yorkshire) and subsequently begins a five-year stint teaching at the university. He attempts to write a doctoral thesis on Samuel Beckett but abandons it, although Beckett remains a life-long interest. During this time he is encouraged to write by Alan Plater. He also continues to write songs and music. Marries his first wife Yvonne Millar in a short-lived marriage. A daughter, Hannah, is born of this union. Attempts to make a medium-length, fiction film inspired by his grandmother, which will eventually be turned into the play, *A Little Like Drowning* (1984). He also writes his first play, *Child's Play*, in 1978. While at the University of Hull, Minghella meets Carolyn Choa who later will become his second wife.

1981   Following the break-up of his first marriage, he abandons his career as a university lecturer. He moves to London to devote himself full-time to writing, and to be closer to his daughter. He writes the play *Whale Music*. He co-writes several scripts with Jim Hawkins for the British television series *Maybury*. In the early 1980s while in London he reconnects with Carolyn Choa and they eventually marry. Their son, Max, is born in 1985. He is a script editor for the British television series *Grange Hill*. He also writes the pilot and several episodes of *Inspector Morse*. He writes all the episodes of Jim Henson's *The Storyteller* and Henson's *Living with Dinosaurs*.

1984 Wins the Critics Circle Theatre Award "Most Promising Play-wright" for *A Little Like Drowning.*

1986 Wins Critics Circle Theatre Award "Best New Play" for *Made in Bangkok.*

1988 Wins the Giles Cooper Award for his radio play *Cigarettes and Chocolate.*

1990 Directs *Truly, Madly, Deeply* for the BBC. It is released in theatres and is critically well received in the UK. It is a modest box-office hit, plays many film festivals, and is released in a number of countries including the US. It garners Minghella a good deal of international attention, and Hollywood begins to take notice.

1992 Wins the "Writer's Guild of Great Britain Award: Film Screenplay" for *Truly, Madly, Deeply.* That same year he also wins the Evening Standard British Film Award "Most Promising Newcomer" for *Truly, Madly, Deeply.* Wins a BAFTA award Best Original Screenplay for *Truly, Madly, Deeply.*

1993 *Mr. Wonderful* is released to lukewarm critical response and poor box-office.

1996 *The English Patient* is released. It is an international box-office success and wins many awards, including nine Academy Awards (1997). It wins for Best Picture and the Best Director award for Minghella. He also wins the Director's Guild of America "Outstanding Directorial Achievement in Motion Pictures" award and the Best Director award from the Broadcast Film Circle Awards for the film. In 1998, Minghella picks up the British Director of the Year award from the London Critics Circle Film Awards, and the film also wins Best Film award from BAFTA.

1999 *The Talented Mr. Ripley* is released and is well received by critics with good world-wide box-office. It is nominated for many awards but does not achieve the same level of acclaim as *The English Patient.* Minghella wins the National Board of Review's Best Director award for the film.

2000 Minghella and Sydney Pollack become partners in Mirage Enterprises. Through their company, Minghella goes on to produce or executive produce a number of films throughout the decade including Tom Tykwer's *Heaven,* Richard Eyre's *Iris,* Tony Gilroy's *Michael Clayton,* and Kenneth Lonergan's troubled, ambitious production, *Margaret*. Also in 2000, Minghella directs the short film *Play*, based on Samuel Beckett's stage play.

2001   Minghella is named Commander of the Order of the British Empire (CBE) on the Queen's Birthday Honors List.

2003   Appointed Chairman of the Board of Governors, British Film Institute, a position he holds until 2007. Late in this same year, *Cold Mountain* is released to decent box-office and reasonable critical acclaim, although there is something of a muted response compared to the acclaim of Minghella's previous two films. *Cold Mountain* is nominated for seven Academy Awards but only wins in one category for Renée Zellweger as Best Actress in a Supporting Role. Minghella wins the 2003 National Board of Review Best Screenplay award for *Cold Mountain*.

2005   Stages Puccini's opera *Madama Buttterfly* for the English Opera Company and restages it in 2006 for the Metropolitan Opera in New York. In 2006 his staging of *Madama Butterfly* for the English National Opera wins a Laurence Olivier Award "Best New Opera Production."

2006   The film *Breaking and Entering* is released to unenthusiastic response and poor world-wide box-office. This same year Minghella is honored with the "Artistic Excellence in Directing" award from BAFTA. In 2006, Minghella is also awarded the Honorary Degree of Doctor of Letters from University of Reading in England.

2008   The pilot to the television series *The No. 1 Ladies' Detective Agency* premieres in both the UK and the US. Minghella directs from a script he co-wrote with Richard Curtis. Anthony Minghella dies, March 18, 2008, in London after complications following surgery.

Filmography

Note: A partial list of Minghella's work as a playwright and television writer can be found in the Chronology.

TRULY, MADLY, DEEPLY (1990)
Producer: Robert Cooper
Executive Producer: Mark Shivas
Director: **Anthony Minghella**
Screenplay: **Anthony Minghella**
Photography: Remi Adefarasin
Art Direction: Jim Holloway
Production Design: Barbara Gosnold
Editing: John Stothart
Original Music: Barrington Pheloung
Nonoriginal Music: Johann Sebastian Bach (from Adagio for Viola da Gamba Sonata BWV 1029)
Cast: Juliet Stevenson (Nina), Alan Rickman (Jamie), Bill Paterson (Sandy), Christopher Rozycki (Titus), Michael Maloney (Mark)
106 minutes

MR. WONDERFUL (1993)
Producer: Marianne Moloney
Director: **Anthony Minghella**
Screenplay: Amy Schor and Vicki Polon
Photography: Geoffrey Simpson
Art Direction: Steve Saklad
Production Design: Doug Kraner
Editing: John Tintori
Original Music: Carole Bayer Sager, Jerry Bock, Michael Gore, and James Ingram
Cast: Matt Dillon (Gus), Annabella Sciorra (Leonora), Mary-Louise

Parker (Rita), William Hurt (Tom), Vincent D'Onofrio (Dominic)
98 minutes

THE ENGLISH PATIENT (1996)
Producer: Saul Zaentz
Executive Producers: Harvey Weinstein, Bob Weinstein, and Scott
Greenstein
Director: **Anthony Minghella**
Screenplay: **Anthony Minghella**, based on the novel by Michael
Ondaatje
Photography: John Seale
Art Direction: Aurelio Crugnola
Production Design: Stuart Craig
Editing: Walter Murch
Original Music: Gabriel Yared
Nonoriginal music: Johann Sebastian Bach (from *Goldberg Variations*),
Irving Berlin, and Richard Rodgers
Sound: Chris Newman and Ivan Sharrock
Costume Design: Ann Roth, Gary Jones
Cast: Ralph Fiennes (Count Laszlo de Almásy), Juliette Binoche (Hana),
Willem Dafoe (David Caravaggio), Kristin Scott Thomas (Katharine
Clifton), Naveen Andrews (Kip), Colin Firth (Geoffrey Clifton)
160 minutes

THE TALENTED MR. RIPLEY (1999)
Producers: William Horberg and Tom Sternberg
Executive Producer: Sydney Pollack
Director: **Anthony Minghella**
Screenplay: **Anthony Minghella**, based on the novel by Patricia
Highsmith
Photography: John Seale
Art Direction: Stefano Ortolani
Production Design: Roy Walker
Editing: Walter Murch
Music: Gabriel Yared
Cast: Matt Damon (Tom Ripley), Gwyneth Paltrow (Marge Sherwood),
Jude Law (Dickie Greenleaf), Cate Blanchett (Meredith Logue), Philip
Seymour Hoffman (Freddie Miles)
139 minutes

PLAY (2000)
Producers: Tim Bricknell, Michael Colgan, Alan Moloney
Director: **Anthony Minghella**
Writer: Samuel Beckett
Photography: Benoît Delhomme
Art Direction: Hauke Richter
Production Design: Roy Walker
Editing: Lisa Gunning
Cast: Alan Rickman, Kristen Scott Thomas, Juliet Stevenson
16 minutes

COLD MOUNTAIN (2003)
Producers: Albert Berger, William Horberg, Sydney Pollack, and Ron Yerxa
Executive Producers: Bob Osher, Iain Smith, Bob Weinstein, and Harvey Weinstein
Director: **Anthony Minghella**
Screenplay: **Anthony Minghella**, based on the novel by Charles Frazier
Photography: John Seale
Art Direction: Maria-Teresa Barbasso, Pier Luigi Basile, Robert Guerra, Christian Niculescu, Luca Tranchino
Production Design: Dante Ferretti
Editing: Walter Murch
Original Music: Gabriel Yared, Martin Tillman, T-Bone Burnett, Lonnie Carter, Elvis Costello, Walter Jacobs, Bob Neuwirth, Sting, and Jack White
Cast: Jude Law (Inman), Nicole Kidman (Ada Monroe), Renée Zellweger (Ruby Thewes), Eileen Atkins (Maddy), Philip Seymour Hoffman (Reverend Veasey), Natalie Portman (Sara), Donald Sutherland (Reverend Monroe), Giovanni Ribisi (Junior), Ray Winstone (Teague)
154 minutes

BREAKING AND ENTERING (2006)
Producers: **Anthony Minghella** and Sydney Pollack
Executive Producers: Tim Bricknell and Colin Vaines
Director: **Anthony Minghella**
Screenplay: **Anthony Minghella**
Photography: Benoît Delhomme
Art Direction: Andy Nicholson

Production Design: Alex McDowell
Editing: Lisa Gunning
Music: Gabriel Yared
Nonoriginal Music: Dado Jehan
Cast: Juliette Binoche (Amira), Jude Law (Will), Robin Wright Penn (Liv)
120 minutes

THE NO. 1 LADIES' DETECTIVE AGENCY (2008) (pilot film for television series)
Producer: Tim Bricknell
Executive Producers: Bob Weinstein, Harvey Weinstein, **Anthony Minghella**, Sydney Pollack, Richard Curtis, and Amy J. Moore
Director: **Anthony Minghella**
Screenplay: Richard Curtis and **Anthony Minghella**, based upon the novels by Alexander McCall Smith
Photography: Giulio Biccari
Art Direction: Vivienne Gray and Cecelia van Straaten
Production Design: Johnny Breedt
Editing: Mary Finlay and Katie Weiland
Music: Gabriel Yared
Cast: Jill Scott (Precious Ramotswe), Anika Noni Rose (Grace Makutsi), Lucian Msamati (JLB Matekoni)
60 minutes

Anthony Minghella: Interviews

Anthony Minghella:
In Conversation (Part 1)

Mario Falsetto / 2003–4

Mario Falsetto: Can you talk about your background and growing up on the Isle of Wight.

Anthony Minghella: My father migrated to England when he was nineteen in 1939. And like many young, slightly dispossessed Italian boys, he was imported by more successful local families who had already immigrated and set up various forms of business. The business of choice in England was ice cream so my father worked for a fairly wealthy family in Portsmouth, which is close to the Isle of Wight. He eventually left that company with one ice cream van to start his own business on the island. He married my mother who was from a neighboring village near Monte Cassino where my father was from. They formed this business and had five children fairly rapidly. The whole focus of attention was around the business and a little café that they opened as well. The Isle of Wight was flourishing at that time so the preoccupation of my childhood was working with my father. My father is unschooled, and my mother was taken out of school very early because there was a great deal of privation in her family as well. So there were almost no books in our house. Ironically, of course, the five children were all rather academic, or became academic in various ways.

My first encounter with cinema was selling ice cream tubs in the local cinema which backed onto our café. The projectionist of that cinema rented a small cottage that was at the back of our building, so I got to know him very well and I was a frequenter of his projection room. The fare on offer in those cinemas was extremely banal and prosaic. There were a great number of "B" pictures around at the time. I would say that my education in film began when I left the Isle of Wight at the age of eighteen to do a drama degree at university. The things around me at home were more musical in so far as my grandfather was passionate about opera, and my mother inherited that interest in music and played music herself. We all learnt to be musicians and played a lot together. In my mid-teens I found that the way to express my particular anomie was to hammer away at the piano, and so I started writing music and songs. I played in various groups and managed to make some kind of living in my late-teens by playing music.

MF: What attracted you to a drama degree at university?

AM: A very significant thing happened in 1968 when I was fourteen. There was a pop music festival on the island and it had a huge impact on me. It began an early fascination with America because a lot of American bands came over and brought with them an undertow of peripheral cultural documents: fashion, magazines, and music. There was this record store that would import American and West Coast music and some of the magazines that attended that music. I started to subscribe to *Rolling Stone*, *It*, and *Oz*, and that was my secret discovery, and then the festival happened three years in a row and that really started to give me a sense of a different world and a different way of thinking.

My interest in drama was very minimal. I thought I was going to paint or play music or maybe go to an art school. Music was the great attraction to me and I was in a band that got a recording deal. As a sort of palliative to my parents, I went through the motions of applying to university. I happened upon this course in Hull (England), which was a brand new course.

I went there because it was away from my parents, although I enjoyed a very good relationship with them. I thought, "Well, that's too far away to have me in an ice cream van on the weekends," and it seemed like an interesting course. For three years I enjoyed this extraordinary opportunity to educate myself because it was a department which had a brand new building with a theater, a radio studio, and a television studio. It was expected of all students that they would explore as many of these areas as they could. Quickly though, everyone got compartmentalized. I was the person who might make some posters and some music for the players, and so I spent the first few years drawing and writing incidental music, as well as reading. I became absurdly focused and even angelical when I was a student there. I discovered the library and the theater, and I was a fairly driven student for the three years that I was an undergraduate. I fell in love with playwrights. I fell in love with plays and read a great deal. I was given the baptism of the theater in a very appropriate way. I was quite innocent.

MF: Is that when you started writing?

AM: I started writing because I wanted to present a series of songs I'd written and the department said it wasn't an appropriate submission. I tried to think of a way of using music that would be acceptable so I thought I'd write a musical. I'd never written anything, but I thought, "Okay, if I can't write some songs, I'll thread some songs into something that looks like a play." I had staged this play that I was in, and although it was probably execrable, it was oddly successful. Within a week of doing it, I'd gotten a commission to write a play from the local professional theater company.

MF: While you were at university, what writers or filmmakers made a particularly strong impression on you?

AM: In my final year I did a film option and discovered the films of Rossellini , Fellini, De Sica, and Visconti. That was the cinema that spoke to me. And that "voice" was not present in any of the plays that I was reading, particularly contemporary British plays, which I still loved.

I recently saw *I Vitelloni* (Fellini, 1954) again, and it has two particular values for me: One, it reflects the condition of my own youth, which involved a great deal of time spent hanging around, looking at the mainland and dreaming of another kind of life. The other thing is that it spoke back to me of my own circumstances, and it spoke in Italian. One of the things that really attracted me to Fellini can be seen in the tonalities of that film. Its flexing between farce and tragedy, its effortless shifts of emotion, as well as its compassion. This is a ridiculous group of guys—ancient teenagers—who are viewed with a great deal of warmth so that their absurdities and vagaries are presented sometimes harshly but always with love.

I was lucky in that my time at university coincided with two particular phenomena. There was an enormously strong British, political theater: Edward Bond, Howard Barker, David Hare—a really interesting group of young writers, coupled with a great period in American cinema. So my cinema-going experiences were films like *Apocalypse Now*, *The Godfather* films, Scorsese, that whole 1970s period. Except perhaps for Coppola, that cinema spoke of a world that I didn't really know, and the theater spoke in a way that I admired but didn't really identify with. The perspective all seemed rather high and looking down at a world and analyzing it in a rather cool way. I suppose I'm talking about emotional temperature. I'd say that the emotional temperature of the British play was much cooler than my own particular instinct. So when I began to write plays, I always felt slightly dislocated from that period.

I also fell in love with Samuel Beckett, and like all people who are late to the table, my appetite was huge. I burrowed into the world of Beckett with a sort of alarming obsession. Again, in terms of language, it wasn't a language that I particularly knew what to do with. But when I watched the cinema of the Taviani brothers or De Sica, I thought, "Well, I know what that voice is, I recognize that voice. It's like the voice of my childhood, it sounds like my family." That's where I belonged, but it was in a language I didn't speak very well, and it had nothing to do with the theater I was studying. Looking back, though I couldn't have articulated any of this at nineteen or twenty, there was a certain amount of autism I experienced in terms of what I was studying, a sense that the compass might have already passed me by or that where I belonged was somewhere else. Even though I started writing plays quite seriously, I was always struggling to know what kind of play I could write, or should write, or was equipped to write. If I was sitting here at twenty-one, I would have talked to you exclusively about the theater—exclusively. I think those things are often connected with the cultural architecture more than the person. If you went around the British Isles around that time, you would've struggled to find anybody who was saying "I want to be a filmmaker," because the opportunities resided almost exclusively in the theater. The whole system of finding writers was conducted by literary managers of theaters, not by film executives.

In 1975, my first year as a graduate student, I got a call from Walter Donahue, who's now my editor. He was then the literary manager of the Royal Shakespeare Company, and he'd read an early play that I'd written, and made me a young writer of the Royal Shakespeare Company. The other thing that happened, which I was not at all prepared for, was that I was offered a teaching job by my department. For the next five years I taught, but that dignifies the experience of what I was doing. I was actually catching up, filling in some of the holes that I'd created as a child because I was really a poor student as a teenager, very unfocused. The students suffered while I tried to grow up myself.

MF: Were you writing at this time?

AM: I was writing a great deal. I was lucky in that every play I wrote was produced, and I was able to learn a great deal in that period. I started to write for the radio, which was another big opportunity in Britain for new writers. And because Beckett had written a great deal for radio, I had a particular interest. I was callow and very impressionable, and in love with language and literature. Beckett was my doctoral subject. Frankly, I had no idea what any of this was going to amount to, but in 1978 I thought I would make a film. I didn't know why, I just thought this would be an interesting thing so I borrowed some money and with three friends made a film.

MF: You hadn't really made any films before?

AM: I'd made a three-minute film for a play, but I thought I could graduate very quickly from that to a feature. So we all took out a mortgage. Calling it a screenplay again dignifies what it was but I did make it. It was about my grandmother, who I had a particular attachment to and who had a very complex and tragic life. I wrote this story about her, and we shot for eleven days. We had about eighty-five or ninety minutes of material. I spent the next two years trying to make sense of it. That sort of put me off being a filmmaker for about fifteen years [laughs]!

MF: It seems clear that you didn't see yourself as an academic for the rest of your life?

AM: I had an experience when I was teaching where I went to the registrar's office to sign some university pension scheme, and he said, "You know, you could be the longest serving lecturer in this university . . . you started young." I remember walking out of there thinking "oh God!" I owe so much to that place and the people who taught me and whom I taught with. They gave me ten years of an education and an enormous freedom to pursue my own interests, as well as a great deal of encouragement. I gave up the job primarily because I wanted to come to London. Also, because my writing was getting enough attention that I thought I might be able to earn a living at it. My parents, who are a huge influence, were somewhat distressed to hear that I was giving up my job, which in that period at least seemed like a job for life.

I started to write for television and I couldn't manage the opportunities that were coming my way, even though I was frightened that I wasn't good enough. There was enough opportunity for me, or incentive to think "I'll try this for a while to see if I can do it."

MF: So in the 1980s you were writing for television, radio, and theater?

AM: Mostly for theater, but I also started to write for television and had some success at that. Again, this doesn't speak particularly well of me, but I haven't always asserted myself very much as an artist, certainly not in that period. I went with the flow a little too much. The flow then was television because most British dramatists found a home in television. It was a very muscular, vibrant, pungent television with people like Dennis Potter and David Hare writing for it. That seemed like a great home. That was where the energy was, that was where the producers were living and working and scouring for talent. I never met a film producer in the 1980s. I didn't meet anybody in the film industry so I didn't get involved with the film business. I thought that I'd discovered my vocation as a playwright.

MF: How did you move towards filmmaking?

AM: Towards the end of the 1980s, my plays started being done outside of Britain. One of them, *Made in Bangkok*, was done at the Mark Taper Forum in Los Angeles, and it brought me into contact with the film industry. It's really as banal as that. I washed up in Los Angeles and stayed with a British filmmaker, Roland Joffe, who I shared an agent with. Somebody bought the option on the play. I got an American agent, and then the calls started to be about writing or getting involved in film, rather than getting another commission to write a television play.

Again, none of this reflects particularly well on me, but one of the things that happened to me at that time, which was of enormous significance, was that I'd started a series in the mid-1980s called *Inspector Morse*. I'd written the first pilot, and then I wrote the two-hour television film. I'd started to adapt this book because the producer was a dear friend of mine and saw a future for this series. I honestly didn't see any future in it, but it was an interesting exercise to see if I could adapt a book. So I adapted the *Inspector Morse* mystery, and it became the most successful drama series on British television. It gave me very little pleasure because it wasn't something I had a passionate interest in. I was delighted by the people involved but I didn't feel like it was personal.

At that time I was very interested in doing my own work. I'd written a trilogy of plays for Channel Four called *What If It's Raining?* which I cared a great deal about. Then I realized that I was working with the same actors in my own work again and again, particularly an actress called Juliet Stevenson with whom I was very close. We'd sort of grown up together in that she'd been in my first television play and I'd worked with her on the radio. We kept talking about things we might do together and there was a convergence. I was trying to extricate myself from *Morse*, and they were very generous to me. They were trying to find ways to keep me inside this show. They knew I had an interest in directing. Juliet or maybe Alan Rickman said, "Why do you do this? Why do you write and then hand the play over when you have these strong relationships with actors. Have you ever thought about directing yourself?" And I said, "Well, I'd like to but I don't know how you do it and where you start? And I've got so much writing to do."

I said no to another season of *Inspector Morse*. But they really wanted me to stay on the series. They knew I was interested in directing and said, "Why don't you direct one?" In the very same week a producer called Robert Cooper, who had done many of my plays on the radio had moved to BBC Television. He was starting a film section called Screen Two with Mark Shivas, who I also knew and who had produced *What If It's Raining?* They were the heads of that new division and they were looking to make inexpensive films. He called and said, "We really want you to write the screenplay for this Screen Two movie." And I said, "Well, I'd like to but I just got this opportunity to direct *Inspector Morse*. I would like to try to direct." And they said, "Well, why don't you direct the screenplay?" I had a few days to contemplate this, and the truth of it is that at that time there were sixteen or seventeen million people watching *Inspector Morse* whereas the scale of the BBC Screen Two films was very modest. It seemed that if I was going to screw up, it might be better to screw up in a quieter way than in front of so many people watching this television show. So I thought I would do an original film, simply to avoid too much attention. It was made for $600,000. It was poor cinema in the best sense. I did the BBC film because I felt more passionate about it.

MF: How has writing for television and theater affected your understanding of cinema and your work as a director now?

AM: The important lessons that I extracted from the theater were social rather than aesthetic, and social in a profound way. I don't mean friends, I mean the culture of making plays or making small, more modest work, which is very actor driven and this has stayed with me. You rely on performance because you don't have the accouterments of resources that are available in the industrial cinema. I'd grown up writing and touring in plays that were performed out of the back of a single truck. The economics of scale were very interesting to me because it made the work more communal, more collective. It taught me to invest heavily in the people that I was working with. The "glue and bits of string" theater has stayed with me. That way of making work has stayed with me.

I also had this marvelous opportunity because I wrote a great deal. When I look back at how much I managed to write in the 1980s, I can't believe it. It's like a different person. The metabolism was so different. I was writing every day, all the time. Plus, I was a script editor at the BBC, and I worked on a series set in a school. I presided over 180 episodes of that series. It meant that I was seeing other writers working, and seeing that work in the studio and then broadcast. I put a lot of miles in, and those miles were very useful. I worked with a writer on a scene on a Friday and it was in a studio on a Wednesday and on television a month later. The discipline was very intense. One thing I inherited from my parents is an immigrant work ethic. I have a great appetite to work. Aesthetically, it's hard to know what you extract from that experience in terms of film. I think it took me quite a long time to understand the values of cinema, what the visual language potential was for myself. Not that I wasn't aware of it as a viewer, but how to manipulate it and use it as a director. I think I had a very fine nib, a miniaturist pen when I first started working in film as a writer. Even now, I suppose, I think of myself as a writer who gets to make films occasionally, rather than the other way around.

MF: Is the writing less important in your understanding of cinema now?
AM: No, oh no.

MF: But it's such an emotional, poetic medium, isn't it? It doesn't always rely on words.
AM: But you write the poetry, and you write the emotion. The banal thing to say is that I realize that the writer in film is the director. The writer has to be the director because the vision is articulated over the course of the film. The ink becomes the camera becomes the editing room. If you want to write film, you have to direct film. It just seemed very clear to me from the beginning, partly because my first real experience in film was writing and directing *Truly, Madly, Deeply* and realizing that I was still writing, sometimes literally, but metaphorically writing all through the process. That's something I understood as a teacher of plays, that writing in theater is architectural. Writers in theater are dramatic architects. They aren't giving words to people to say, they are creating *mise-en-scène*.

When I talked about plays with students, I became obsessed with the degree to which language mattered in the way that it related to action.

If nothing else, I learnt in that period of being a teacher and playwright that my job was not about putting words into people's mouths. It was about creating action, creating *mise-en-scène*. That continues to obtain for me and my interest in writing has not been to write dialogue but to write circumstance. If you looked at the screenplay of *Cold Mountain*, nobody says very much. It doesn't mean I don't feel that it's an extremely "written" film. It's a film of some scale, and heavily reliant on its visual iconography. In fact, we cut most of the film on silence.

MF: Since *Truly, Madly, Deeply* was your first film, how prepared were you when you went into that situation? Were you fearful of directing your first film?

AM: I just did the DVD commentary for *Truly, Madly, Deeply* and I hadn't seen it since I first made it. They gave me the production notes and some continuity sheets from the film when I was doing that commentary. This will tell you more than any rhetoric that I can create. They gave me a sheet of continuity notes that was something like six or seven pages. By contrast, the continuity notes for *Cold Mountain* take up two volumes! Basically it said "Shot One, Take One: Print"; "Shot Two, Take Two: Print"; "Shot Three, Take One: Print." It was as far away from the creation of a piece of cinema as you could imagine. We had twenty-seven and a half days of shooting. I didn't know what coverage was. I did two days of second-unit shooting, none of which was used in the film because it wasn't usable. I was terrified. I had no way of preparing, except to invest heavily in my belief in the actors.

I remember one particular day sitting in my living room. My wife is Chinese and we had a wooden Chinese god about four feet high. I borrowed a viewfinder and I sat with the viewfinder at one end of the room, put the statue at the other end of the room, and changed lens size and tried to draw the difference in. I mean, I'm ashamed that I'm telling you this story, but that's what I did to kind of teach myself so that when the cinematographer turned up and said "what lens do you want?" I could at least pretend I had an answer for him.

The making of that first film was completely apart from any subsequent experience I've had. One of the things that defines the cinema experience as a filmmaker is the degree of negotiation involved. The managerial elements of making a film are as significant as the artistic ones: managing the scale of crew, the number of people who peck at you in preproduction and in postproduction. The industrial elements of filmmaking, which can be so suffocating and defeating when you're officially a filmmaker, were completely absent when making *Truly, Madly, Deeply*. I wrote a screenplay. I think probably two people read it by the time we went into production. I didn't rewrite it. I shot the film, showed it to them, and we released it.

MF: Was it a difficult shoot?

AM: It was absolutely joyful, and that was largely because it felt like I was making a home movie. I had my friends in it, even some of my family. It was about a world that was as close to the world I was living in as to make no difference. Its ambitions were minuscule. I assumed that I would make it, and it would be seen for two seconds. I would then have served an apprenticeship as a filmmaker and I'd see how I had done. I didn't ever imagine an audience for it, so there was no pressure on me to make anything. I didn't have any aspirations for it at all. You could argue it's not even a real film. The film was very honest, there was very little guile in it. I still believe that films are actor driven, that no amount of weaponry can compete with a single moment of truth an actor gives you. The films and filmmakers that I love have loved actors, and so they give you these moments of performance which are indelible. When I was talking to Juliette Binoche about working with Kieslowski, she said that film was precious to him, they had so little film. He felt you had to earn the film, you had to earn the right to shoot the film. That an actor standing against a wall and telling you the truth was more exciting and more poignant than any swoop of a camera on a crane or a thousand soldiers running across a field. None of it added up to the power and authority of an actor exposed in the way that film can expose them.

MF: People seemed to either love *Truly, Madly, Deeply* or really dislike it.

AM: I would say it has been the best received film I've made and the worst received. I remember seeing some film journal and *Truly, Madly, Deeply* was number two or number three on this critic's list of all-time favorite films, and then three pages later it was number three on this other critic's all-time least favorite films. It's very odd because its ambitions were so miniature and its intentions were so modest. It seemed bizarre to me that it would incite such extremes of reaction. In fact, I would say that more people have written to me and made contact with me about that film than anything else I've done.

MF: I can understand why people would be affected by it, but I'm not sure why people would reject it so strongly.

AM: I think the degree of emotion that's available in it offends some people. They don't trust it, and resist it. Again, *I Vitelloni* was very badly received and probably for the same reasons. It's a much better film, but it excited the same kind of consternation. It was seen as a betrayal of the work Fellini had done with Rossellini and the neo-realist cinema. Whatever trend you want to assert as being prevalent in the late 1980s in Britain in fiction film, it was never interested in the emotional life of characters. Traditionally, in Britain, we don't like emotion in films. I wasn't even conscious of what it was that I was collecting when I was making the film. In a prosaic way, I was just focusing on whether I could get all of it shot in the time that I had. My intentions were largely directed towards the actors.

You can't elect your voice as a filmmaker. You might want to, you might want to design the kind of filmmaker you could be. You might aspire to be a particular kind of filmmaker, but you can't elect it. You might want to be a baritone, but if your voice is tenor then your voice is tenor. It took me a long time to make peace with the fact that your taste exists. You can learn to harness your taste, you can learn to make the material that you create adhere closely to your taste so you can better articulate yourself, but you can't alter your taste. You have to embrace it, make peace in some way with how you write.

MF: The style of that film is a little different than your later work. It has an excessive number of close-ups, it's really in your face all the time, and there are lots of long takes, which I guess your work still has. I assume you're the kind of filmmaker who feels that the material dictates the form.

AM: Well, I think you're being kinder than you need to be. First of all, I don't want to apologize for that film because I loved making it, and I loved the people involved in making it. In some ways, I'll never make a film that is as meaningful to me as that film. When you say there are an excessive number of this or there are long takes, none of that speaks to my experience of it. I didn't know enough to plan the results, to know enough about what it meant or what I was doing. I didn't have any experience of shooting. I didn't know the impact of the shot size I was selecting. I was just winging it. I don't apologize for that. I know that the film found a very vocal and supportive audience who understood the intention, even if they might have quarreled with the execution of it. When you say there are long takes in it, I didn't know what a short take was. I wasn't familiar enough with the grammar of film to engage with it. There was no dialectic involved in making it. I wasn't saying, "Well, you might think that this sequence should be shot this way, I'm deliberately going to subvert that."

MF: But you knew what a big close-up was. I mean, if you're holding on a big close-up for three minutes, you know that that's going to have a particular impact, or at least when you're cutting the film.
AM: Let me say this. What I've learnt is that a film sentence requires vocabulary. It requires five shot sizes, ten angles, and then you can elect a style. If you've got one shot for the scene, then that's what you cut. There was virtually no editing in *Truly, Madly, Deeply*—there was just assembly. There were times when I had one shot for a page. I didn't say, "I think I'll use the close-up all the way through." That's what I collected. My obsession now with film vocabulary is one that I've acquired, rather than was innate to me.

MF: What was the most important idea to explore in *Truly, Madly, Deeply*? Was it this issue of how to deal with loss, or was it something else?
AM: The obtaining idea in *Truly, Madly, Deeply* came from a tension in my work as a playwright, which was primarily made out of a vocabulary of naturalism where I thought the job of writing a play was to harness the fractured expressions of idiomatic language. I'd written a radio play, which was a very important play in my work called *Cigarettes and Chocolate*. That play is a torrent of language where meaning has almost extinguished itself from the language. Characters are trying to speak but find that language impedes what they want to say rather than supports it. If you analyzed it, it's full of appositional clauses, eroding clauses, and qualifiers in the language. I found myself unable to write a single uncomplicated line because I was trying to examine the tension between meaning and speech, and what we do with language, how language is often used to obfuscate meaning as opposed to making it transparent.

That experience of trying to work language, and use the most domestic architecture to support language, was going on simultaneously while I was working with Jim Henson for two years writing the television series *The Storyteller*. The thing that struck me when I was working on *Storyteller* was that the narrative expressions were bold. The people [doing the series] had no interest in naturalism whatsoever. It's a world where giants woke up and found their heart had been stolen or people turned to stone. There was much more interest in how you told story, the thrill of storytelling, and the thrill of quite fundamental rhythms of storytelling, fantasy, and dreams. So on the one hand I was working hard at this series—I wrote nine films in that series—and at the same time I was writing my own plays about adultery or sexual tourism or whatever it was. I think what you see in *Truly, Madly, Deeply* is some sort of merger of the narrative excursions of *The Storyteller* with the style that I developed as a playwright. Instead of writing a film about the breakup of a relationship, or people coming to terms with the loss of a relationship, which is what I originally intended to do, the narrative assertion was more extreme and bold. Rather than saying "How do you get over a relationship that's broken up?" I thought, "Well, why not push it further and say that it's not only about a relationship in which there's a bereavement, but the bereaved lover actually returns." So it has a fable element, which comes directly from *The Storyteller* experience. I was trying to use some of the joy I had in writing *Storyteller* episodes, but in a contemporary, quasi-naturalistic setting.

MF: Can you talk specifically about working with Juliet Stephenson on her character and performance? What kinds of discussions did you have? Did she get the character right away?
AM: Well, the character itself was invested very heavily in what I knew about her. Not in a literal sense. She hadn't had the experience of the character in the film, and she's not like the character in the film. But I did feel like I was the equivalent of a tailor. I did think, "Well, I know how she'd wear this dress, I know what kind of dress I should make."

MF: You specifically wrote it for her?
AM: Oh yeah. There was a lot of interest in the screenplay when I wrote it, and some quite tempting offers to relocate it to America, but they all involved recasting. So it was a much less interesting prospect because it was all about her ability to express character through language, her ability to turn a line, to hear a line. It called upon aspects of her life that intrigued me: a single woman living in London, a great befriender. Whenever I went to visit her, for example, there were all sorts of strange people who attended to her in some way. And Alan [Rickman] and Juliet had been friends for many years, and he's an extremely interesting man who has a very strong, quite formidable personality which everybody gets enthralled by in some way. The dynamics of the relationships I already knew informed the way I was writing, and the rehearsal process was really investigations of tone.

I think Juliet Stevenson is one of the great actors that we have. When

I met Juliet, there was an extraordinary event that took place. She was reading a play I had written for the BBC, and when she read she sounded exactly like the voice I heard in my head. It was as if I'd been writing for an instrument and the instrument showed up. The way she approached a line, what she heard in the line, what she saw in a character, was so close to what I'd imagined that it was shocking. And I clung to her because I felt like I'd found an external agent of my writing. I also felt that she was an undervalued spirit, in the sense that she was known in Britain at the time as a rather formidable, classical actress. She was a star of The Royal Shakespeare Company, but nobody knew she was funny, nobody knew she was contemporary and larky. So I approached the film rather like a tailor. I thought I'd make her a part that would show off her range. Again, I think my ambitions were not much greater than that, which was to make a film where you'd see all her colors. We rehearsed in my car driving to set, it felt very private as an experience. It didn't have that enormous elephant of production sitting on it.

MF: I can't remember who it was, maybe it was Robert Bresson, who said that the more tears on the screen the less tears in the audience. I mean there's always this suspicion of emotion if it's all too visible.
AM: Maybe you're pushing me to arrive at why some people received the film so well and why some people rejected it because the volume controls are turned up on the skittishness of it, the tragedy of it. If you looked at every knob, they're turned up full, and that's what we talked a lot about, this "going for broke" in every area, and also just trying to tell the truth about it, and the pain of it, and the joy of it. Taking it and not judging the narrative events at all. So that if you're in the bath and this man has come back from the dead and says he's brought some friends back and they're watching videos, rather than allowing yourself to play into the absurdity of it, play into the reality of it. That seemed to me to be fun and we did have fun. How could we get the most pleasure from all of these elements? I've probably spent more time talking to you about this film and what it's about than I spent talking to myself or with the actors when we were shooting it.

I think Bresson is completely right, by the way. What you're describing is first of all a manipulation of form and a clear understanding of the dynamic between the image and the audience, which I've become very interested in. I was trying to tell the truth about something. For example, the scene in the psychiatrist's room where Juliet breaks down had one element which I believed completely and that was the rage in it. That's what I was collecting and thought was fresh. Traditionally, we're supposed to believe that if you love somebody and they die, you're heartbroken. What we were trying to explore was the degree of anger involved at being bereaved. I suppose when the film is successful, it's the anger that's being heard, and for people that don't have those experiences or don't have that connection, they just see the degree of emotion. A very important phenomenon of film is that the more the audience is asked to fill in—the more it's dealing with ellipsis, either narrative or emotional—finally, the more pleasure there is, the more reward there is.

MF: *Truly, Madly, Deeply* in some ways is also a kind of reaction to the Thatcher period, is it not? Its liberal humanism, you could call it.
AM: Oh yeah, completely. I thought I was writing a great deal about London, about the fact that there was a new underclass in London that had replaced the British labor class. We thought we'd become a classless society but we'd created an invisible class of migrant, dispossessed workers. I was in contact with a great number of those people. The Thatcherite world simply swept everything under the carpet, and talked about dismantling the class system. I was very interested in the failure of the Labour Party to get elected, and tried to work for the Labour Party. So a lot of my own interests were percolating around.

The fact of the matter is that I'm a Catholic, Italian immigrant with a very prescribed view of the world. I want to believe in the potential of people for good. I do believe in it. But it's a conscience-orientated fiction, isn't it? That fiction, if it exists, has to exist with some aspirational elements. I have to believe that there is a role for fiction to play, over and above giving me employment. It's got to be about something, and it's got to earn its keep as a meta-document. Also, it has to be subject to scrutiny, so it can't just exist for its own sake.

MF: Juliet's character, Nina, represents the first in a repeated pattern of very damaged individuals in your work, and charting their journey.
AM: Damage and healing, because healing is more interesting to me than the damage. Everybody's damaged, so there's nothing interesting about recording damage. I suppose I have been interested in how people heal themselves, what heals people. I saw that film much more about the way people can move on rather than the way people get trapped. It's an extremely affirmative film. That's the other thing which meets resis-

tance, the fact that it's affirmative. Maybe it's too easily affirmative, but it wants to believe that people are capable of change, and that there is a system of support that is available.

MF: I think we want to have a sense that film characters are in a different place by the end of the narrative.

AM: Yeah, although I don't subscribe to the idea that every character has to be on a journey. One of the things that's happened, I think, is this hegemony of three-act structure and character arc. Many great pieces of fiction have no interest in classical structure or indeed in character arc.

MF: I couldn't agree more. I'd say that film has a lot of musical rhythms in it. Not just the playing of the music, because obviously music is really important in the film, but it's almost like a chamber piece.

AM: Absolutely. I talked a lot with the actors that it was like making a chamber piece and it was essentially a duet. I started *Truly, Madly, Deeply* with some notes about a couple who met once a week. I didn't know what the story was going to be, but I had one image with a Bach cello and piano piece, and two people would meet on a weekly basis to make a duet. That's how I began. All my early notes were about this duet and why they are making it.

Bach, I suppose, has been the biggest influence on nearly every part of my life. What most intrigues me about him is the degree to which the line is austere, but the content is volcanic. Pablo Casals said that Bach is a volcano. When I was learning to play Bach with a cello, I always rejected it because it seemed so desiccated and tactful and austere. Then I realized that Bach was this painful, emotional torrent contained within this very tight line. That's something I've learnt to do better in my films, to sit on the log of emotion rather than express it, and that tension can become very interesting and extremely potent.

Music is at the center of every film that I've made in some shape or form. I also think editing is musically oriented, rhythmically oriented. One of the things that interests me is the idea of visual rhythm. I realize what the power of those visual rhymes is. I've always felt that music and architecture are the twin reservoirs to me of how film is made. At the most simple level, everybody's trying to make films like the ones they loved. It's not really much more complex than that. I've tried to create for other people experiences like the ones I've had myself as a viewer where I've had enormous pleasure.

MF: When you finished *Truly, Madly, Deeply*, did you feel that you wanted to keep directing or did you feel that you were still a writer?

AM: Both. I didn't understand this because I wasn't surrounded by people with similar experiences. When *Truly, Madly, Deeply* was shown in Los Angeles, it was sold five minutes later, and ten minutes later screenplays started arriving in my hotel. I thought, "Well, this is interesting." People were cornering me and saying, "You directed that film?" Nobody was asking whether I'd written it. There was the vacuum cleaner sucking and in I went up the tube. So I chose between a batch of screenplays that I'd been sent, and was certainly seduced by a very powerful and persuasive producer named Tom Rothman, who now runs Fox and who has become a close friend. He had a passion for this material and I listened to it and bought into it and got caught up in that development. I thought when somebody offered you a film it meant they were going to make it. What it meant was that they were going to start you on a journey that might or might not arrive at production. I'd never experienced the idea of "green lights." I didn't know what any of this meant and how this industry worked. I had no real contact with it. For *Truly, Madly, Deeply* somebody said, "We want to make a film that starts shooting in September," I then went away, wrote a screenplay and started shooting in September. Now I went into this limbo of trying to rewrite, trying to understand what they would require, re: budgeting, cast, everything.

MF: Your next film, *Mr. Wonderful*, is viewed as your biggest failure. Was it a totally negative experience?

AM: I actually think that experience was probably more important than any other I've had, and I see that more clearly as time goes on. That film made me a filmmaker, irrespective of its content and its result. When I came home from America after making it I was very clear that I was never going to make another film, even before it was released. I don't mean as a result of its reception or its achievement. When I came home I thought, "Okay, well I'm either never going to do this again or I'm going to do it the way I want to do it. There's going to be no compromise in the way I work." *Mr. Wonderful* is the sum of a series of very benign compromises. I went into it with such absurd innocence about Hollywood and what it meant to be a film director. I never thought of myself as a director at all, then suddenly I was seen as a director and went through the motions of directing a film. Here's an anecdote. My wife had gone to Bali and she is a very particular soul and extremely trusting. She'd gone to buy some cloth at a market, and at the market the vendor said, "It's ten rupiah for this cloth." My wife took the amount from her purse, and the woman said, "No, no, no—you say two rupiah, and I say eight and you say four, and then you pay five." The *Mr. Wonderful* experience for me was the "ten rupiah " experience, where I just paid the ten every time, not realizing that the whole discourse is designed to be a barter discourse. You're supposed to say, "I'm not shooting there, I'm going to shoot here. No, I'm not going to give up that actor." I just paid the money, you know, all the way through the experience with varying degrees of success. It was really like going to film school. I filmed every day as if I were in film school.

MF: Did you write the screenplay?
AM: No, I didn't write it but I did work on it. And I learnt first of all that I'm not a director of other people's work. I'm a writer of films. I'm an author of films for good or bad. I'm not somebody who has an interpretive skill at all. Also, the degree of rigor and courage and sense of self that's required to survive, the armor that's required, the obduracy that's required, the conviction that's required, were all lessons that I learnt the hard way by showing up like many other callow directors have shown up in Hollywood. It was not an atmosphere where I was surrounded by bad people, but the reverse, where I was surrounded by very good people. But the process just chews and mangles and spits out as a matter of course. Either you learn how to operate in that world or you're destroyed by it. I was ready never to direct again, and thought probably I wouldn't. I thought, "Well, I'm not equipped. I don't have the armor to survive this world."

MF: Was it such a painful experience?
AM: Painful in that I don't think I made a good film.

MF: It's not unusual for filmmakers to make a film that's not so great.
AM: No, but it was painful and I think if you're going to fail you better fail on your own terms. I'm not frightened of failing but I want to be able to defend passionately what I'm doing. I want to take responsibility for what I'm doing. I haven't seen *Mr. Wonderful* since I made it, so I don't have any opinion about the film. I know that in almost every part of it, the compromises I made were not proper ones. They were not sane ones. They were not ones that were going to feed me as a filmmaker. It doesn't

mean I don't believe passionately in collaboration and in working in a team. In fact, I've done everything I can to create a team to work with, and they've all stuck with me, thank God. A lot of the team I found began on that film, so in almost every respect it was positive because it was absolutely galvanizing. First of all, it made me want to make films; and secondly it made me fear that I couldn't make films. Nothing that happened in making *Truly, Madly, Deeply* prepared me for what I was going into, no part of it.

One of the most important lessons from *Mr. Wonderful* was knowing which battle to win, and not to spend so much time attending to every hint of smoke when you've lost the war going on behind you. I can't sustain that metaphor, but it was Film School 101: scouting, casting, crewing, shooting, editing, dealing with the studio, every part of it.

MF: What was good about the experience?

AM: I felt I had a very good bunch of actors. I loved being in America, and shooting the movie with an American crew. It's just that the stuff of the film, the noise around the film was louder than the film itself. Now I try and focus my attention on what I'm achieving, as opposed to just achieving anything.

MF: When you looked at the material itself, did you not think that there was something wrong with it, or that it was too formulaic and unconvincing?

AM: I was always trying to push the screenplay towards an area which intrigued me. It just so happened that the area that intrigued me didn't intrigue the studio. They'd bought a high-concept film that they saw as a "straight down the road" romantic comedy. I was interested in something else, and probably what I was interested in wasn't sufficiently muscular to overwhelm the conventionality of it. That's what I take away from that experience. I thought I wanted to write about a community. The reason why I attached myself to it was because I thought, "It's about Italians in New York. I probably know something about that. It might be a bit like Italians when I was growing up." And the idea of "aspiration" appealed to me because I felt like that was a journey that I'd been on. I made the film more about a woman who was trying to get out to see if she could survive in a world in which the mind had triumphed over the presiding culture in some way. She just wanted to get out and redefine herself and was never able to.

MF: How did the producers interfere in your process?

AM: I had never even been in a development process before. I didn't even know what it was. You sit in a room and twenty people or five people or two people would say, "You should do this or do that." I'd never experienced that before. It was very compelling and passionately held, and came from experienced people who worked in an industry I knew nothing about. I listened very hard to the conversations. "This casting idea is a terrible idea, this person never works. I can show you chapter and verse about how every movie they've been in has been catastrophic. This is a person that will be much more suitable." It was that sort of thing.

MF: How about on the set? Did you have producers sort of hovering over you?

AM: No, but I had a lot of deconstruction at night from Los Angeles. I was shooting in New York and had a great deal of feedback at night, and a great deal of pressure to simplify and get the film shot in the allocated time. There was enormous pressure on the budget, reducing the shooting days. Also, I've never shot on location in that way. I'd never been to New York so trying to shoot in New York with all the difficulties made that film as hard to make as *The English Patient*. There was constant noise. Being able to turn over [the camera] was a feat in itself. It was hairy as an experience, but it was enormously valuable. That's what I'm saying. I felt that what I know about film I learnt in the failure of that film.

It's not that I think making *Mr. Wonderful* was a negative experience. It taught me something about myself, which was that I couldn't live in Los Angeles and be a studio filmmaker. I'm not equipped to be. I've got an office in Los Angeles. I go there once a year and look at all the mail on my desk and come home again. I would be hopeless in that environment because I know that I flourish best when I've got control of the perimeters of the world I'm in, and I'm not held hostage to the imperatives of the industry.

MF: *The English Patient* was your first literary adaptation for cinema. Can you talk about the way you adapted that novel? You have a very specific method, which is a bit unusual.

AM: Well, it's a method that grew directly out of my relationship with the novel. I didn't have a method that I applied to a book. I had to find a method which made sense of the novel, and then subsequently it became a method that I've used. It felt like it could be a way forward with any adaptation but it was one that evolved because of the struggle I had with the architecture and characteristics of Michael [Ondaatje]'s book. In a way, *The English Patient* is a poem disguised as a novel. It's not really a novel in the conventional sense, it's very much a product of a deconstructive, postmodern commentary on the novel rather than being a novel. It's certainly not driven by any narrative concern. Story is the least significant element of the book as far as Michael is concerned, and as far as the reader is concerned. It's much more an engagement with fractures of chronology. It is a book in which archaeology is central, in the same way that archaeology is this collocation of fragments and shards and mosaics. You piece together something by examining tiny pieces of the past. The novel is a mirror of that. In other words, the structure is just little tiny fragments and you have to stand quite a long way back before it resolves into any kind of pattern, rather like a mosaic.

In film there is such a narrative imperative, story seems to be the primary preoccupation. There is such an obvious disjunction between the *English Patient* material and the film medium that I found myself marooned for a long time trying to work out how I could tell the story on film. Also, because I was so in love with the book and its construction and its beauty, it was disabling. I found the closer it was to me, the more disabled I was. I found myself wanting to copy every contour of each page. In one page of *The English Patient* you get changes in chronology, location, and perspective, which in film would just implode. You would be loathe to try to burden it with so many points of view. Film is inelegant in its ability to handle too much information. It's rather prosaic as a medium in some respects. A novelist can conjure a time with a few brush strokes and a few sentences, get a perfume of a place very quickly with a bold brush stroke. For example, "London in the early part of the century was bleak and growing bleaker by the second." There's one sentence but how do you transpose that into a film sentence? It's almost impossible. You can say, "At this moment London is bleak." But iterations are really difficult and *The English Patient* is full of these iterations.

The long and the short of it is I didn't know how to go about conveying some of the poetry of the book on film, and the more I labored the harder it seemed to go, the more resistant it became. Finally, I came up with this notion that what I would do is leave the book alone. I went down to a friend's cottage with a trunk load of books because obviously one of the problems with doing a period adaptation is that it's not your speciality, it's someone else's. I didn't know about archaeology, I didn't know about Egypt or North Africa, I didn't know about Italy at the end of the war, I didn't know what Sikhs were doing in the British army. All of it was news to me. So I went armed with a whole trunk load of stuff, none of which included *The English Patient*. And then my job was to write my way back to the book in some way. I had to imagine that there was no book, and I was going to make the film from the same kind of source materials that Michael used. Somehow, I had to arrive at the film story, which emerges from exactly the same reservoir that Michael's book emerged from. It has to tell itself using only the devices and gestures of film. So I didn't open *The English Patient* book again.

Michael and I became friends very quickly, and he is the most gracious and empowering person. I would send him a draft of the script—the first draft was over two-hundred pages—and we would discuss it. He was so encouraging of this process that it sort of amused and appealed to him, and somehow felt like there was no danger of the film being some kind of "CliffsNotes" to the book. It was liberating for both of us. He described his method once in terms of writing novels as rather like a jazz musician riffing on a few notes from a familiar song. And then he would riff a character and a situation, and just improvise. In a way, I felt that I was doing the same thing. I would take my memories of the chord changes of *The English Patient* and improvise upon those chord changes. It resulted in a script that had as much invention as it had deletions and omissions.

MF: You must have made a lot of notes when you were reading the novel.
AM: I made notes but I didn't make a lot of notes. I knew the book very well and also I had Michael as a kind of reference point. Just jumping ahead, it's now got to a point where I'm so superstitious about this process that when I was writing *Cold Mountain*, I would call Tim Bricknell, who was helping me do the research for the film, and say, "Could you open the book and somewhere towards the end there is a passage. . . ." I didn't want to open the book myself. It's become something of a totemistic process. It's absolutely silly, and I know it's silly, but it's how we all develop as odd human beings. It seems if I violate that rule then I will just turn into a more conventional filmmaker or get too conventionally allied to the shape of the books.

MF: That helps explains why there are some significant differences between film and book.
AM: Just bad memory [laughs].

MF: Some criticisms of the film complain about how you deemphasized the Kip and Hana relationship.

AM: That's an interesting point. When I wrote the first draft of *The English Patient*, the Kip and Hana story was the center of the film. I probably wrote fifty pages on Kip alone in the first draft, maybe more. I was obsessed with Kip and I'd invented a lot around him, trying to extrapolate from the novel. I'd invented a lot of "Kipness" in England. That was some of my favorite writing. There were all these strange British characters like bomb disposal people, and I invented a whole community of them in the west country. Walter Murch is always saying that you can't deal with the film you want to make but the film you have made. Always deal with what you have rather than speculation. The film then knows what it is quite quickly. The character of the English patient had to be the fulcrum of the storytelling, otherwise it just started to fragment too much. The necessary hostages to that were England and the back stories of lots of characters. The backstory of Kip and Caravaggio all sort of fell away. It was already an ambitious piece of storytelling. It could really only handle what happened to Count Almásy before he showed up at the convent and what happened once they were in the convent. It didn't seem to want to hold any more information.

MF: Was there something central for you to retain from the novel apart from this notion of poetry?

AM: It's a while ago, so almost anything I say about it is a lie as I try to remember what I felt, but most of all what struck me about the various relationships in *The English Patient* was how many kinds of love were articulated: love of country, love of friends, carnal love, innocent love. There is a quote in the book which I will now burglarize in the act of telling you: "The heart is an organ of fire and new lovers smash everything." I think the dominant idea is that notion of what people get up to under the flag of love in all its various colors.

MF: Were you thinking of any cinematic models when you were making the film? You've got this grand, epic scale, an almost *Lawrence of Arabia* thing, plus these very intimate love stories.

AM: To be honest with you, I think I made a film that was closest to my sensibility. I felt I had been sort of aping filmmaking before this, and I felt I had to try and make a film that reflected my sensibility more.

MF: So things like the nonlinear structure?

AM: Yes, absolutely. If you look at my plays or the original work I've done, it tends to be much less preoccupied with narrative transparency.

As I made that film I got more and more confident. I also found my film family. Walter [Murch], John Seale, Ann Roth, Gabriel Yared—a very, very important element of this—all clicked into place on that film.

MF: Can you talk about your relationship with some of those people.

AM: Notwithstanding the fact that these are all much more experienced and distinguished workers in film than I will ever be, nevertheless, what's happened is that we've fed each other. Now, what I think of as a natural way to construct a scene reflects both my working with Walter, and to some extent I think I've influenced Walter. It's hard to know where his taste ends and mine begins, or where John's taste ends and mine begins. It's become quite a virtuous circle in a way. We like working together, we help each other. I think I've done better work because of them. I like the work they've done in my films often more than I like what they've done elsewhere. There is something that we've done together that seems to be greater than the sum of the parts of our individual skill.

There has never been any score that Gabriel has worked on for other movies that is as good as *The English Patient* or *The Talented Mr. Ripley*. The *Ripley* score is profoundly good as a piece of film music. He's certainly made my work better because it's so intuitive and so in tune—if I can use that pun—with what I'm trying to do as a filmmaker. Walter, of course, who has a brain as big as a house, is a rigorous and demanding collaborator. He is the most rigorous and the most demanding person I work with, and the one I spend the most time with. John will have a hundred days of shooting and then we see each other for a couple of weeks before and that's it. With Walter, it's all the time in preproduction, all the time during shooting, and then a year in postproduction. And during postproduction we're practically living together. I spend more time with him than I do with my wife, practically. He feels, to some extent, as if he's making the film and I'm providing him the material.

There's been a lot of mutual support in the process, which I'm really grateful for and feel honored by, I really do. I feel like I've had this incredible, intense education about what's possible. They don't just show up and do their job. They expect me to be good, to be ambitious, and to challenge them. They've been challenged by great people in the past. I often feel when I'm sitting with Walter in the cutting room that I'm getting his experience and then the experience that he's gleaned from Francis Coppola, George Lucas, from all the other great people he's worked with.

Saul Zaentz began that in the sense that he had such confidence in me at a time when I had very little confidence in myself. So much of what we do is based on our confidence to go out and collect images and trust the way we think a shot should look, trust the way we think a scene might develop. When you don't have many credentials, confidence is hard. You think, "What right have I got to be in that situation?"

MF: Were you confident on the set of *The English Patient*?

AM: I was pretty terrified most of the time because I realized what was at stake. I felt when I was making *The English Patient* that it was as much a manifesto as a film. If this doesn't work then I shouldn't do this job, because I'm not going to try to compromise. I'm not going to try and be a good boy and please everybody. I'm going to do this film the way I think it should be done, with the cast I think it should have, with all of the particular characteristics it's got. I insisted on this way of making the film. I insisted on this material that nobody believed in. Saul [Zaentz] was the only person who thought there was a movie in this book, apart from me and my crew as it assembled. No studio, and I mean nobody, believed in this material. I thought, "Well, if this doesn't work then I've got to accept that what I think as a filmmaker is not really in tune, and not constant with, what is out there and I should just go back and be a playwright." And I would have been happy to find that out.

MF: Can you talk about working with the actors on this film because the level of performance is quite spectacular, with Ralph Fiennes and Juliette Binoche and Kristin Scott Thomas, everyone. Can you describe the kinds of discussions you might have with them on their character? How did they approach their roles?

AM: These are the vital questions. These are the hardest questions to answer.

MF: Obviously you listen and you're sympathetic, and try to give them emotional support and those kinds of things, but why do they do such good work in all of your films? All of your films have this level of performance that is spectacular.

AM: [long pause] First of all, I like actors a lot. And that may be a crass thing to say but it's very important. I like actors. Some directors don't really like actors, and are intolerant of their process. It has always been clear to me that the movies I like, I like because of the actors in them. Finally, I'm not somebody whose nose for a good film is connected to the director's work. It's often about one moment with an actor, the fragility of an actor, the skinlessness of an actor makes me want to walk into the screen. Most people see movies because they want to see an actor's performance. They don't even know the actor, they just fall in love with an actor sometimes because they feel this incredible connection with them. I'm no different than that. So I've always wanted to create those moments with actors myself in my own films. I think every film that a filmmaker makes is a sort of poor rehearsal of what they've fallen in love with in other people's movies, what they've fallen in love with as an audience member. I trust certain things about myself as a filmmaker, and one of them is that I have this reliable jealousy. When I look at a film I think, "Oh God, she's great. I wish she was in my film." Or, "Oh my God, that is a great shot, I wish I had that in my film." It's a sort of awful, greedy but very reliable instinct. I remember watching *The Unbearable Lightness of Being* (Kaufman, 1988) thinking, "I want that person. I want to put my hand through the screen, grab hold of her and throw her into a film. I want that, whatever that is." Within a second of seeing Juliette [Binoche], I had that instinct.

MF: But as Arthur Penn once said, "Film is a director's medium," and when I look at say the work of Fellini or somebody . . . yes, Marcello Mastroianni is incredibly important, but I want to be in the creator's imagination, Fellini's world.

AM: Of course! And so do I. It's completely true. It's also the case if you're a film lover, you can take three shots of a movie and probably identify the director. In terms of the great directors, you can probably spot a Kurosawa or a Fellini movie. Here's my perception of it. I think that performance in film is not unmediated but quite the reverse. What the audience sees of an actor is what the director is seeing. There is some uncanny chemistry that occurs if I see something in you when I'm shooting that the audience then sees. If I don't see it, they won't see it. If I want something from you in a scene and I work hard on my purpose, the audience will feel it. If I want you when you're hoisted up into the rafters of this church to feel this bliss, to feel this unadulterated joy [referring to a scene in *The English Patient*], if I want that feeling and I manage to convey that want to you, the audience will feel it. I don't need to put any subtitle in to explain what's happening, they'll know it. It's chemistry. I don't mean chemistry between actors. I mean chemistry in the sense of real chemistry, there is some sort of event that goes on that is connected to the way that I look at an actor and the way the audience looks. If I'm connecting to them in some way, if I'm communicating my want to them, then the audience will feel it. And it's so mysterious to me that that happens. It's so mysterious that I know that what I am thinking when I'm looking at Nicole Kidman will in some way bounce off her and into the audience.

MF: Do you know when you have that on set?
AM: Yes. I don't want to convey to you that I show up, see what's going on and go home. I'm not going to stop working on something until I feel that I've got what I want. And I can be tough on an actor if I'm not getting it. Sydney [Pollack] taught me something which I think is really important. I got to know Sydney really well during postproduction on *The English Patient*, but it's still implicit in *The English Patient*, which is that film is rude to actors insofar as the director can steal whatever they want from an actor in a film. The actor doesn't need to know how they got to a place, they don't need to participate in their achievement of a moment, they just need to deliver it. There are some things in *The English Patient* that are not a violation of an actor's performance but where I've taken a moment from fifty scenes later, a look, because it was better or more appropriate than I got in the scene I'm in. I'd never addressed that before, that you didn't need to observe the unities of time and place matching a performance to get what the film needed.

In the theater, you rehearse in order to be able to vault to exactly the same height or thereabouts night after night. You need to get to five-foot-eight at that moment. How do I get there? How do I prepare? What's my preparation for that emotional moment so as an actor I can plant my feet correctly for the performance. In film, these bets are all off. All you need is for that moment to be available somewhere in the mass of footage. It only needs to happen once. So that has taught me a great deal, and the one thing I've always said to actors is, "You can't be wrong on film." You have no need to worry about being wrong. There is a level of relaxation that is possible because, first of all, there's never going to be another version say of Almásy or another Hana on film. So you are, by definition, correct.

It begins with casting well. One of the only conflicts that Saul and I ever had was not about casting but about casting methodology. When I finally got to a script that worked, to a place where I thought you could make the film and he did too, we sat down and I said, "Okay, I want to start casting." And he said, "Good. I'll come to London." And my response was "No, I want to start casting. I don't want to cast with you." And he said, "Well, then we don't have a movie because I've been on every casting session of every film I've made. It hasn't hurt those films as far as I can remember, and it hasn't hurt my relationship with the directors as far as I can remember, so I'll come to London and we'll start casting." And I said, "Well, no, we won't do that. That's not going to happen." And that was a difficult moment because Saul is extremely formidable.

MF: So you did all the casting yourself?

AM: I did it by myself. Again, I suppose I felt that the *Mr. Wonderful* experience was most important in terms of showing me how I wouldn't flourish. I'm quite easily browbeaten and I'm not a banger of tables, that doesn't work for me. I'm not good in those environments. I yield quite easily. I knew that Saul had an incredibly strong personality and I couldn't imagine how I would flourish in a room where I was trying to make decisions and trying to look at an actor with this quite solid force around. It seemed like a controlling environment. I held out, and to Saul's great credit, he allowed me to pursue my own instincts, which was a very important moment because, really, there was a point where there was an absolute inertia between us. I just knew that I couldn't do that.

So I meet actors, I don't read with them. I like to be with them and feel whether I believe they will make me better and that I might make them better, that we can connect and see something in them that makes me think, "Here is what I want and can relate to." I feel like they might relax into something special, they may find a place of relaxation because I think most things to do with film have to do with relaxation. One of the only jobs a director has is to still the noise of the clock so that there is no clock, and no reason to feel threatened, no reason to do anything other than to relax into this work. That's easily said when there is only you and me here talking, but it is an incredibly hard thing to pull off on a set. "There's nobody else, it's just us. We can do what we want, it's all fine." There's this quiet work that has to happen and the set must be very still and quiet. That's what I've managed to do in the last few films, to make actors feel that they can't be wrong and that they're fine.

Sometimes I make mistakes in casting and don't know how to help. I let actors know my regard for them all the time. I remember speaking to a director once who said the important thing is to wrong foot an actor, never let them get comfortable. There is that whole theory. I don't feel that discomfort or chaos or pressure helps people's work.

MF: Subtext is obviously very important to your work. Many things are communicated indirectly, which is definitely a more subtle approach to cinema and results in more complex work.

AM: What I've come to understand is that the preparation for moments in films are as significant as the moments themselves. The deflections and inflections of context are everything. The place an audience is in when a moment occurs is as significant as the moment itself. In Chekhov, a groan or the failure to speak can acquire an enormous moment because of what the expectation of that gesture is. The profundity of any particular moment in a film or a play is as much determined by expectation and context as the particular event itself. The choreography of that becomes as significant as content.

Subsequently, I suppose, film language is what I've tried to grapple with. Walter [Murch] and I spend hours and hours talking about this stuff now, about how you speak to an audience. We were talking yesterday about the degree to which intention, however mangled in execution, however imprecise—you know, the failure of the light, the failure of the location, the failure of the performances, the failure of the writing—is all forgiven or absolved if intention is clear. The audience has this enormous ability to excavate intention if it's present and to identify the absence of intention, and enormous dissatisfaction occurs when the audience adjudicates there is no intention in the moment, there's simply a rehearsal of it. I've come to see more clearly that if you have purpose in a shot, if you have purpose in the movement of the camera, if you have purpose in the writing, the audience will extract it from you, however painfully or inefficiently it's presented. If there is no purpose, if it's simply the rehearsal of narrative or the rehearsal of character, then finally it's an unsatisfying experience for the audience.

Talking about actors, subtext is of course the thing they love. Actors love not playing the scene, working against the text, although understanding that the text maybe supports the scene's meaning. That's the most glorious thing you discover when you start studying someone like Chekhov. You realize that what people say is not the issue. It's what they fail to say, it's the smokescreen in the dialogue. I've been teaching recently a little bit. I find myself showing up in places to talk to writers and one of the things I always want to do is to make them think again about the value of dialogue. The movie is not the sum of what people say to each other, and what people say to each other is not necessarily the point. Dialogue is not about communicating. When people use it simply as a communicating device, it's often at its most thin point. Dialogue is action. Dialogue is action in the sense that my failure to say what I want to say, my lie, my obfuscation, is much more fascinating than being able to say it. Interviews are bizarre because interviews—this kind of interview, maybe not a press interview—is trying to get at the heart of something, whereas most of the time we're not using language in that way at all. We're using language as a way of defending ourselves and our emotions. Somebody said that animals don't have language because they don't need to disguise what they're feeling and thinking.

The Patient Englishman: Getting Personal with Anthony Minghella

Tomm Carroll / 1997

From *DGA Magazine* 22, no. 2 (May–June 1997). Permission to reprint courtesy of the Director's Guild of America, Inc.

After ten years of writing plays for Britain's stage and radio, and then television scripts for such English programs as *Inspector Morse* and *The Storyteller*, Anthony Minghella was given the opportunity to direct his first film, *Truly, Madly, Deeply*, from his own screenplay in 1991. Thanks to the acclaim of that small BBC-financed feature ("the thinking person's *Ghost*," it was proclaimed by enthusiastic critics), the British-born Italian suddenly found himself known—and in demand—in the US as a director. He next was hired to helm the script for *Mr. Wonderful*, shot in New York, two years later. That romantic comedy proved to be a learning experience for him—in more ways than one.

After that, Minghella labored for two years adapting Michael Ondaaje's allegedly unfilmable novel, *The English Patient*, into a screenplay. With the help of noted producer Saul Zaentz, and then Miramax (which stepped in when original distributor Twentieth Century Fox bowed out), he was able to complete *his* vision of the film—but not without a grueling four-months-plus of production on two continents. The result, as we all know, was critical and popular acclaim for *The English Patient*, as well as several guilds' and Academy Award honors, not the least of which was a Directors Guild of America Award and an Oscar for Minghella's direction.

A few days after his DGA Award win, the *DGA Magazine* caught up with Anthony Minghella over breakfast at the Four Seasons Hotel in Beverly Hills for a long chat about *The English Patient*, his career, the role of a writer-director, his philosophy of filmmaking, and the importance of remaining true to one's personal voice.

Tom Carroll: First of all, congratulations on winning the DGA Award for feature directing.

Anthony Minghella: Thank you. It was great for me. I felt so honored, so blessed by that award. It's exasperating the way it gets parlayed into Academy Award significance, whereas for me, the significance was to win that award. I was just thrilled. And I can't tell you what it meant for me as a validation of *The English Patient* and the work in the film. I'm a firm believer in guilds, and this recognition from the Directors Guild means a huge amount to me.

TC: Did you ever think that you'd receive such recognition on only your third feature?

AM: When [producer] Saul [Zaentz] and I began talking about this film four-and-a-half years ago or longer, we dreamt, as all filmmakers dream, about making a film that would excite us and move us and be the kind of film we would enjoy seeing ourselves. In terms of what my expectations were, my expectations were of surviving. I felt like I was clinging to the edge of a precipice nearly every day on this film—as a writer and as the director and then in the postproduction phase. It was such a monumental task that all I thought about was what was in front of me the next day, which was always, for me as an inexperienced director, a new and testing obstacle.

TC: I know you started out as an academic and as a playwright and then moved into television and radio writing and then, suddenly, you were a director on a feature that you wrote. How did that come about?

AM: Let me work backwards, rather than forwards. One thing is very clear to me—that the writing process in film is a continuous one, and I mean that in a literal and a metaphorical sense, insofar as that not only does the writer need to work throughout the film process and into the cutting room, but also that the director is a writer in film. Essentially, the director is the author. I know that's a contentious remark. I'm a writer first and foremost, but it's quite evident to me that the camera is the second pen at work in the film. So, if you're interested in being a filmmaker, it seems imperative that you continue that writing process with a camera.

It's an absolutely organic process to go from being a writer to some-body who writes and directs film. There doesn't seem to be any disloca-tion to me in that role.

TC: Were you a fan of the cinema?
AM: I've always been entranced by the cinema and I've always wanted to work in it. And I suppose what happened was that I discovered, as a writer, that I had an affinity for working with actors. It seemed a neces-sary process to become involved directly with them in filmmaking. Also, before I became an academic, I studied in music, art, literature, and his-tory, and those elements seemed to me to make up a great deal of what is required for filmmaking. So, I've been able to find an activity in my life which harnesses all the things I'm interested in; a place where I think more of my passions can be corralled than in any other activity.

I don't mean to dilute the role of screenplay writing, I just know that as a director, I'm able to direct from the first day I start writing. And as a writer, I'm able to write on the last day I'm directing. That, to me, is a wonderful opportunity and I've grasped it with as much skill as I have and as much commitment to it as I can muster.

TC: Why did you begin working in theatre?
AM: I suppose there's a very simple answer to that, which is that there was nothing else available to me when I started writing in the early eighties. There was no film industry to speak of in England. And what little there was was so remote that I think nearly all writers, directors, and actors in England begin their careers in the theatre because that's the dramatic arena available to them.

It's not accidental that Danny Boyle [*Trainspotting*] directed one of my early stage plays, and that my first experience of Mike Leigh [*Secrets and Lies*] was to walk onto his set as a young writer when he had a play on at Hampstead, and I was just about to have a play done myself. The theatre was our training ground.

Obviously, for film, that's a mixed blessing because theatre and film are very different forms of dramatic expression. What they both share, however, is a freedom of style that television hasn't embraced, in the sense that there's a fluidity of scene and transition and expression. Tele-vision favors naturalism. And film, in its structure, is not naturalistic. Nor, on the whole, is contemporary theatre. A great deal of what I've learned in the theatre is very valuable to me as a filmmaker. Not least is a real celebration of what actors can bring to both media, and how significant performances are.

Although I'm delighted to make cinematic films, and I desperately want to make films on a large canvas, I think that ultimately, I'd rather watch an actor against a wall opening up to the inner life, than to look at any ravishing vista.

TC: Tell me about *Truly, Madly, Deeply*, your feature debut.

AM: Well, I'd worked with the same group of actors again and again— particularly Juliet Stevenson, but also Alan Rickman, Michael Maloney, Colin Firth, and a whole group of actors who've become part of a loose repertory company, and I'd started to write specifically for them. Juliet is somebody I think of as being, without question, one of the most talented actresses working. I felt she had been adjudicated as a formidable, classical Shakespearean actress and, although it's true to say that she's a remarkable actress on the stage, the sense of her being quite severe and cerebral as an actress seemed to me to be so far from the person that I've worked with and from the joy that she has as a human being, that I wanted to write something for her which showed the whole range of her skills.

The reason that I directed *Truly, Madly, Deeply* had a quite prosaic and revealing history. I had started a television series as a writer in England called *Inspector Morse*, which had become very successful and, as much as I had enjoyed doing it, it wasn't personal and I was struggling to make personal statements as a writer. With each successive year, the producers would come to me and ask me to do some more scripts, and I would always try to find some way of not doing it. The fifth season, they came again and I said, "You know, I can't do any more of this." And they said, "Well, what about if we ask you to direct one?" They knew that I was interested in directing and, incidentally, had begun as a director in the theatre before I became a writer.

So I was very, very tempted, but *Inspector Morse* was so popular in England, and so many people watched it, that I felt very nervous of being exposed in such a way.

Then the BBC had called me and said they were starting a film division. They wanted to know if I would I like to write—and direct—the first screenplay. And the truth is, I felt that if I directed a small BBC film, it would be a much safer place to begin than in the glare of *Inspector Morse*, so I made the decision to make *Truly, Madly, Deeply*—not out of some act of bravery, but out of modesty in wanting to make my first film quietly.

And the irony is, of course, that that film then became the passport for me to become a filmmaker. It was seen by many, many more people than ever saw an episode of *Inspector Morse* and introduced me to America—not as a writer, which is what I'd been all the time, but as a director.

So, I became one by default, really. It's an interesting story of how fear can be as much of a compass as courage in these things. And it's also a testimony to the power of a working relationship, because I've always understood that in dramatic work, you ride on the shoulders of your collaborators and you're only raised as high as they can carry you. And I think that I've been incredibly lucky to work with people who've dignified my writing and my directing.

TC: I find it interesting that of your three features, your first was an original screenplay, your second was from a script by other writers, and your third was adapted from a novel. Which of those situations do you prefer, and how do they affect your directing the material?

AM: Well, *Truly, Madly, Deeply*, which is a film that means an enormous amount to me as a personal statement, was a summary of the kind of work I had been doing as a writer—which isn't to say that I don't perceive it as a film, but I think that it's celebrating an actress [Stevenson] and the nature of our working history together. I would be quite forlorn if that were to be the last personal film I'd made.

When I made *Mr. Wonderful*, I was delighted to have the option to make a film in America, to work in filmmaking on a slightly larger—although still modest—scale, in which I was able to learn some more of my craft. The studio [Samuel Goldwyn Company] had a perception of what the film should be, which wasn't entirely the same as my own. In a confrontational way, there was a certain amount of give-and-take in terms of trying to connect my vision with theirs, and I think there was some loss involved because ultimately, the dilution of the filmmaker's voice—good or bad—is unfortunate. In the compromise and the negotiation, there's an inevitable move towards the general and away from the particular, and I think that it's in the particular that films live or die.

I don't want to apologize for a film I'm happy to have made. But I know it's not a personal film, certainly not as personal as I would have chosen it to have been, despite the fact that I had a wonderful producer, Maryann Maloney, and a very good working experience. I worked hard on [developing] the script and, obviously, found ways of insinuating a great number of my own interests into the project. I'm of Italian origin [like the Annabella Sciorra character in *Mr. Wonderful*], and I wanted to try and bring some of that immigrant experience to bear on the material that Vicky [Polon] and Amy [Schor] had written. I also wanted to introduce an element that was very personal to me, which is the struggle to escape one's roots and the irresistible tug of one's roots. So, Annabella's character, who moves away from a blue-collar environment to try and live in an academic one, absolutely parallels my own struggle with my father—who's a great man; he's an ice cream seller who didn't have any education at all and came [to England] from Italy without anything—and my own experience growing up living in an extremely blue-collar world, which I tried to get as far away from as I possibly could as an adult, only to find that that's my home and my world and my family in every sense. The ironies of wanting to escape, only to arrive back precisely where you came from, but perhaps changed, is my own experience and I tried to color in the character of Annabella in that film with my own reconciling of a life of the mind and of one's roots.

So the whole story in the film—her university life, her collision with the academic world, then her return and her attempt to marry the past and the present—is something that I see as a personal journey as much as a fictional one in that film. But at the same time, the story structure and the impulse of the film doesn't belong to me at all, and I wouldn't want it to. When I look at the film, it seems to me to belong much more to the studio than it belongs to me.

TC: What do you think you learned from that experience?
AM: Perhaps that I'm not as good at making studio films as I am at making my own films, and that there's something to be said for nursing my own passions, wrongheaded or otherwise, and reconciling myself to my own voice. One of the things that we all struggle with is, first of all, identifying what our voice is, and then reconciling ourselves to it because often we want to be other filmmakers, other directors, other writers. This instinct to try to be somebody else, to try and trade in your voice for one that you admire more, is one that you ultimately have to resist.

TC: What about adapting *The English Patient*?
AM: One of the things that characterizes *The English Patient* is how idiosyncratic it is to my own taste and judgment. I think you have to live or die by that, and I made a very conscious decision to be more steely about pursuing a vision. And I was lucky to work with a producer like Saul [Zaentz], who not only supported the vision I had of the film, but he insisted on it, which is a very different thing. He didn't just defend it,

he attacked me to insure that I had a vision, and for that I'm so much in his debt.

Although *The English Patient* is an adaptation, it feels by far the most personal film I've made because it doesn't have the reticence of *Truly, Madly, Deeply* in terms of its directing ambitions. And at the same time, despite the fact that I was adapting somebody else's book, there was so much space in that project for me to work, there was so much opportunity for me to write as a writer, and not as an editor, that I see as many of my preoccupations and follies at play in *The English Patient* as I do in *Truly, Madly, Deeply*. I think that, despite the differences in scale, surface quality and production value in the two films, they seem to be intrinsically related. They have the same preoccupation with healing and damage and the capacity that people have to hurt and heal each other in the name of love. The same focus on small details of behavior, the same investment in what an actor can tell you in a film. They both give over a great deal of the weight of the event to performance and they're also, I think, ultimately more concerned with the humanity of cinema, than with anything else.

They're human films, and I think that's true with *Mr. Wonderful* as well. I've tried not to judge the behavior in the work that I do; if a writer or director judges behavior, it gives nothing for the audience to do. It closes the moral circle of the film, and presents and demonstrates feeling and emotions, rather than asking you to participate in the struggle that people have.

TC: Do you think you ever would direct another screenplay that wasn't yours?

AM: It's very unlikely that I'll direct anyone else's screenplay in the future, because I think it's inappropriate, ultimately, for the director to trample on the vision of the writer, or to try and appropriate that vision. It's forcing material into places where it naturally doesn't want to go, forcing a genre perhaps to accommodate more than it's able to. It seems to me to be a much more sensible and sane route to develop material that either comes directly from me, or from a source other than a screenplay.

TC: You prefer being a writer-director.

AM: The advantage I have when I walk on a set with my own writing is that I know every beat and impulse and nuance of it because it's come directly through me, and so there's nothing I don't know about the screenplay. It means I'm free to let go of it completely.

I was talking to [actor] James Woods, and he said that he's always found that writer-directors are the least preoccupied with the writing because they know that the writing is transitional, that it's part of a longer journey.

But I also think there are lots of incredible directors out there who can direct screenplays, who know what it is to animate other people's writing. I don't have that experience and I don't know if I have that skill. I think it's a very different skill from directing your own work. I'm enormously respectful of those directors who know how to respect the writer and still leave their signature on their movies. And I think of directors like Sydney Pollack and Mike Nichols—directors I admire very much working now who have a very particular style as directors, and yet know how to bring the best out of the writers they work with. That's what they're good at. I think that my small piece of ground to plow involves generating the material myself.

TC: You spoke of the similarities between *Truly, Madly, Deeply* and *The English Patient* concerning love, healing, cruelty, and betrayal. In watching your films again, I realize that *Mr. Wonderful* fits in with that theme as well. In the first film, you have Alan Rickman coming back from the dead and Juliet Stevenson is truly, madly, deeply in love with him, but it turns out he came back to push her into continuing on with life, and with Michael Maloney, at the end. In *Mr. Wonderful*, you've got the premise that Matt Dillon is trying to marry off ex-wife Annabella Sciorra to avoid the alimony payments, only to come around and fall back in love with her. In *The English Patient*, too, Kristin Scott Thomas's husband kept allowing these situations to occur where she would be alone with Ralph Fiennes. All three deal with the idea of pushing the women characters into a kind of healing betrayal . . .

TC: You've done your homework. It's very disconcerting to realize how narrow a vein one is investigating as a writer and as a filmmaker. I probably shouldn't know too much about those things.

But I think fiction has some obligations. It's very hard to explain why it is that human beings sit in dark rooms and watch other people pretending to feel things and do things and say things. And it's a very rare moment when anyone ever questions why there are films, why there are plays, why there are pieces of literature. The only answer that made any sense to me is that we have fiction in order to enlarge experience. We only have a very small series of relationships ourselves, so we look to fiction to give us some way of measuring our experience against the way that other people may respond in similar circumstances, or in circumstances we can't hope to experience ourselves, so that we become larger in some ways as individuals.

Stories exist in order to do two things: to enlarge experience and also to force us into perspectives that we're not otherwise afforded. We can't be the jilted husband, the wronged wife, the dying woman, the detective, and the murderer in our own experience, but we can be through the prisms of fiction. So if films or plays or novels are working, we're forced to inhabit perspectives we could never experience in our own lives.

What you would want from a piece of fiction is for it to make all of us less misanthropic and more generous toward the experience of being human, which isn't the same thing as endorsing adultery, or murder or cruelty. But it's a reminder that there is no secure moral framework that is available to us, that we are the sum of our choices and that our choices, on the whole, are made for the best possible reasons. The cruelty of being alive is that in the pursuit of our own morality, we seem so easily to trample over other people's. We seem so efficient in damaging others. And that's the world I feel I live in and I want to rehearse it for others.

I feel strongly that the one obligation that makers of fiction have is to try to tell the truth as best as they understand it about the experience of being alive.

TC: What was it that drew you to make *The English Patient* into a film?
AM: First of all, it's the richest piece of literature I can remember reading in recent times; rich in its ideas, its images, its meditations, and its journey, which is so transporting. I love the book, and that's a very useful emotion to have when you're setting off on a complex project.

There's such a striving in the novel to make connections between the sum of individual action and history. It says that history is not something going on outside a room, it's the sum of the personal action and choice. In times of impending war, the membrane between personal behavior and the public world in history is much finer and so it's much easier to detect the relationship. Obviously, in this story, the personal betrayals and the historical betrayals are the same thing, so that really intrigued me because it's a preoccupation I've had for a long time before I encountered Michael Ondaatje's writing.

That seems to me to be the perfect material for filmmaking because the sentence of filmmaking is not made up of nouns and adjectives and verbs and adverbs, it's made up of shots and sizing and positions. So you're able and obliged to make connections between the small and the large, between the contraction and expansion of the iris, which is what the sentence of filmmaking is.

Also, I thought [*The English Patient*] was such an opportunity to work on this [larger] scale because the danger is that you get compartmentalized so quickly that people think they know who you are from the first piece of your work that they come across. Every piece of work I was offered or encouraged to pursue after *Truly, Madly, Deeply* was miniature because that was what that film is. It's a miniature film, but my instincts have much more do to with the cinema of film.

I think it's evident in *The English Patient* that storytelling with images is as exciting to me as language, but because I'm an academic, because I'm a writer, the quite natural estimation of me would be that I would be interested in literary films or films in which language is most potent. In fact, as a writer I always thought that dialogue is the least interesting part of the job. It's often in the lapses between language, in the distance between what people want to say and what they do say, between the emotion and the stated position [that I find most interesting]. Those things preoccupy me a great deal more than epigrams or fine writing. Not only that, but I think that the architecture of writing—what scene happens next, where a scene begins, who's in the scene—excites me more to talk about and to investigate than any one line in a film.

What I loved in this project is that I knew that I would have to go away and bring back visual material that would tell the story at least as powerfully as anything that anybody said. That opportunity to make a film on a canvas which was a painter's canvas and not a writer's one was a real thrill and a real challenge to me.

TC: The visuals and the entire look of the film were outstanding, but what stood out the most for me was the editing, the production design, and the cinematography. Did you work very closely with Walter Murch, Stuart Craig, and John Seale, respectively?
AM: Yes. The most exciting part of this film was in the cutting room because, first of all, I was working with a master: Walter Murch. It's very hard not to bow down in the presence of someone like Walter because his challenges and his arguments were so exciting and so rigorous that it was a constant education and joy to me. The struggle to make sense of a film is the best reason to be doing it. We focused on transitions almost every day—what the film required and how to best braid the different narratives so that they felt seamless. The work he did on the sound with

his collaborators—Pat Jackson and the other people there—to make up the sounds was fabulous also.

I think Stuart's work in the film is unsung for the best possible reason—because it's invisible. This is a man who is absolutely involved with every set-up; there's no accidental detail in the frame. You're not conscious when you watch *The English Patient* of how designed the film is, but it's *completely* designed in the strictest sense. Often what appeared to be location shots were actually constructed. There is no world, so you're constructing. There is no Cairo, 1935–36 to go and find. There is no desert with a cave of swimmers that we could get to. And so we had to make everything. We made a church. We made a monastery. We found a garden we liked, we found a set of stairs we liked and we found some trees we liked and then around that we designed a building on the stage and on location. I felt often in this film as if he were teaching me that the responsibility to directing is to create a world. His work was vital.

With John, you have the luxury of having a cinematographer who literally becomes your eye. We met many, many times and scouted the film together with Stuart. We were able to come up with some quite solid ground rules for the filmmaking and those were largely connected with color and palette, whereby a certain set of colors were reserved for the desert and all scenes connected with Cairo and Africa, and another set of colors and light was reserved for Italy. The rule of thumb we came up with was to imagine that the desert was made by a graphic designer, where the images were simple and bold and reflected in some way the purity of the desert where there are very few colors and very few lines. There are very strong horizontals, very few verticals and a starkness of look. John had to produce those images.

One of the things that kept occurring to me while I was making the film was that in a novel, you have this great facility at your disposal, where you can write a single line and the audience fills in [the rest]. That's the joy of reading—one sentence can evoke pre-war Cairo. It has to mention a scent or describe a piece of architecture, or the way a woman walks, and the mind develops that into a full-fledged image.

Film is the most prosaic medium around because you turn the camera on and if there's nothing in front of it, it doesn't record it. There's nothing suggestive about the camera. It's literal. It records the information available with the lighting. And so we had to create from scratch a world that was as transporting to the viewer as Michael's book was to the reader.

John was responsible for that. It was 124 days of principal photography; it was relentless. We were moving the whole time. We had very few facilities. We were trying to make a huge film on a modest budget. He was the operator as well as the DP, and it was an enormous test of his determination to pull the film off. He's absolutely indefatigable as a co-worker.

TC: The film certainly has an amazing look to it . . .

AM: What's great, of course, is that all these people are being recognized. The various guilds have been very quick to celebrate the work and I think it's marvelous that John and Stuart and Walter have won their respective guild awards. There's one person's name in the front of the film, who is the filmmaker, and then there's a whole lot of credits at the end—and they are the filmmakers as well. The orchestral analogy is the perfect one. Every member of the orchestra is a vital element in the music, and the job of the conductor is simply to bring the best out of all of them. My job is to give them a score, but I'm not playing anything.

TC: A lot has been written about the struggle to get *The English Patient* done with Fox, and then Miramax stepping into the breach and saving the day. What is your take on that?

AM: I have a very strong take on all of this. It's untrue to say that Fox pulled out of the film. I think what happened was that there was too much distance between our view of the film as filmmakers and what they saw as their responsibilities as film sellers, which was ultimately that their evaluation of the film was lower than ours. They wanted to give less money than we [needed] to make the film with. It was a divorce on irreconcilable differences; and I think it was a mutual divorcing rather than an abandonment, which is how it's been characterized in the press. And I feel badly in a way that Fox has taken unnecessary and injudicious flack for that. It's just this fight between this scale of budget and what the studio thinks it's getting for that investment.

As far as I'm concerned, the mistake was that they underestimated two things. One was the appropriateness of my casting choices. Our mantra was, "Don't use a star to introduce this film to an audience. Make the film the star." And that's exactly what happened. It didn't need a film star for the film to work. In fact, in many ways, Saul and I both felt a film star would puncture the skin of the film, that it would become personality-oriented and people would be viewing our film with the obstacle of a film star rather than the blessing of a film star.

And the second thing is that there's no button on their calculator for emotion. When they're doing their numbers, it's very hard to imagine the emotional impact of the film at the point where it exists only on 120 pieces of paper. I was convinced that the film would not only be ravishing to look at, but emotionally ravishing as well, and that the audience is hungry for that and desperate to be treated as grown-ups. I think the idea that you make films that appeal to you as a filmgoer got lost somewhere in the Hollywood equation because, understandably, they've had such marvelous results when they've let go of that equation. Ultimately, the awards and accolades are secondary in their minds to the accounts at the end of the year—and their accounts are very healthy.

Thank God, they were wrong.

TC: What about Miramax?

AM: Thank God for Miramax, because what's absolutely extraordinary about Bob and Harvey [Weinstein] is that they have no fear. They're not looking over their shoulders to account to anybody, not even Disney, for what they want to do. They don't work from fear, they work from excitement and conviction and they were excited and convinced by the screenplay and by our plans for the film. They focused their energies on how to introduce the film to an audience, which they've done magnificently. They've been marvelous colleagues. And they're being amply rewarded for that faith.

I think that's a lesson—if you invest in filmmakers, there's potentially a great reward. The Barton Fink scenario doesn't have to apply, which is that you take your Barton Fink and try to make him into somebody else. On the whole, it seems better if you take your Cameron Crowes or your Scott Hickses or Mike Leighs and say, "Oh, good, I'm working with Cameron Crowe or Scott Hicks or Mike Leigh, and that's why they're here." And not to be surprised when you get a Cameron Crowe or a Scott Hicks or a Mike Leigh film back, which is what so often happens. There's no point in investing in an Anthony Minghella and saying, "My God, I've got an Anthony Minghella film. What do I do?" Miramax's great triumph is that they invest in filmmakers because they want their films.

TC: Speaking of an Anthony Minghella film, what is your next project?

AM: I'm looking to make a film of a radio play called *Cigarettes and Chocolate*, which I wrote about eight years ago. It's about a woman who stops talking. It's the one piece of writing that I'm most proud of, and it's also the most personal piece of writing of mine. The idea of the film is that one day this woman stops talking, apparently for no reason. And all the people around her come to the conclusion that it's something they've done, only to find out that the reason she's stopped talking has nothing to do with any of them.

I'm also working with Sydney Pollack's company, Mirage, on *The Times of Mr. Ripley*, which I've adapted from Patricia Highsmith's book. That's a film I want to make very much. Sydney's been a great mentor and guide to me. He was very supportive through *Truly, Madly, Deeply* and I became friends with him. I invited him up to the cutting room with *The English Patient*, and he read every draft of the script and I felt delighted in his wisdom.

And there are all kinds of other things on the horizon—the utmost of which, to be honest with you, is to go home because I have this obsession with the fact that home is the only place where you can make proper choices. And I haven't been home for over two years, so I don't know what is a good step for me. I think the one thing I must not do is become paralyzed by *The English Patient*, because I think somebody's written quite cogently about the phenomenon of directors becoming marooned by success. And given that I'm so early on in my filmmaking career, the best thing I can do is to make some films and not worry too much about the other end of the process; just keep learning about the business of filmmaking.

TC: Who would you cite as your influences as filmmakers?

AM: Billy Wilder recently told me how much he admired [*The English Patient*], while I was able to tell him at some length how much I admired him and how much he had led the way for so many directors of my generation. I think he's a wonderful filmmaker and I'm a great fan of his. And Fred Zinnemann's *From Here to Eternity* is a film which has a great deal to say about the way I made *The English Patient*.

But chiefly, I would say that the films which have influenced me have come out of Italy, the ones that I was brought up and raised on—the films of Fellini, Visconti, DeSica, Rossellini, and the Taviani Brothers I think are wonderful filmmakers. *The Tree of the Wooden Clogs* is a film that I've gone back to again and again in my life. *I Vitelloni*, Fellini's biographical film, is probably my favorite film. I've discovered that I've always gone to Italy as an inspiration, and also it's where my sensibility resides.

And finally, the cinema I find to be the most exciting at the moment is Chinese. And I think the greatest living filmmaker is Zhang Yimou, the director who made *Raise the Red Lantern*, *Ju Dou*, and *Red Sorghum*. He is a masterful director of image and actor.

TC: From your brief but celebrated experience, do you have any advice to give to young filmmakers today?

AM: Well, one is to make peace with your own voice. That's one thing I've learned. The other one is that perseverance furthers, as the Chinese say. Your will is your best ally. If you try to second guess what will work, you're lost. The minute you surrender your taste to the taste of others, it's over. It's the deaf ear and the hearing ear; you have to have one ear that is so wide open to advice and to other people's wisdom, and one ear that is so deaf to invasion. It's just learning whom to let in the deaf ear and whom to let in the hearing ear, and that's a trick I don't think any of us ever learn.

I Don't Have a Speech. I Look Terrible in a Tuxedo. What Could Possibly Go Right?

Anthony Minghella / 1997

Monday 17 March

This isn't really a proper diary, of course. I've never kept one. Rather, this is penance for missing my advertised *Observer* interview at the Barbican on a day when I found myself scheduled to be in three different countries at the same time. It's a problem I have, saying no. And there's rampant expurgation here, too—not simply because I am currently so starved of an inner life, nor to dignify myself, nor to protect anybody; it's just that otherwise I would be recording an unholy catalogue of pampering, anxiety, solipsism, hubris, exhaustion, and despair. The gnomic version of this account is that I am being made a fuss of. My parents, who make ice cream on the Isle of Wight, have graduated from Golden Globe Delight and are busily concocting Oscar Orange. Flavor of the month. How apt. I've spent my whole life being reminded that everything will melt away. A taste, then, of Minghella ice cream.

I don't have my old job any more. I have surrendered to some virus which renders me incapable of the most mundane tasks. Nice people escort me everywhere. I am handed sheets of paper which tell me my day. I am collected, groomed, briefed, watered, driven, led to a chair. This has been going on for months. In the past two weeks alone, I have criss-crossed the Atlantic three times. My life is measured out in airport lounges and hotel rooms and column inches. I no longer have conversations. I'm interviewed. I have suggested to my friends at Miramax that they stop publishing the box office grosses of the film in favor of my air miles. I am intimately connected to my suitcases. I know my suitcases well. When this is all over, I am retiring them, battered servants. Then I am taking a vow of silence.

I'd love to stay immune, of course, from the puff, from this rosary of award ceremonies, but I am not. Instead, I am grossly inflated by winning the Director's Guild of America award a week ago, suitably punctured by failing to win at the Writer's Guild ceremony last night, delighted by the triumphs of the other members of the production team, while reciting the mantra that we're not horses in a race, but filmmakers blessed by the resounding welcome *The English Patient* has received. Meanwhile, the betting is on, the odds are printed, and preparations for the main event are in full swing.

My hotel room here at the Four Seasons is part delicatessen, part florist, part off-license, part souvenir shop. This morning, I received a basket of hair and body unguents from my "new friends" at a salon in Beverly Hills. Jewelers send over brochures, optical specialists offer sunglasses, the concierge drops by with a pair of possible shoes, a massage therapist is standing by for a complimentary rub. Flowers from strangers. Telephone calls from strangers. I listen incessantly to Bach and the new Van Morrison. Great solace, both. "This weight—it's bringing me down," Van moans on my behalf. "Hollywood, it ain't no good." Although, in truth, Hollywood is being very good to me. I'm Bottom the Weaver granted a glimpse of life as King of the Fairies. And, of course, I like it. I could get used to it. But I am most definitely wearing an ass's head.

These have been strange days since the film's release. My notebook conjures some indelible occasions: fetching up late one night at a tiny bar in Old Tokyo—La Jettée—where Juliette Binoche and I decorated a bottle of whisky which will remain there alongside the collection of similarly adorned bottles, all by filmmakers, until somebody else from our crew visits and can drink from what is now the official *English Patient* bottle (we tippled from Kieslowski's *Blue*); a reading with Michael Ondaatje at New York's Town Hall, where fifteen hundred people crammed in; live fish and crabs being carried, flapping, in paper bags to our dinner table in Hong Kong; an all-night procession of interviews on John Seale's rainy terrace in Sydney the night our nominations were announced, when I was so humbled by my seventy-six-year-old producer's stamina that I determined to match him phone call for phone call until 6:30 in the morning; hiding in a reeking alley by the Curzon Mayfair in London with Ralph and Kristin on the night of the British premiere, waiting to be rescued from a terrifying pack of photographers; a young Taiwanese critic so moved by the film that she begins to weep during our live radio interview; hanging out on a street corner in Madrid with a jovial Almodóvar as he set up for a night shoot; an audience with Billy Wilder at the Producer's Guild Awards in Los Angeles, where his enthusiasm for the film sent me scurrying to a phone so that I could ring all my cronies and recite exactly what he'd said; and, most fun, being repeatedly mistaken for Billy Bob Thornton (writer, director, and star of the remarkable *Slingblade*), for whom I've signed autographs and given interviews, until the hapless questioner realizes there's something seriously amiss with my accent. At the Oscar Nominees Lunch, we swapped name tabs and I wore his trademark cap—throwing the photographers, who this year have had to learn a whole lexicon of new names, into confusion.

Tuesday 18 March

Went last night to see a rough cut of a new movie, *Home Grown*, by my friend Steve Gyllenhaal. Billy Bob is in it, of course. And so we ran into each other again. He wants me to be in his next film. I love this idea. Acting is so much faster than directing—I've spent over four years writing and making *The English Patient*. Then back to Steve's house with his wife—the writer Naomi Foner—and Steven Soderbergh for a long, exhilarating dissection of the film. America is so good at this sharing of skills. Sydney Pollack came several times to Berkeley when I was editing and gave me an invaluable chunk of his experience, challenging our cut and sharing his wisdom. I try to be half as constructive with Steve's film.

Today I had lunch with Bill Horberg, who's one of the producers on the film I'm supposed to be making next—an adaptation I've done of Patricia Highsmith's *The Talented Mr. Ripley*. Bill's smart enough to know that I have a bag of Liquorice Allsorts for a brain at the moment and that the prospect of ever doing this again is terrifying.

In a day punctuated with interviews, I spend a couple of hours with my agent, Michael Peretzian, and my lawyers, Barry Hirsch and Marcy Morris. They are benign counselors and longtime friends who have grown accustomed to my career vacillations. I leave with some clear advice, but by the time I get back to my room it's fractured into riddles— don't make a small film next, don't fall into the trap of making a big one, it would be a good idea to work with an American movie star, better to stay home and write something I believe in, important to grasp the opportunities suddenly on offer to me, work from the heart, money's not important, it's about time I earned some money. . . . I'm still thinking of this when I go with Cheryl Maisel, my shepherd, for A Fitting. Cheryl works with the PR company who organize my days here, and she has minded me, protected me, beaten me into shape, escorted me, and generally kept me out of trouble. She has arranged for Donna Karan to make me a tuxedo for Monday. The tailor, a Russian woman whom I know only as Laura of Beverly Hills (from the sign on her store), is a genius. She suffers my body with dignity, chalking and pinning. I have a rare ability to make fabulous clothes look disgraceful. Cheryl frowns, but insists I'm going to look fine.

Then it's precious night off and dinner with my friends Julian Sands and Evgenia Citkowitz, who have provided me with an oasis during this craziness. I go to their beautiful house above *The English Patient* billboard on Sunset Boulevard. Julian humbles me with accounts of his exploits. He is a real-life Almasy (the Ralph Fiennes character in our film), who revels in exploration and adventures, and who is in obscenely good shape. As always, I leave promising myself to get fit, to go trekking, to learn about gardens, to get a life.

Back in my room, I collect my e-mail messages and write my nightly note to my family. I am evangelical about this new technology. I swear it's kept me sane. I write down all my fears and press a button which sends them to Hampstead. In exchange, I receive Carolyn's constancy and scraps of news from home—Max's day at school, a bulletin on the state of our house and its predilection to rival the tower at Pisa.

Wednesday 19 March

John and Duncan, who try forlornly to manage my financial affairs, visit the hotel to explain to me that I must stop spending money until I earn some. I go back to my notes from yesterday's meeting. It's a strange phenomenon that I can have made a film which will shortly gross $100 million and still be broke. My last pay check was in September. I promise myself that I will leave the room the next time someone suggests I defer my salary to get a film made. I must have a sign over my head which says "Will Defer."

More interviews. Another Fitting. Laura of Beverly Hills is disturbed by the folds in my suit. I explain that there's only so long a man can suck in his stomach.

I meet Lindsay Doran for lunch, new head of United Artists, and an old pal. She wants to know what I'm doing next. Not deferring, is my considered response. Mindful of my trousers, I resist the fantastic pasta at Toscana and pick sourly at a salad. Laura of Beverly Hills would be proud of me.

David Cronenberg had invited me to a screening of *Crash*, and so I turn up in a tracksuit top and jeans, only to discover it's an incredibly glamorous premiere, there's a press line, and I'm suddenly quizzed on camera about my attitude to censorship, my response to a film I've yet to see. The Liquorice Allsorts rattle about. I buckle up carefully on the drive home. No sign of Billy Bob today, although I did manage an autograph on his behalf.

Thursday 20 March

Meetings, interviews. The Four Seasons is filling up with arriving nominees. I love the staff here, who are unabashed *English Patient* fans, and spoil me rotten. It's 95 degrees. I drive to a meeting at Sony and pass a hundred signs reminding me that the Academy Awards are looming. The whole town is dizzy with Oscar fever. I can't bear to pick up a paper or turn on a radio. I get lost in the bowels of Sony Studios and arrive twenty-five minutes late. John Calley, who recently took over, is my friend and mentor. We spend a jolly hour discussing a book they have which is on offer for me to adapt and direct. It seems impossible to me. Just up your street, he suggests mischievously. John is a longtime partner of Mike Nichols and I tell him of Mike's message to me about the Oscars: "If you lose," he told me, "you will experience real magic. When your name isn't called, you become instantly invisible. This will last for several days." As I recount this observation, it absolutely ceases to amuse me.

On the way back, Van the Man is growling in my car. This weight is still weighing on his heart. I sing along with the windows down. The William Morris Agency is throwing a cocktail party for me at the Bel Air hotel. Johnny, my best friend from London, has turned up hugging a stack of letters from home.

I fish out the back copies of the *Portsmouth Football Mail* and devour them in a corner. Kristin has arrived from London. She looks dazzling, and I marvel at the transformation the success of the film has wrought on her. She has become a movie star. The room swivels with her every move.

Later, I take Johnny to another reception, this time for Frances Mc-Dormand, nominated for her brilliant performance in *Fargo*. About half of the nominees are at this bash. We end up on the terrace in various permutations.

I run into Eric Fellner, one half of Working Title, the company which produced *Fargo*. I have never been anywhere in Los Angeles without running into Eric. This would be a strange thing even if he actually lived here, but he doesn't. At this point, Billy Bob shows up. There are only twenty-eight people in my world at the moment. Johnny gets into a deep tryst with Gillian Anderson of *X-Files* fame. She tells us that she once lived in Crouch End, my old stomping ground. Naturally.

Friday 21 March

Another fitting. More pins, more chalk. I swear to Laura that my body is exactly the same one I brought in on Wednesday.

I have a television interview. The interviewer wants me to confirm that Miramax have bought the grosses on the film (meaning that they've spent so much on advertising that the public feel obliged to show up), have somehow extracted the nominations with a clever marketing campaign, but that no one in Hollywood will actually vote for us because of their irritation that we're not a studio picture, and how many Oscars do I expect to win. The Liquorice Allsorts jumble around. I point out that Hollywood is a district not a group of people, that it was members of the Academy who voted for the nominations, that these same members will vote for the winners, that it's a testimony to the generosity of the movie business here that they are so prepared to embrace filmmakers from all over the world, that Miramax have worked miracles on a modest publicity budget, that the film didn't get any better for having twelve nominations and won't get any worse if it doesn't win any of them. Then I go back to my room and call my agent and tell him that nobody in Hollywood is going to vote for us because they hate the fact that we're independent and foreign.

I ring my parents and advise my father to cancel Oscar Orange because we're going to be a statistic, that I have it on authority that we can't win anything. Then it's off to a party for Diane Keaton, who arrives as I'm leaving, and a dinner for Madonna, who appears to have left just before I arrived. "Hollywood, it ain't no good," laments the unhappy Mr. Morrison as I drive home.

Saturday 22 March

My family are arriving today, along with the rest of the *English Patient* contingent, including my partner-in-crime, Saul Zaentz. This is a good thing. Saul and Carolyn are the two people who know how to sort me out. Saul achieves this by settling me with his indomitable confidence, Carolyn with her indomitable sweetness.

Someone once described a pessimist as a person forced to live with an optimist. I've lived with Saul for the past four years and he has turned me into the most negative person imaginable, but like all depressives I long for a bit of yang to go with my yin. He has no truck with my predictions and reminds me that I've taken the dim view as a matter of course throughout our adventure. His typical retort to my downcast musings is "That doesn't make any sense." This is his favorite phrase, and hearing it makes me feel instantly chipper.

Carolyn is altogether different balm, and her appearance has the effect of turning the strange life into a familiar one. I unravel. The children are very excited. Hannah comes flushed with the delicious prospect of turning eighteen on Monday, eleven-year-old Max with a list of parties he wants to attend after the Oscars and an autograph priority. Nobody loves movies more than my son. His latest passion is for Baz Luhrmann's *Romeo + Juliet*, which, in Max's opinion, is without doubt the best film of the year. His most important mission is to meet Leonardo DiCaprio, Gwyneth Paltrow, and Quentin Tarantino. He arrives sporting a *Romeo + Juliet* cap, which I ask him to remove. Carolyn has her own outfit anxieties and we repair to Laura of Beverly Hills. My jacket is now crooked. Laura glares at my waistline. Carolyn's dress is dazzling, but this doesn't interrupt another bout of chalking and pinning. Strange undergarments are donned and discarded. I am struck by the appropriateness of this metaphor for the event. Practically every nominee will be turning up at the awards in borrowed clothes.

I attend a lunch for foreign directors and am moved to tears by the discussion at the table. In what seemed to me to be a horribly contrived formality, we are asked to speak in turn about our experiences filming in countries other than our own, and about language in cinema. But after a glorious hour listening to twenty distinguished directors from all over the world, culminating in Ronald Neame explaining that his story about the problems of language would refer to the introduction of sound on the first movie he worked on—Hitchcock's *Blackmail*—I find myself delighted to be invited to drink in the collective wisdom on offer. Film is such a new thing and, at that table, Billy Wilder its uncrowned king. I was reminded of my great luck, and that what I'm doing only began in a time still retrievable by living witnesses. Whatever happens, I've been allowed at the table.

I hurry off to a BAFTA tea and am instantly plunged into gloom by the gauntlet of journalists, all pressing me for my predictions of Monday's outcome. I have nothing to say. Nor does there seem to be any tea.

Sunday 23 March

It's open house at the hotel all morning and we receive a torrent of visitors, faxes, flowers, bottles of champagne. The eve of a wedding or a funeral. The Liquorice Allsorts have congealed into a sort of glob in my head. I am, to be blunt, in a funk.

Later, Miramax hold their own pre-Oscar ceremony, where we are all winners and receive chocolate statues. I would be content to let it go at that. The event sees Harvey Weinstein at his very best and we are forced to earn our awards with party pieces. I have first to read a speech from *Slingblade* as Carl and then to direct Juliette and Kristin in an improvised scene from Miramax's upcoming film of *Absolutely Fabulous*. The women bring the house down. These charades are the closest I've come to working in months and I derive ludicrous pleasure from them. I interrogate Billy Bob about the size of my part in his movie. I don't want a cameo. Michael Ondaatje arrives with his family. If nothing else, the Oscars have allowed us the most glorious reunion. Saul, Michael, and I huddle together and remind ourselves that the film has succeeded beyond our wildest dreams, that we're friends for life come what may. This is all completely true and, right now, no comfort whatsoever. I get back to the hotel and discover my dinner jacket hanging on the door. It looks like a sad man.

Monday 24 March

The next time I go to bed, it will be over. I wake up at dawn and stare at the ceiling. We have a plan to escape Los Angeles tomorrow at the first opportunity. I grope for the Advil and my daily fix of vitamin B. We have a long breakfast with Hannah, who is radiant and relaxed. How did she get to be eighteen? This is the proper thing to celebrate. My wonderful daughter. I refuse to get dressed. If I don't get dressed then I won't have to go. I haven't allowed myself to write out an acceptance speech. This casts an additional pall over the morning. What happens if I actually have to go and stand in front of a billion people and have nothing to say?

The ceremony, which begins at seven, requires us to be there a couple of hours earlier, so that we can be grilled along the course of the red carpet by the army of international journalists—a tradition I'd hitherto only enjoyed mocking on television. Working back from this, and the fact that there will be a thousand limousines heading to the same destination, means that we have to be ready to leave the hotel at 3:30. At three, I'm still in my dressing gown. Hannah and Carolyn emerge in all their finery. I put on my clothes and we get in the car.

As we wind towards the Shrine, we can see helicopters hovering. The children tell me that people have been camping out for days to catch a glimpse of the event. I want to say that I've been working for years for the same privilege. It's not that I need to win, it's that I need to finish.

We arrive, it's mayhem, and I'm suddenly calm. I cheerfully negotiate the press line, see all the familiar faces, good people all of them— Mike Leigh, Brenda Blethyn, Billy Bob, Scott Hicks, Joel Coen, Cameron Crowe, Milos Forman, and my lot—Ralph, Kristin, Juliette, Saul. And then we're inside and Billy Crystal is on stage and they're opening the envelopes . . . and I didn't know what to say, and it doesn't matter, and the next time I go to bed I'm on an island a thousand miles from Los Angeles and the blessings keep coming.

The Talented Mr. Minghella

Richard Stayton / 2000

From *Written By*, February 2000. Reprinted by permission of the author.

Revered mystery writer Patricia Highsmith has challenged numerous filmmakers throughout the decades, from Hitchcock's *Strangers on a Train* to Wim Wenders's *The American Friend*. Her most challenging creation is not a story so much as a character: the deadly chameleon Tom Ripley. In his first film since earning a Best Director Academy Award for *The English Patient*, Anthony Minghella takes on the challenge of adapting and directing Highsmith's murder mystery *The Talented Mr. Ripley*. Also an award-winning playwright and university drama professor, Minghella employed an intellectual approach to the emotional task of writing the screenplay. Here he explicates a few of his methods.

Richard Stayton: Patricia Highsmith died just as you started the script. You never got to consult with her. But previously with *The English Patient*, you practically—co-writing is the wrong word—but really collaborated with the author, Michael Ondaatje.

Anthony Minghella: It certainly wasn't the co-writing process, but it was a commitment to Michael that wasn't ever contractual. I was such an admirer of his writing and became such close friends with him that it would have been a terrible thing if the only person who wasn't pleased with the adaptation I made was the author. There was nothing to fear about ensuring that he was alert to the way that the screenplay was developing by simply showing him every draft as I wrote it, having him call me or meet with me and tell me what he thought. Particularly in the case of *The English Patient*, where I was making such huge structural reevaluations of the material and real departures—not only in terms of the omission but also in terms of commissions. There were many new characters and new situations. I felt that to just cut Michael out of that

57

process would've been foolhardy. He was the greatest resource I had and the other person in the world who knew as much about what I was trying to do as I did. So why be nervous about it? It seemed to me a marvelous reservoir of information. I would've liked to have exactly the same relationship with Patricia Highsmith because she's another novelist that I really admire and a book that I really admired.

RS: How is it different without the author?

AM: It's hubris to say that filmmaking is a solitary activity. There are many other people involved in this process with me, all of whom are very quick to voice their opinions, attitudes, and so forth. But it doesn't have the comfort of knowing that I was doing something that, with each step, she understood and approved. I found a way of working—I'm not sure if it's a good way or bad way, it's the way that I've happened upon—which is not to have the book with me when I'm adapting. It began with *The English Patient* because I so loved the book that I thought that if I had the book next to me, I'd be genuflecting through it the entire time. My job was not to appropriate the book and put the dialogue in quotes. It was to reimagine the book as a film. It's very hard to do that if the material is right in front of you. It's easier if you're trying to write your way back to what you understood as a reader. And so I tried to do the same thing with *Ripley*. I'm not advertising it as a great method. I'm advertising it as a way that made sense for me to work in order to feel free to go on my own adventure with the film.

RS: Once you began actually writing the script, you didn't refer to the novel? It's very close to the book.

AM: Well, it's close, but . . . I was talking to someone the other day who had read the book some time ago and said, "Gosh, it's a very, very faithful adaptation." Then they reread the book and said, "It isn't such a faithful adaptation." I think it's both. What I would like to feel is that it's an adaptation in which the author would absolutely understand every choice that I've made. It has certainly two substantially new characters. The character of Peter Smith Kingsley is alluded to in a paragraph, and that's all. He became a very significant character in the film. The film is populated with Italian characters who are not mentioned in the novel, and they become in the making of the film very substantial. But the actual ideas and rhythms of the novel I tried to maintain in the film. My job is to try and be the best possible reader of the novel and then be somebody who some time later tries to tell a friend as enthusiastically as possible about all the things that he loved and the things that were exciting and extraordinary and tense and suspenseful. Necessarily, if you are somewhere away from having read the book, then you tend to emphasize things that perhaps are not emphasized in the book. You find yourself reinterpreting, reimagining certain moments. You find yourself dropping characters and inventing new ones because the story's passing through you. That's the place I need to be in when I'm writing a screenplay. I'm saying all this while very wary of thinking that there's any great method in it. I'm sure there are many other saner and more successful ways of doing this. It's just that this seems to work for me at the moment.

RS: Your Ripley is much more—not compassionate—but he's sympathetic. With the Ripley in the novels, there's something alien about him.
AM: I have to say this carefully, but it seems to me that I'm most spurred on by the curiosity of what it means to be human. If the character is so distant from anybody that we know or understand, it's very hard to learn anything. You adjudicate rather than recognize. You feel right from the beginning that you do not inhabit the same journey that the character is going on. Dramatic fiction has always intrigued me because it gives us the opportunity to reevaluate and reconsider the world from all manner of different perspectives. But if the perspective is one that so alienates us that we can't join with it, then it's not very interesting to me. I want to *feel* in film. I want to understand, and I want to see the parallels. In some ways this is just a very vivid version of what many of us know and understand. I think many of us anyway know what it's like to feel on the outside of things, to feel our nose pressed up against the window of a world we don't belong to, to feel longing for somebody or for something, to feel in the wrong class. If it's a journey where you recognize every step that the character takes, then it becomes a kind of moral fable. That's the only reason to make any movie.

RS: You began writing *The Talented Mr. Ripley* while waiting for *The English Patient* to begin production.
AM: That's when I did the first draft. What happened, as you probably know, is that we had this great deal of difficulty getting *The English Patient* financed, and we lost our money a few weeks before we actually started shooting, and the whole production was put on hold. There was a longer hiatus because Ralph Fiennes had a commitment to be in *Hamlet* in New York. I found myself with several months—I hoped it would be several months, it could've been forever—that I wasn't going to be

making the film. It coincided with Sydney Pollack calling me and mentioning this project. At first I took the job on as a writer, and it was only subsequently that I was attached to it as the director.

RS: So you wrote with the idea that you would not direct it.

AM: It wasn't as simple as that. At that point I didn't know what I was going to be doing. It had been many years since I first read the book, and when I read it again, I found myself increasingly absorbed and fascinated with it. It got to the place very, very quickly where I didn't want anybody else to do it.

RS: Is there a difference writing a script you intend to direct and writing one for someone else to direct?

AM: What happens is that after *The English Patient*, when I went back to *Ripley*, there is a process that you begin. It's very hard to know when you hand over the baton from being the writer to being the director of the film. But you begin to look at the architectural drawing of the building and think a lot more about building than you do about designing it. I think all writers should direct their own scripts because it means there's an organic process from the first day of writing to the last day in the cutting room. It's a great place for a writer to be on duty.

RS: Is editing a film similar to rewriting a script?

AM: I think so. You're finding the great and often exciting disjunction between what you thought you were collecting and what you've brought home with you. That's the metaphorical rewriting insofar as you then have to try and make sense of this new landscape that you've discovered. There's also, in my case, actual rewriting insofar as postproduction is a wonderful place to continue writing ADR lines and reimagining scenes. There's a great deal of postproduction writing that can really enhance and maintain the fabric of the film after it's been torn. You can have it stitched in postproduction in many ways. It's a way of healing any of the wounds of production. So I'm really interested in the writing process in the cutting room.

RS: In your version the sexual identity of Ripley is insignificant in why he does what he does.

AM: It's not the study of a homosexual killer in any shape or form for me. It's not about denying Ripley an emotional life. It's just an extremely erratic and mysterious internal life. It's a study of what happens to anybody when they lose faith in themselves and when they so long for a life and an identity that isn't their own, that they annihilate themselves in the process. It's a story about identity, so to reduce it to a story about serial killing or any of the headlines in this narrative seems very unfortunate to me.

RS: Did you study other films that were based on Patricia Highsmith novels?

AM: Yes. I mean I didn't look at them specifically for this film because I've looked at them many, many times before. I love *Strangers on a Train*, and I'm a great Hitchcock fan. I thought *American Friend* was a really interesting movie. What's fascinating to me is how they've all been, in some ways, improvisations on the novel. Each film has been like a jazz riff on the novels that they've been adapted from, which I think is fair enough. They all tend to speak very loudly of the period in which they were made. Perhaps I'm luckier in this period of being able to not duck any of the issues, which are in the film. I've had more license to get close to the book in this period than perhaps was available to a filmmaker forty years ago or thirty years ago.

RS: It's not a Hitchcock thriller, but it has a unique suspense rooted more in character than plot.

AM: The obligation is to try and find your voice as a filmmaker. Sometimes your voice is really irritating to you, no matter to anybody else. You have to make peace with what it is that you're doing. I've realized that my job is to try and find a way of most clearly expressing my own take on things and my own taste, and then people will have to bear with that in some way. I can't apologize to myself or to anybody about the noise I make as a writer. You find the sound that you make, and you have to live with it. Of course, I'm interested in the suspense in the film. Of course, I'm interested in the energy that a thriller gives you. But most of all, I'm interested in these people.

RS: That's obvious on the page in the script.

AM: One of the things that annoys screenwriters is the distinction between the director's visual ideas and the writer's literary ones. But good film writers are making or writing films. They're not writing dialogue. They're writing situations; they're writing scenes that may have only visual information in them. As a writer who's been allowed to direct, I want to say, on behalf of the writers who don't direct, that most writers are not infatuated with dialogue. They're infatuated with how to construct a moment in a film. You can sometimes make that entirely visually, and you can write that. So it's been an appropriation sometimes by directors of what writers do.

RS: You also wrote a lullaby.

AM: It's sung over the opening sequence. I was looking for something that Ripley could be playing at the very beginning of the film, and we were listening to all kinds of arias. In the end it just seemed like it would be more organic if [composer Gabriel Yared] and I could write something together and have it speak, however obliquely, about what the film was about. I've always thought the film had a primal quality that seemed so much like the Cain and Abel story on some level. The man who gets mocked, followed by covetousness and then murder in the desert. All those themes seem to be somewhere, however obliquely, in *Ripley*. I just imagined what it would be like if Eve was forced to sing a lullaby to the son who murdered her other son. Sinead O'Connor sings it in the film. It's again quite primal in sound.

RS: The screenplay's last moment on the boat when the closet door swings open, and you describe the ocean breeze and the swells, and Ripley was sitting in the cabin. It's very powerful. And inexplicable.

AM: That's the one part of the film that stayed intact from the get-go. It happens sometimes that you're writing and you feel like your compass is pointing true north and you just follow it, and the reason takes second place after the intention of true emotion. Then you find yourself in the process of rewriting, refining, and refining, but you trust that the destination is the right one. It gets harder and harder as you turn from writing into filming because more and more logic is applied to the way that the narrative developed. But I trusted in my instinct for how the end would function, and I hope that it will pay off.

The Talented Mister: An Interview with Anthony Minghella

Daniel Argent / 2000

From *Creative Screenwriting* 7, no. 1 (January 2000). Reprinted by permission.

Daniel Argent: What initially interested you in adapting Patricia Highsmith's novel *The Talented Mr. Ripley*?

Anthony Minghella: The character of Ripley is one that once you've encountered him, he never really goes away. I think it leaps away from the actual text of the novel and from any questions about the quality of the novel. It's such a creation, it's such a pungent example of the alienation of people in postwar society. Ripley is an index of how far from the center people feel and how much at odds with their own personality that people are led to feel and do intrinsically feel. And I also remember the absolute claustrophobia present in every one of [Highsmith's] novels I read, the sense of there being no air in the writing at all. In a way you feel that the sensibility of Ripley colored almost every other character she ever wrote. She said herself she felt Ripley had written his own novel. And I think that having found the sound of his sensibility, she never gave it up. Literally, in the sense that he went on to be the protagonist in a clutch of other novels, but also in almost every other novel she wrote there was a Ripley sensibility at play. And so that's what I took with me.

DA: Ripley's talent is for improvisation—there are several scenes where he practices mimicking people, honing his skills. Does he know what his talent is, and does he know how his actions affect those around him?

AM: I can't answer that question. I think there's something essentially unformed about Ripley that's very much a young man story. In many ways, it's a rather nightmarish rites-of-passage story. It's a film which constantly plays with the idea of journey and of travel, and the biggest journey that's made in the film is Ripley's own voyage of discovery. So, when you say, does he know what his talents are, I think the annihilation of self that he is so fixated with, the idea of trading himself in, almost by definition means that he does know himself, he doesn't value himself in any way. But whether he knows what his talents are, I couldn't say. He is tormented by himself and tormented by his own personality, so I don't think he'd be quick to recognize any of his own virtues. One of the hardest things for him in the film—and it happens at the most tragic moments—is to hear finally somebody advertise his talents and his qualities, at the very end of the movie.

DA: There's a philosophical discussions between Ripley and Peter Kingsley-Smith about the locked room that contains your past, and later Ripley gives Peter his room key. Do you think that Ripley knows what's in his own room, and would he unlock the door if he had the key?
AM: I think he's terrified. He says himself, "If anybody knew how awful [I was]. . . ." His view of his own personality is so distorted and so childlike. I constantly talked to Matt Damon about the fact that Ripley is very much the child who makes a small mistake, tries to cover it up, and in the process, sets off on a journey of bigger and bigger mistakes. And the way he deals with what happens to him is very much with the lack of responsibility that a child learns to grow from. Part of the way that we adjudicate somebody moving into adulthood is their ability to take responsibility for themselves and for their actions. I think that Ripley doesn't confront that until the very end of the film.

DA: So when you were working with Matt Damon [who plays Tom Ripley in the film] on the character, you two approached Ripley with the attitude of "here's what's on the page, and in these pages we find everything we need to know about Mr. Ripley?"
AM: I think there are certain circumstances which formed his character, most of them to do with class. The way we began was to investigate the architecture of class in this period, to talk about what it meant to feel on the outside of things, to feel an anomie that predisposes Ripley to feel outside of everything. There's an innate sense of shame in his disposition. That informed every page for me and therefore was a very big reservoir to investigate when we were working. It's a feeling "to the manner" in terms of a sensibility, but not "to the manor born" in terms of an inheritance. So there's an essential conflict in Ripley between his sensibility and his [inheritance].

DA: Is it Marge who comments, after seeing the "new" Ripley [after he has killed Dickie Greenleaf and taken over Dickie's life], that Ripley is "to the manor born"?

AM: Yes. "Look at you now, to the manner born." But he's not to the manor born, and that's his problem. In some ways, it's a very modern character. It's a character that is representative of the circumstance that many people find themselves in. Every message we get from the print media is to try and discover ways to change ourselves, that who we are and what we have is not enough, that we require transforming. Ripley to me is, in that sense, a barely mythological character, the character who has no access to the life he wishes to lead.

DA: Ripley is the pauper who has a chance to trade places with a prince.

AM: I think so. It always seemed to me a rather dark Cinderella tale. One of the things that I tried to do was to work from references away from the source material, as well as the source material itself. I was very intrigued by the correlatives in the story with other characters in fiction—Albert Camus' *The Outsider*, also *MacBeth*—because there is a story of somebody who through a whole series of circumstances finds himself at the mercy of his own ambition, facing the consequences. There's certainly that aspect to Ripley, and it's not an accident that he has Dickie write out a passage from *MacBeth*, because I feel that he has a real sense of connection with MacBeth's story. I also thought that at some level there was a Cain and Abel-like quality to this narrative, it's about the kissed brother and the unkissed brother, the envy and the longing that one brother feels for the other, and the consequences of the poison of that love. I was very much raiding the themes of those stories to see if they would help me give some resonance to this tale.

DA: You've said that, in your childhood in England, you felt tattooed with all the wrong identifying marks. You could draw some correlatives between yourself and Ripley. What's the difference? What kept you from becoming a Ripley?

AM: [Laughs] What I've been trying to do, as a writer, is to make a connection directly with the character myself. The writing has to become personal for me in some way, humanized. In some ways, Ripley is just an extreme version of everybody, as is often the case in fiction. Fiction gives back to you a distorted version of yourself, but recognition is the key element. So I suppose I tried to borrow from within myself what seemed to correlate with Ripley, and that is the feeling that I certainly had as a child: that there were several membranes between me and the host child that I was living in, in the sense that my family's from another country. I was living on an island off the coast of the mainland, as we called it, and so there was always a feeling of not quite belonging. And also because I come from an extremely blue-collar family, and I found myself as an academic as a young man, feeling my own upbringing was very much at odds with the upbringing of the people around me, who had come from more established and educated classes than I did. Particularly in England, where those striations of class are very keenly observed, I was always conscious of where I'd come from. There's a special pleading in that. I don't want to say that I had a tough time. I was conscious, always, of being on the outside of things; which is a very useful place for a writer to live, by the way. I don't see it as some torment that I have to suffer. I felt there was a way to use that feeling to help me write the character of Ripley. And obviously what stops most of us from becoming Ripley is the tight cinch of morality which we belt around ourselves.

The thing that happens with Ripley, which is incremental, is that starting with a little lie he ends up in an absolute web of lies which gets increasingly insidious and destructive. What's interesting to me is for the audience to see how that small lie develops into actions which they couldn't possibly contemplate at the beginning of the film.

DA: That ties into another point. You talk about Ripley being "unformed," and about missteps. Ripley has been referred to as "amoral." Is he? Would you consider Tom Ripley amoral, and is he any less amoral than Dickie Greenleaf?

AM: I don't know if amorality is just a gloss that you can put on any behavior which doesn't conform to public mores. Dickie's actions are almost as reprehensible and careless as Ripley's are. It's quite possible in the way that I've staged and written the sequence on the boat that Dickie could have ended up murdering Ripley. And in that sense, they're not dissimilar. Ripley is certainly human insofar as he's alert to the suffering of others and troubled by it. So in that sense, he isn't amoral. In a way, the film is as much about morality as it is moral. I've tried to turn the actions of the story into a cautionary tale, but ultimately, it's as much about morality as it is a cautionary tale. It's an argument about morality, because all of the characters find themselves in some moral bind to the film.

DA: And very few of them take what we'd call the "moral way" out.

AM: Well, they are careless people. That's not true of everybody. It's true of the father in the film, it's true of Dickie, and it's true of Ripley. Marge's character is a moral compass in the film, as indeed is Peter Smith-Kingsley. So it's hard to generalize. But there's something about the license to travel and the license of being in a foreign country which enables people to imagine they have a clean slate, and that they can make themselves up again. A lot of the dynamic in the film is about people in the process of trying to reinvent themselves in all kinds of ways.

DA: Peter Smith-Kingsley seems to be the one male in the screenplay that helps redeem the gender, after Hebert Greenleaf, Dickie, Ripley, and Freddie.
AM: Yes! And he's an invention, obviously. He's not in the novel.

DA: Why did you insert him into the screenplay?
AM: He throws into sharp relief the chaos of the other personalities in the film. He's somebody who has a center and is rooted. There seemed to be a very interesting irony to explore there. And it seemed important to separate out sexuality from Ripley's own disturbance. He's not disturbed because of his sexuality. He's disturbed, and therefore is disturbed about his sexuality.

DA: It seems Ripley does not, per se, focus on his sexuality. When Ripley's visiting the various Italian historical sites, the screenplay's descriptive tells us that "This is the real Ripley, the lover of beauty."
AM: Ripley is looking for love, and looking for love in all the wrong places. Part of the film seems a rosary of love stories, of Ripley trying to find a place where he's accepted. There's so much longing in the film—longing for beauty, longing to be accepted, longing to be admitted to a club Ripley feels he's never going to have access to, longing to collide with culture. There's so much yearning in that character. And the film is also full of other characters who are looking for love, and again, potentially in the wrong places. You feel that Dickie is bashing around, so acclimatized to being envied and to being admired, but not able in any way to return [the feelings]. And the Meredith Logue character—which is another character that I invented for the film—is also trying to make herself up in Europe and trying to find somebody who will relish her. There's a searching, you feel everybody's scouring Italy for something.

DA: That's most blatantly set up by Herbert Greenleaf sending Ripley to scour Italy for his son. Herbert Greenleaf is yet another person who is trying to get Dickie to return emotion: it seems he feels that if Dickie was in close proximity—in the States—that love might have a chance of happening.

AM: I've reimagined the relationship between Herbert Greenleaf and Dickie in the film from the novel, because it seemed that part of the tragedy of the story is of a father's misjudgment of his son. So many of the things which happen in the film come about because of an essential suspicion and lack of trust that Herbert has for his own son. He's blind and deaf to reality because he's already viewing every event through the prism of this trust and fear of what his son is capable of. He can't see the truth, even though it's right in front of him, because he's already prejudged what kind of person his son is, and I think that's a terrible, terrible feature of the film. As he says at one point: "People say you can't choose your parents, but you can't choose your children." There's such a disappointment in his own son, and you feel that is the key to Ripley's escape: Herbert Greenleaf thinks the only person who is capable of behaving badly in the world is his own child.

DA: And that allows Ripley to move on. But—much like that unformed child who's not yet matured to adulthood—Ripley has this tendency, when confronted with something dangerous, to lash out with the simple and easy answer of violence, rather than deal with confrontation using nonlethal means. We see this in his confrontations with Dickie, Freddie, and on to Peter.

AM: It becomes a solution to him. I think he's terrified of violence, in fact. I think that on the boat he is in fear of his own life, and that then he discovers a solution rather than it being something he's predisposed to.

DA: That was a change you made from the novel. In the screenplay, Ripley doesn't plan on killing Dickie. How does that form the character of Ripley?

AM: You're nosing around in all the characters which most interest me. I think that if Ripley had premeditated Dickie's death, then it turns him into somebody that we can't possibly recognize because most of us don't go around planning to kill other people, and so in a sense it pushes that audience into an adjudicative position from the get-go. It means that you can write Ripley off as somebody who has no resemblance to your own personality, and it's impossible to do anything other than to confirm all of your preconceptions from the outset. Whereas in seems to me that if you can see the humanity in a character and see how that humanity gets corrupted, it's possible to inhabit the journey of the character, not walk away from it. And it's possible to see fiction, therefore, as a way of addressing instincts that we all share. There's something so distancing about a cold-blooded killer that it becomes a very different activity to watch them at work. Whereas if you can understand a character, and if you can travel with him on an increasingly dark journey, it's possible to see fiction as a way of offering up versions of the consequences of action. I don't mean that we can therefore rehearse what it would be to kill somebody, but rather rehearse what it was to give up on yourself, and the punitive consequences of that. So I'm looking for ways of keeping the audience inside Ripley's journey rather than outside.

DA: Not allowing the audience to build that protective wall, make an objective viewing experience more subjective.
AM: Exactly right. And the story is told exclusively from one person's point of view, so it's pretty important that the audience can get inside that point of view.

DA: You've said that the film has a moral imperative, another difference between the novel and the film. How does that inform the journey that you take the audience on? And do films have to have moral imperatives?
AM: Well, films don't have to have anything. I think there's room in fiction films for all kinds of stories. All that betrays is my own preoccupation, that I'm not particularly interested in films which have no moral argument. It doesn't mean that I think that morality is an essential element in filmmaking. It's just that I am interested in the fact that there's been such a shift in the function of fiction in society. In its original forms, fiction was intended as punctuation to real life, it was connected with high days and holidays and festival and was an opportunity to try and explore man's relationship with the gods and with himself and with his fellows. It was very much a comma in the paragraph of a daily life. What happened in this century, and increasingly, daily, is that people's lives are made up of a lot commas in their paragraph. There's much more fiction invading people's consciousness than there is reality, we learn a great deal more through the stories that we tell each other than we do from our own interactions. There's such a deluge of fiction that people collide with. It's inevitable that, when we first encounter fiction, we're able to separate it from reality, it all goes into the same place in our minds. I think, over time, our memories find it difficult to distinguish between what happened and what we've encountered in fiction, and so

I would like to feel the very least that—if I'm adding more mess to the big mess—it has at least some consideration. I'm not saying that it's one that has to obtain in every bit of fiction that's made.

DA: That's particularly good because, whether or not the audience agrees with your particular viewpoint expressed in that piece, it allows them something to push off of.

AM: Exactly. In the end you make films that you want to watch yourself. In some ways, I try and remove my own adjudication from film because I think that if I've adjudicated Ripley as being a premeditated pathological character, an amoral character, there's nothing for the audience to determine, you know? Whereas, I think that what I want to be as an audience member is a participator. As an audience member I want something which stays in my mind and forces me to enter some dialogue with the film, and so inevitably I'm helpless about also trying to make films that way.

DA: It's a very difficult path to take.

AM: But it's not an elected path, I don't think. You can't ultimately elect the voice that you have as a filmmaker. Your voice is betrayed in every frame and your sensibility is betrayed and you have to make peace with that in some way. Just say, that's the noise that comes out of me when I make films and so be it.

DA: It seems that philosophy underscores the issue of the Hadrian statue, which goes from classically beautiful to damaged during an act of violence. And later, when Ripley is putting on his glasses, he sees both himself and Dickie reflected. What is the corollary analogy between the drowning of the Madonna del Mare [an annual Italian festival of the Virgin Mary] and the discovery of Silvana's drowned body occurring at the same time?

AM: Well, the drowning of Silvana is another presentiment for me in the film. Just as the words that Ripley speaks at the beginning of the film— they are a warning—I think that the idea of the drowning of Silvana was a presentiment of the violence, and of the consequences of action. Because Silvana is somebody who is victim to Dickie's carelessness, just as ultimately Dickie ends up overboard as the victim of Ripley's carelessness. And the sea is a very big element of this film. Ripley's at sea at the end of the film in a boat going nowhere, as it were. Dickie drowns at sea.

I was trying to indicate the level of ritual in Italy. The fact that that is the moment in the film where the Americans are most American, the Italians are most Italian, and also it's where the difference in cultural moral values is most clearly and acutely marked. Because for Dickie, his promiscuity is without consequence for him. It's part of the privilege of being a wealthy young American in Italy. In Italy, the cost of being a single and unmarried mother is dire, particularly in that time. It's just not acceptable in Southern Italy. And so what for Dickie is a dalliance without real cost, is to somebody else of huge consequence. It's the mis-reading of the culture that is so evident in that scene.

DA: It also underscores the fact that Dickie is concerned with himself, and the fact that he has irrevocably changed someone's life is without consequence to him.

AM: Yes, but I think he's in a phase. Dickie's in a place of thinking that it's appropriate to sow his wild oats in every possible way and then go home and take the responsibility that's waiting for him, of running a business. It's a particularly western idea of travel, which is that we annex all of our morality. We think we can behave badly as long as we're outside the perimeter of our own lives, that we can go somewhere else to behave in a way we'd never believe in behaving at home.

DA: The traveler feels invulnerable.

AM: You feel that Dickie is on holiday from his life, and therefore doesn't feel he has any responsibilities for the way that he behaves.

DA: The damaging thing about holidays is, if you don't have a specific return date you can get lost in your travels.

AM: Yes! The other thing about the film is that it is very much about the American in Europe. It's about a period where the idea of the grand tour—of going to Europe to remake yourself or to take time off from the circumstances of home. With something which has much more reso-nance than it has today, when we're all so much more traveled and where you're not going on a boat for five days to get to Europe. That's why the film couldn't possibly be set in the 1990s. It's not by accident that Patri-cia Highsmith went to Europe in this period, and why it was a haven for all kinds of people who were trying to remake themselves or live in a way they couldn't possibly have lived at home.

DA: And your filmography follows that travel.

AM: Journeys. The fact is that journey is a wonderful dynamic for film, journeys of one sort or another. The next film I'm going to make, *Cold Mountain* [based on the novel by Charles Frazier], is about a man literally walking back from the Civil War. But the character he's going home to goes on her own journey, which is as profound as his but it takes place over a couple of hundred yards. And I think that it's a very good energy, because you want the character to be transformed and to go on a journey, an interior journey in the film, so often journeying itself is a very interesting way to describe that.

DA: As a writer, a creator, and a filmmaker, what journey are you on? Where do you think you're going, and what surprises have you come across that have changed your path?

AM: [Sighs] Well, I am on a journey and I feel I've happened later than perhaps would have been useful to understand that being a film director, being a filmmaker, is a way of lassoing all of my interests and dreams. As long as I'm allowed to make films, as long as people allow me to and finance the films, I think I should try to make as many as I can. And also understand something that you've pointed out, which is that the scale of a film is less important than the journey of it. Much as I'm loving making films on a big canvas, I don't want to get myself into a place where the only way I can learn more about film is to make bigger films. So I hope that there's going to be some way that I can flex. I want to feel that I can work on the biggest canvas and the smallest one without making any qualitative difference between the two films. I want to feel also that I'm able to write original films. I don't want to get stuck into the trap of thinking I always have to adapt source material to have my say. I never imagined and never anticipated being an adapter. That's probably why I have such a strange relationship with other stations [laughs]. But where it takes me, I have absolutely no idea. I think that there's been such a radical change in my life because I've gone to other places to make films, in every sense. And there's a toll in that, in that it takes you further and further away from home. And I suppose that part of me is yearning to see whether it's possible to step out of my front door and make movies as well as always having to get on a boat or a plane or a camel. Or a gondola.

DA: When did you start calling yourself a writer?

AM: I think that when anybody asks me what I do, I always say that I'm a writer. I think of myself as a writer. Because if tomorrow you said, I have to give everything up except one thing, I would have to keep writing. Because filmmaking is a luxury and a privilege, and writing is a necessity.

My Bloody Valentine

Nick James / 2000

From *Sight and Sound*, February 2000, published by British Film Institute. Reprinted by permission.

On a hot day in July 1999 at the Jim Henson studios in London's Camden Town, Anthony Minghella is, he tells me, about to do something "tentative and experimental." Here he is, the shorts-wearing, Oscar-winning director of *The English Patient* (1996) inviting *Sight and Sound* into the cutting room of his latest film *The Talented Mr. Ripley* to see a few sequences. He and his collaborator, the revered editor Walter Murch, are properly genial and accommodating, yet there's an air of nervousness. On their side, it's because having previewed an early cut of Ripley to largely approving colleagues and advisors, they are now confronted with the US marketing people. "There's a concern that there are pansexual relationships in the film that might be unattractive to some Americans," says Minghella. It's at this point that he and Murch have decided to have their first formal press conversation and Minghella is worried their thoughts are only half formed. For my part, I'm anxious that Minghella may be simmering quiet resentment at his past treatment by critics, perhaps *Sight and Sound*'s in particular.

For is this magazine not the epitome of the anti-Minghella tendency? I assumed so until I checked the reviews. Paul Tarrago, it's true, was pretty rude about Minghella's only "Hollywood" movie *Mr. Wonderful* (1993), saying his "authorial ethos" was, "when emotions run high, make everyone act endearingly young" (to which anyone might reply, yes, but isn't that what people do when emotions run high?). However, while the *S&S* reviews of Minghella's first film *Truly, Madly, Deeply* (1990) and *The English Patient* were not exactly raves, they did quietly admire. This was a surprise because there remains a question mark over Minghella among British critics. Certain early lapses of taste—such as the unbearably fey

73

scene in *Truly, Madly, Deeply* where Michael Maloney and Juliet Stevenson do indeed come over all childlike and start hopping along the South Bank promenade—earned him a vigilant antipathy among some commentators that's hard to shift.

This background of critical enmity was only partly deflected by the evident talent Minghella brought to *The English Patient*. Michael Ondaatje's allusive and slightly absurd novel of damaged souls thrown together by the backwash of World War II gave the director the chance to prove he could handle scenes as grand and imposing as the soaring emotions he was trying to describe. Yet though well written and superbly put together, the film rarely lets you forget its glossy packaging of international stars and exotic locations. You're always aware you're watching a prestige work, designed to dazzle. And for all its dark centrality to the film's explosive outcomes, the affair told in retrospect and performed so sensitively between Almásy the Hungarian explorer (Ralph Fiennes) and his English colleague's wife Katharine (Kristin Scott Thomas) is only slightly sour cream.

Which is not something you could say about *The Talented Mr. Ripley*. The most compelling reason for wanting to talk to Minghella was this choice of material. Patricia Highsmith's unnerving 1956 psychological thriller may be about enviable lifestyles but it is not about enviable emotions. It tells the story of Tom Ripley (played by Matt Damon), a striving, affectless young itinerant mistaken for an ex-Princeton student by a Mr. Greenleaf, a rich shipyard owner. Ripley goes along with the mistake, pretending he knew Greenleaf's only son Dickie (Jude Law), who is now living it up on the Italian coast and refusing to come home to New York. Greenleaf commissions Tom to go all expenses paid to Mongibello to persuade Dickie to return. Enraptured by Dickie's playboy lifestyle, Tom ingratiates himself and confesses his arrangement with Greenleaf. But Dickie is fickle, and when, after weeks of what for Tom is exquisite intimacy with the high life, he shuts Tom out, Tom realizes his desperate need to become Dickie Greenleaf himself. He does this in the only way left to him, by murdering Dickie and taking his place.

It's a cold subject, though it has plenty of "hot" scenes for nervous Hollywood studio types to get nervous about. In particular there's a strong homoerotic tension between Tom and Dickie, despite Dickie's ever-present girlfriend Marge (Gwyneth Paltrow). Minghella and Murch show me four sequences, each of which immediately demonstrates how far from the novel the director is prepared to go. The first starts with Dickie and Tom larking about on a Vespa, then has Tom singing *My Funny Valentine* à la Chet Baker to Dickie's sax accompaniment in a basement club, then Tom getting Dickie to do his signature so Tom can forge it, then Dickie in the bath playing chess with a bathside Tom.

This is probably the sequence that troubled the marketeers. Tom suggests he'd like to get in the bath, but when Dickie suspects him of some sort of sexual intent, Tom says he meant to get in it after him. The scene is filled with slightly sinister erotic tension with plenty of nudity and flashes of confused anger.

The jazz buddying is Minghella's own idea (the pair are not musicians in the novel) predicated on the irony that poor-boy Tom—who learns classical music because he thinks it's refined and only explores jazz to get closer to Dickie—turns out to be much better at improvisation than the rich dilettante. A second sequence reprises the jazz theme: Tom, in Rome for the first time, is standing in the doorway of a record shop waiting to visit the Coliseum, while Dickie is inside grooving to the latest jazz releases with his Rome pal Freddie. Dickie eventually emerges from his booth and suggests that Tom goes ahead, though Tom has heard him arrange a club visit that evening from which he is clearly excluded.

A third sequence shows an Italian religious ceremony where a statue of the Madonna is borne out of the sea, during which the corpse of a local girl suddenly bobs up. She has committed suicide because—as only Tom knows—of Dickie. Last comes the violent encounter between Tom and Dickie aboard a boat. Without the context of the rest of the film, the religious-ceremony sequence lacks something, but the fluent ease of the first sequence makes it clear that Minghella and Murch are crafting something powerfully inventive and the shock of the last confirms it. One thing Minghella and Murch are not prepared to do at this point is show me anything of Matt Damon as Tom playing Dickie after the murder (see the postscript after the interview for a view of that). Please be warned that the interview which follows reveals much about the plot that might spoil your enjoyment of the film.

Nick James: What has been your approach to adapting Patricia Highsmith's novel?

Anthony Minghella: The film opens in New York with a title sequence, but unlike the novel it's then centered on Italy. The screenplay began with forty-eight or so pages of America before Ripley went to Italy, but with each successive draft that gradually receded. I wanted to make sure the audience couldn't extrapolate what was going to happen. A lot of the novel is taken up with the police process, and if you strip away Highsmith's marvelously airless and claustrophobic treatment of it, her narrative beats don't stand up to scrutiny. They're covered with a wonderful prose gloss that makes you experience things without question which wouldn't work on film. Tom Ripley is a fascinating, complex, Camus-like character. But what I didn't respond to in the novel is its seeming lack of dramatic structure.

Then the end looks past its last page to the return of Ripley in sequels. Unlike in the 1960 René Clement film from the same source *Plein Soleil* in which Ripley gets caught, I was charmed by the idea of a central character who could commit murder and get away with it. It's not that I enjoy the amorality of that. I wanted to say that getting away with it is his punishment.

NJ: What have you added?

AM: There's a character called Peter Smith-Kingsley, played by Jack Davenport, who warrants a couple of mentions in the novel but in the film Ripley falls in love with him. He's a musician who is capable of loving Ripley for who Ripley is. In the screenplay Ripley says, "I'd rather be a fake somebody than a real nobody," and that's like a mantra around him. Then Ripley meets Peter, but in pretending to be Dickie Greenleaf he has already annihilated himself. I've added the killing of Peter at the end, and it's as if you've seen Ripley killing lust or desire or passion with Dickie and then killing the possibility of love with Peter. Ripley's ability to extemporize, to invent plausible stories in implausible situations, is his blessing and his curse. He can never be like he is.

NJ: The book is an intriguingly chilling choice for a director whose films are thought of as highly emotive.

AM: In the days when I was writing plays—in particular the last one, *Made in Bangkok*, which coincided with a series I'd written, *What If It's Raining?*, on Channel 4—people said I was dark and acerbic. But I didn't feel that way any more than I now feel unduly committed to large gusts of emotion. Obviously I gravitate towards material in which there's a free articulation of feelings—I'm not ashamed of that. And Ripley's feelings seem to me to be volcanic: a constantly bubbling emotion that's suppressed but extremely present. In many ways he's the most feeling character I've been connected to.

You can only assume that your own taste largely collides with other people's. And I've always found it very likely to want to trade myself in for somebody else—I've often wished I was a different kind of writer, that the music I made was a different kind of music. So there's certainly common ground between Ripley and myself—the feeling that there's an easier, less fragile world being enjoyed by other people. Then when I met Matt Damon he said, "I know who this guy is." And many other people connected with the film have said, "I'm Ripley."

NJ: Matt Damon seems a good choice to play someone so hard to pin down.
AM: Matt Damon is a revelation in this film. For an actor on the verge of being a big movie star to choose to do this part is already extraordinary, and then the absolute guile with which he approaches the character is amazing.
Walter Murch: You never feel him peeping out from behind the character and saying, "It's Matt Damon behind here just doing a part."

NJ: Why did you choose an English actor to play Dickie Greenleaf?
AM: I was obsessed with Jude Law being the right person from the beginning. It's rather the way Ralph Fiennes was cast in *Quiz Show* as someone who could play a well-to-do young American in the late fifties and early sixties. Most good young American male actors don't play that social territory very well, whereas a lot of British actors go there very naturally. There don't seem to be many Brahmin American actors in the way that, for instance, Gwyneth Paltrow is so clearly able to essay that territory.

Patricia Highsmith hated Marge. I read a letter in which she referred to someone as "a vile creature, a Marge Sherwood type." She didn't care for Dickie either, but for me films which adjudicate are very dull. I've always been allergic to them. So I've always tried to force audiences to come to their own conclusions about characters. In the film Dickie and Marge are, by their own lights, perfectly agreeable people.

NJ: In the novel there's a sneaking feeling that Ripley might be interested in Marge.
AM: It's not the relationship in *Plein Soleil* where you feel Ripley wants the girl rather than the guy. Here you don't think he's in love with Marge, you know he thinks it would serve him well if she thought well of him. If we're going to have trouble with this film I know it'll be because of its darkness rather than its light—I mean, nobody will say we treat this movie with a light hand. I have this notion of it being a tragedy, purga-

torial and about descent. We unravel this person, I hope with a certain amount of compassion, but it's a bruising event. It's not an easy film to watch—which may be the kiss of death for its commercial prospects.

NJ: There's a lot in the novel that's reminiscent of Hitchcock, particularly the emphasis on suspense.

WM: I don't think there's anything like it in Hitchcock. *Strangers on a Train* is maybe the closest. I thought about the suspense in terms of a tower of teacups. The film stacks cups and saucers on top of each other—sometimes you think they're bound to crash one way, then something happens and they lean in the other direction. In the end the tower is leaning as far as it can, but the film is over and you never see it fall.

AM: I've never written or been associated with something where there's such a singular point of view. But you can't avoid yourself whatever you do. When I was writing plays I wanted to be Howard Barker or Edward Bond, somebody really stern and analytical with a certain coolness. Whatever I did, though, you could always stick the thermometer into the bit of meat and it would be 68 degrees. Whatever its surface noise and whatever the bruising and remorseless tone, I'm sure this film betrays my chemistry at every point.

NJ: Why did you make Tom and Dickie jazz fans?

AM: In the novel Dickie is a not very good painter and has various discussions with Tom about painting, which made me wary of "as interesting as watching paint dry" pitfalls. So because I'm obsessed with music and think that sound in film is as important as image, I made their argument a musical one. It's also a way of lassoing the period in that a lot of jazz players were living in Europe in the late fifties. Dickie has gone to blow his alto sax in Europe away from the claws of his father and Ripley is a classical musician who tries to learn jazz in order to have something to share with Dickie. But while Dickie sees himself as an existential beat person who lives by his own law and Ripley worries that he's a straight conservative who doesn't understand anything, in reality—just as it's Bach and Beethoven who were the great improvisers, not Charlie Parker and Miles Davis—Ripley turns out to be a great improviser while Dickie is a rather conventional guy sowing his wild oats. It's Ripley who has the jazz chops.

NJ: I remember a quiet Italy of ease and comfort in the novel—not a jazz fan's Italy.

AM: Because of my Italian blood I didn't want to go to Italy and just have lots of postcard views. And Italy in that *La dolce vita* period of *il boom*, as it's called, had changed. Ten years after the war they'd started to escape poverty and discover style and Vespas. So the film had to buy into that. The novel is based partly on Henry James's *The Ambassadors*, which is all about the idea of Americans becoming marinated in civilized European culture, whereas to me Italy, and particularly the south, is hugely pagan. So I tried to weave into the story a sense of Italy as a character acting on these people.

Actually Highsmith writes almost nothing at all about the places. There's much more about how you make a Martini, or adjudicating people by what drink they order in a bar. Where the bar was, who was there—so much about the striations of class and personality by choices of costume and hair.

NJ: What did you decide about Tom's sexuality?

AM: That's very interesting territory that I can't really work out. I decided Ripley is both. I think he's a virgin and a lot of what he's feeling is to do with a terror of what it means to feel physical interest. Also he tries to have a relationship with a woman and can't really carry it off. Whereas you do feel that when he meets Peter he could have a proper relationship. Even though there's nothing like that in the book, there are parallel episodes. That to me is what you have to do when you create material—create stuff that could have been in the novel. When you haven't got it right and there's something that's treacherous to the novel it feels as if you've begun to lose faith with what you started from.

Postscript: January 2000

Having now seen the completed film, I can say Minghella's overhaul of Highsmith is comprehensive. And he and Murch must have won their marketing discussion to some extent since the bathroom sequence is not materially altered, though I have the impression there's less of Jude Law nude than there was. The film grips you with claustrophobia; the plot is a narrowing of options for Tom always down to murder. It certainly does chill. But best of all is its tackling of a matter some claim doesn't exist—the American class system.

Despite his brilliant improvising, Ripley can't get it right. In a *tour-de-force* moment for which the Academy should post him a statuette right now, Philip Seymour Hoffman as a suspicious Freddie trips around what is meant to be Dickie's apartment (but is really Tom-as-Dickie's), flipping up his hands at the decor and braying viciously: "Tommy, Tommy, Tommy, Tommy, Tommy, this isn't Dickie, this is so bourgeois." It's here the film moves back through the novel to its own inspirations in Henry James. In *Why Read the Classics?* Italo Calvino says of one character in James's *Daisy Miller:* "He has been living in Europe too long and does not know how to distinguish his 'decent' compatriots from those of low social extraction. But this uncertainty about social identity applies to all of them—these voluntary exiles in whom James sees a reflection of himself—whether they are 'stiff' or emancipated." This is the tragedy of Minghella's *The Talented Mr. Ripley*—that Ripley, who fears sex as James did, could not find his place as the stiff among the emancipated.

Italy: The Director's Cut

Anthony Minghella / 2000

From the *Guardian*, February 26, 2000. Copyright Guardian News & Media Ltd 2000. Reprinted by permission.

Last year I spent a great deal more time in Italy than anywhere else, but on reflection it's clear to me that I wasn't really in Italy, but in a country of my own imagination. Film directors are thieves; magpies. They resemble barbarians bringing home the spoils, ransacking each city for its treasures. They plunder landscapes, corrupt geography, redraw maps, and invent villages. Screenplays, too, are notoriously hieroglyphic. They resemble architects' blueprints and collide with many of the same practical obstacles when translating ideas into reality.

In my screenplay of *The Talented Mr. Ripley*, adapted from Patricia Highsmith's mordant 1950s novel of the same name, Tom Ripley (played by Matt Damon), a young American misfit, is sent to Italy to persuade Dickie Greenleaf (Jude Law), the errant son of a wealthy industrialist, to return home to New York. Instead, he becomes obsessed with the glamorous life Dickie is leading in Mongibello and stays on, first befriended and then rejected by Dickie and his fiancée, Marge Sherwood (Gwyneth Paltrow). Eventually, Ripley assumes Dickie's identity and takes himself to Rome and Venice where, as is often the case with holidays, he samples the life he's always wanted.

His catastrophic adventure begins innocuously enough with a blue Fiat bus, 1940s vintage, puttering along a coast road, Ripley inside, having hauled itself up from the harbor at Naples where the Queen Mary has just delivered him from New York.

Collecting the half-dozen shots that create this sequence was less straightforward. The Queen Mary is long becalmed, the New York skyline irreparably altered by fifty years of vertical aspiration. The once-majestic Arrivals Building in Naples is derelict and—most exercising to the filmmakers—Mongibello, Ripley's destination, notionally situated on the Amalfi coast, is a figment of Highsmith's imagination. But there it all is on film. A departure from Manhattan, an arrival in a teeming hall of passengers, a short bus journey, a picturesque fishing village complete with villagers, fishermen, fish. And none of it, except perhaps for the fish, is real.

So the Italy I explored for the past year is available to the traveller only through the distorted frames of a movie. I lived in the land of Ripley, and that mosaic of dream images, half-remembered moments from Italian movies, photographic references, travel diaries, documentaries and anecdotes, was my guidebook as I explored modern Italy and reimagined it in the service of the film.

The shooting of *The Talented Mr. Ripley*, set in the Italy of 1958–59, was continuously confounded by progress: buildings mentioned in the adaptation were no longer there, or were hemmed in by modern neighbors or decorated with the ubiquitous green canvas of Rome's makeover for the millennial celebrations. In the 1950s, travel was largely the privilege of the moneyed class, and this had particular significance when it came to shooting in Italy's landmark locations: there were simply fewer people then. We were faced with the problem of clearing piazzas swarming with tourists.

By locating the movie a year or two later than the novel, there was an opportunity to explore a significant moment in Italian history, *Il Boom*, where a thin veneer of the modern, the sophistication of *La Dolce Vita*, had glossed but could not entirely hide the more primitive mores of the country. Italy is a place I love above all other places, but it's always possible to detect a darker note sounding under its breezy melodies. And this dissonance seemed to speak of the film itself: apparently sybaritic, but lounging on a volcano. Mongibello, as it happens, is a local name for Mount Etna.

As Dickie, Ripley takes a suite in the Grand Hotel. This hotel has one of Rome's few genuinely impressive hotel exteriors and lobbies and so, for once, we were able to shoot an only semi-modified reality. But for Ripley's hotel suite we used the breathtaking interiors, frescoed and ornate, of the Palazzo Tiburna. The same building has a staircase of grim beauty, austere and colossal, like Escher's Möbius etchings. Here we filmed the halls and stairs of Ripley's Roman apartment, where bad things happen; while its evocative courtyard served as the exterior of an apartment belonging to Meredith Logue (played by Cate Blanchett), a young heiress with whom Ripley has become improbably involved. It was possible, then, to walk out of a door, down some stairs and go outside, and have passed through three of the film's most significant locations, separated in the movie by weeks and miles. And so it went on. We filmed Roman locations in Naples, Neapolitan locations in Rome, Venetian locations in Sicily, sometimes by choice, mostly by *force majeure*.

A key scene in Ripley's stay in Venice is a visit to his conductor friend Peter's rehearsal of Vivaldi's Stabat Mater in the composer's own church, La Pieta, a scene I wrote specifically because of the location. In fact, an earlier visit to a concert there actually gave me the idea for Peter Smith-Kingsley's occupation. Naturally, then, when it came to filming, the church became mysteriously unavailable.

With the schedule tightening on us, we were faced with the prospect of having to shoot the scene in Palermo, Sicily, the next stop on our own journey. I couldn't scout a replacement church myself, and had to rely on a hastily assembled selection of photographs. My eye was taken by images of the astonishing Byzantine gilt mosaic work in one of them, the fourteenth-century Chiesa Martorana. Its dazzling iconography of golden saints and angels seemed to offer a perfect backdrop to one of the film's few genuinely romantic moments.

We arrived in Palermo the evening before we were due to film, only to discover that the mosaic work was confined to the rafters above the brooding monochrome of its walls. The church rehearsal would have photographed as if it took place in a large garage. The only solution I could think of, to the dismay of the production design team, was to take the performers to the mosaics. We built a terrifyingly rudimentary plat-form, and musicians and instruments were hoisted up. The camera has one eye; geography is only what the film establishes. Ripley enters the church, looks up to see Peter rehearsing Stabat Mater in what appears to be an organ loft. The audience can't see the glue and bits of string creating this illusion.

Sometimes, of course, there is no simple line between fiction and fact. An elegantly dressed woman approached us as we were preparing a café exterior in Rome's Piazza di Spagna. There has never actually been an outdoor café there, but I'd had an idea about Ripley observing his con-nivances from a high vantage point, and the architecture of the Spanish Steps, with its view stretching past the piazza, lent itself perfectly to the mechanics of the scene.

The woman ducked under our work ropes and sat at one of the prop tables, indifferent to the fact that there was no café, that the facade con-cealed a dress shop, and insisted she had arranged to meet her friend at

Dinelli's. As I attempted to explain that the café was in reality a film set, that Dinelli's had been the name of my aunt's café at Ryde Esplanade, on the Isle of Wight, her friend arrived and they sat down and had their meeting, a little irascible at our failure to serve them coffee but otherwise perfectly content.

This seems to be the contract that Romans have made with Rome generally. They have made accommodation with a city bristling with facades and gestures from Nero to Mussolini. They perch on the statues, argue at the fountains, slouch against antiquity, and eat lunch on steps that might have been carved by Michelangelo.

As Italy reconciled itself to our foibles, we tried to reconcile ourselves to Italy's. Filming was often fraught. You can't shoot in this street on Monday morning unless you restrict the field of view to 180 degree. The building is undergoing sewerage repairs from 7 AM to 10 AM and the owner has a birthday party in the afternoon. That pneumatic drill can't be silenced until after 6 PM. A key location in Venice is suddenly not available when the clergy discover there's a murder in the film (hard to imagine how they view the Bible). Every day, to quote our wonderful Italian crew's shrugging words of explanation, is a casino.

And yet I would rather spend an afternoon with an Italian than anybody else. They know certain things about the world. They know how to lean. They most certainly know how to eat. They stare particularly well. They mostly know how to dress.

The search for Mongibello took me and Roy Walker, the film's production designer, on a loop around the perimeter of Italy, tracing its coastline with increasing frustration for the necessary constituents: a house with a terrace giving directly on to a harbor; a pungent sense of life unchanged for centuries; good beaches—in short, an undiscovered Italy. Starting at Portofino (too self-consciously glamorous), then taking the train that winds through the Cinque Terre, that rosary of vertical medieval towns on the country's outer thigh, exquisitely colored like so many Klee landscapes, we eventually strayed as far south as Sicily. Italy has not cherished its past and has been cavalier, particularly on its coastline, with postwar building. The Amalfi coast, the obvious choice for Mongibello, was not suitable. The whole region is scarred by development, some of it excruciatingly misjudged, and many beautiful medieval towns, flanked by a single clogged road—Positano, Amalfi, Ravello—are suffocating under the accretions of garish holiday homes clustered round them like cheap baubles on an elegant neck.

I was excited by the neighboring volcanic islands of Lipari and Salina, off Sicily's northern coastline, but their inaccessibility, and the lack of a house or terrace sufficiently ostentatious for Dickie or of a real focus to their harbors, led us to surrender their austere charms for two other islands off the Gulf of Naples, Ischia and Procida, less admired sisters of glamorous Capri. From their complex geographies, we created a map of a small village, with Dickie's and Marge's respective houses at either end of a harbor, a beach, a church, a small piazza. The houses themselves were on Ischia, but the funneled alleys and cobbled streets which connected them were shot on Procida.

The process of witnessing, which I think of as a particular duty of the director, extends beyond observing the work of the actors in the film. A choreographer once told me that he began each day in the studio by writing down everything in his head and tossing the results into the bin, a kind of mental spring cleaning. I try to observe the same exercise when arriving on set, abandoning the meticulous planning that preproduction has until that moment demanded, and telling myself that any obstacle is useful, every curse contains a blessing. This happened on several occasions in *Ripley*, not least in the circumstances surrounding an important scene in the movie, where a local girl, Silvana, secretly pregnant with Dickie's child, drowns herself for shame during a religious ceremony.

While working on the screenplay in a monastery in Cetona, Tuscany, I had had a dream in which I had seen a statue of the Madonna surfacing in the sea, followed by the body of a young woman. From this image a whole strand of the screenplay had developed, a calm surface broken by a death in the water, prefiguring what would happen later with Dickie. Now we were in Ischia, there seemed no appropriate place to stage the festival in a way that the American characters could have vantage of the event while remaining appropriately isolated from the rest of the community, whom I wanted present in the scene.

During our location scouting, Roy Walker and I stood on Dickie's terrace and decided to make the best of an eroded slipway that poked into a narrow cove next to the house but was altogether too small. On the back of an envelope we devised a plan to enlarge the scale of the celebration by surrounding the cove with fishing boats, imagining a festival in which the Madonna was blessing the harvest of fish, as if this Christian event had been written over a pagan one, an idea consonant with the notion that the American interlopers were reading only the surface of the world they had found themselves in and not its darker currents. The location seemed a necessary but unhappy compromise.

• • •

A few weeks later, our art director arrived back in Rome with photographs and a painting, which corresponded almost exactly to the sketch on our envelope. When I asked where he'd found these references, he told me they'd come from Ischia, that the slipway was the very same we'd felt obliged to select.

But I also examine the equivalent of the choreographer's trash. A year before filming, I had been invited to Capri to receive an award for what seemed no better reason than being in possession of an Italian surname. I went on the basis that it would be a good opportunity to visit the Amalfi coast and do some exploring. Afterwards, I was cajoled by the producer to go to a club on the island where he assured me there would be a terrific party. He introduced me to a young friend, darkly handsome and effervescent, who had turned up during the evening and together we drove to an extremely unprepossessing building.

Inside we found a cave, throbbing with people, who burst into applause as the producer's friend appeared, chanting his name—Fiorello! Fiorello!—and practically carrying him on to the stage. It transpired that Fiorello is a national star. Struggling through the crowd, he jumped on to the stage, began a writhing impression of Michael Jackson, sang, and danced. "And now," he shouted, "all the way from America [sic] to sing for you tonight, Anthony Minghella!"

I would love to report that this social wallflower declined, but I didn't. The atmosphere was contagious, and I found myself sharing a microphone, singing my heart out to a medley of songs. Somewhere during my intoxicating stint in the club I had found myself talking to a coven of Italy's celebrated singers, listened carefully to their advocacy of a famous 1950s song whose composer was also present, "Tu Vuoi Fa l'Americano."

It had long occurred to me as I struggled with the screenplay that at the heart of Tom Ripley's unease is the fear of not being chosen. It's one of the things that makes him human. I think everyone knows this feeling or its correlative, knows too that for each of us as we pass from child to adult is the essential recognition that we are alone, the essential desire that we yearn not to be alone.

Music was to play a huge role in the film of Ripley, and here—in the incident at the Capri club—I had found a way for Ripley to make the first significant claim for Dickie's affection, through music, through being chosen to come up on stage in a jazz club in Naples. And so my own experience, barely mediated, literal even to the extent of casting Fiorello in the movie, having him use the same form of words for inviting Tom

Ripley up on stage, found its way into the film in a moment of unadulterated pleasure, as he and Dickie and Fiorello jump and jive their way through "Tu Vuoi Fa l'Americano," a song about Italians wanting to be American, in a film about Americans wanting to be Italian.

In a sense, the blatantly fictional landscape of Italy created to serve Ripley's story provides only a more noisy broadcast of what each traveller experiences. Just as a reader projects an internal and unique film of the novel he or she is reading—imagining rooms, faces, gestures—so the traveller brings home from each journey a landscape that is selective and personal, influenced by expectation, mood, the weather, a romantic encounter, a great meal, a terrible one.

As tourists, we pay attention with a rigor that would paralyze us at home. The man who passes Trafalgar Square every day without looking at it is the same man who carefully photographs the Bernini sculpture in Piazza Navona. And what is it about, this endless snapping and videoing, if not to prove we were there, to say that this is what we thought beautiful or significant, this is what we want to remember? Similarly, if the adapter of a novel aims to be the ideal reader, a passionate advocate of the source material, then the film director must attempt the same function as a witness to the world he finds himself in, collecting and marveling, abandoned to subjectivity, the ideal tourist.

Behind the Eyes of a Killer

David Gritten / 2000

From the *Daily Telegraph*, February 12, 2000. © David Gritten/Telegraph Media Group Limited 2000. Reprinted by permission.

When the writer-director Anthony Minghella sets about adapting a novel for film—a task at which he is astonishingly skilled—this is how he goes about it. First, he borrows a country cottage; for his last two films, he has used one in Dorset owned by his friend, film producer Duncan Kenworthy. It was here that Minghella brilliantly molded Michael Ondaatje's *The English Patient* into an Oscar-winning big-screen epic, and where he also wrote his latest film, *The Talented Mr. Ripley* (released on February 25), based on Patricia Highsmith's unsettling psychological thriller from 1956.

He drives down to the cottage from his Hampstead home with a "truckload of books." For *The English Patient* it was "a lot of stuff about Cairo in the early thirties," he says, "about map-making, explorers, the Resistance in Italy, letters from soldiers in Anzio. Anything that fed the novel back to me."

For *The Talented Mr. Ripley*, Minghella's books included the works of two photographers: William Claxton, the portraitist of jazz musicians, and the great Henri Cartier-Bresson. He took *Remembering Denny*, Calvin Trillin's memoir of a dazzling young man who after Yale spent the fifties struggling with his sexuality; books about the New York jazz scene; and the diaries of Chet Baker, the legendary jazz singer and trumpeter.

These volumes offer clues to his filmic vision of Highsmith's novel. Its antihero is Tom Ripley (Matt Damon), a young upstart of humble origins who craves gracious living. In New York he encounters Mr. Greenleaf, a rich shipbuilder who wrongly assumes Tom was at college with his son Dickie (Jude Law), a dilettante living it up in an Italian coastal town.

Greenleaf pays Tom to go to Italy to bring Dickie home to take over the family business; but Tom falls in love with the charismatic, insensitive Dickie and becomes part of his clique, which includes his girlfriend Marge (Gwyneth Paltrow). When Dickie tires of Tom and rejects him, Tom kills him and assumes his identity, at last living the high life he always wanted. In other words, he reinvents himself. Minghella has stressed the homoerotic element of Tom's attraction to Dickie; it remains coded in Highsmith's novel, for all its dated references to "sissies" and "fairies." A barely talented painter in the books, Dickie hopes to play sax in a jazz group in the film. Tom feigns enthusiasm for jazz to impress Dickie, but his tastes are loftier; in New York he works as a humble lavatory attendant at an opera house, though in Italy he makes it to a box seat.

Highsmith made Tom Ripley a nihilistic, calculating petty criminal, but the film softens him; rather he becomes enmeshed in deceptions of his own making.

Minghella also invented a major character for his film: Meredith Logue (Cate Blanchett), an heiress trying to jettison the trappings of her privileged upbringing, and therefore Ripley's opposite. And Peter Smith-Kingsley (Jack Davenport), mentioned briefly in the book, is fleshed out significantly; he and Ripley enjoy an affectionate but doomed relationship.

Lastly, Minghella sets the scene a few years later—making it 1958, when Italy was in the fleeting, heady, pleasure-seeking period known as "*Il boom*," captured unforgettably by Fellini's classic film *La Dolce Vita*.

"You take enormous liberties with the novels," I tell Minghella, whom I meet in an appropriately bookish setting—the reference library of Kenwood House in Hampstead Heath, north London, near his home. "I know," he says firmly. "I don't think you can be over-reverential. The novel will remain the same after I've made the film, so you don't have to genuflect." And what's an authentic adaptation of a book, anyway? A book on tape is the closest you can get to it. Other than that, you have to do something different."

Intriguingly, he travels down to the country cottage without the source novel. "When I adapted *The English Patient*, I was so in awe of it I couldn't have it near me while I worked. There would have been such temptation to corral chunks of material from the book and shove it into the script.

"Part of adaptation is that you're trying to write your way back to the book, to those things that arrested you in the first place. You have to find your way through the thicket of writing to what's essential about the story. It's just like when you retell a joke—you emphasize those elements that move or excite or amuse you."

Before becoming a big film name, he worked for a spell for Jim Henson's company adapting Grimm's *Fairy Tales* for a TV series, *The Storyteller.* "It was a lesson to me in how essential stories get changed from region to region, while remaining recognizably the same story. I try to make that an apologia for my adapting methods."

Minghella, forty-five, is an amiable, courteous man. He's also dazzlingly articulate, so it's predictable that he has a plausible rationale for his changes to *The Talented Mr. Ripley.* He repeatedly refers to his "argument" with the novel; in other words, modifying those elements that do not appeal to him.

"I suppose I wanted to emphasize what's familiar and human about Tom Ripley," he says. "That way you can gauge the extent to which extreme action is linked to lying and other small sins of omission. For me that's more interesting than to judge him as a sociopath and watch him behaving badly."

As for substituting music for painting in the story, music lover Minghella is unapologetic. "Painting on film isn't dynamic in any form. It's literally watching paint dry. Music is such a pungent way of taking you to a particular time and place."

He mentions a scene in which Ripley sits in with Dickie's jazz group, crooning *My Funny Valentine* in the style of Chet Baker. "Tom can speak to Dickie through that song. He could never say that lyric, 'Your looks are laughable/Unphotographable,' without the music. And later he goes to the opera to see *Eugene Onegin,* about a man who kills his best friend, and understands the reality of his actions for the first time. He has made his way to the box at the opera, but it's all hollow."

He and the novel go back a long way. When he was a student at Hull University, dramatist Alan Plater commissioned him to write his first play, and wrote the program notes for it, observing that Minghella's writing reminded him of Patricia Highsmith. Minghella had never read a word of her, but rushed out and bought *The Talented Mr. Ripley.*

He also identifies with Tom Ripley. "The fascination I have with him is about the tendency we have to jettison the very things that characterize us. When I was growing up on the Isle of Wight [his Italian parents made and sold ice cream in Ryde], I couldn't wait to leave. Now I can't wait to get back. It's a special, marvelous place to have been raised."

His young cast—Damon, Paltrow, Blanchett—are quite a collection of stars, the first time Minghella has worked with such a constellation. "It's also the first time I've worked with actors who aren't my peer group," Minghella says. "I was dad. When I cast them, they were all promising. Gwyneth was just about to do *Shakespeare in Love*, Matt hadn't opened in *Good Will Hunting*, Cate hadn't quite finished *Elizabeth*.

"The shadow of their celebrity started to cross the film before it even started, and the expectation level for the film grew. But all of them are actors before they are movie stars. And Matt Damon is the most responsible and collaborative actor I have ever worked with. He was an incredible ally." Damon, one of America's most bankable young heart-throbs, had to play a killer with openly homosexual tastes—a formula to make studio executives apprehensive. I tell Minghella I heard rumors during production that Paramount wanted him to downplay the gay content in his script.

"Maybe the stories you heard had some accuracy," he says, choosing his words carefully. "But no one tried to invade the process. I had the final cut, and there's not a frame of the film that isn't as I wanted it to be.

"It's not surprising the studio would be nervous. It was a lot of money for them to lose. And I'm astonished by what's happened to this film." (To date it has grossed about $80 million in the United States.)

He fought to persuade Paramount that Englishman Jude Law should be the patrician bohemian Dickie. "It may be easier for British actors to essay issues of class," Minghella says cautiously. "But I also wanted something specific. Jude has such effervescence. I feel he lives life with the volume controls turned up. I wanted someone who could be a satyr, the absolute opposite to the tonalities Matt would bring. Jude was in a category of one. And when I get obsessed with actors, I don't surrender them easily."

Indeed he doesn't. Fox famously pulled out of *The English Patient* because of his stubborn insistence on the then little-known Kristin Scott Thomas in the lead female role. Beneath his expansive cinema, that's how Minghella is nowadays. After his success with the 1990 British film *Truly, Madly, Deeply*, he went off to America and directed the amiable romantic comedy *Mr. Wonderful* with Matt Dillon. It disappointed him: "It made me understand what I had to be if I were to survive. On that film I had no power, no muscle to see the film home.

"At the time of *The English Patient* I thought, I'll only survive in this job if I stand or fall by my own lights. I have to follow my own compass. If people don't like the films I made, they'll just take my check away. Now, of course, I feel I must pursue a vision of what a movie should be."

After *The Talented Mr. Ripley* runs its course, that's just what he'll do. His next film, for Miramax and United Artists, is his adaptation of Charles Frazier's bestselling American Civil War novel *Cold Mountain*. He hopes he'll be able to use many of the Ripley cast.

"I've made films in Africa and Italy, and for this one, I imagine I'll be in North Carolina," he says. "But I have to write it first. We have a new cottage lined up, in Hampshire this time, on a farm." All he'll need is a truckload of the right books to take with him.

Happy Days

Ted Sheehy / 2001

From *Film Ireland* no. 79 (February 2001). Reprinted by permission of the author.

At the launch of the Beckett on Film season in Dublin, Anthony Minghella, Damien O'Donnell, and Neil Jordan spoke with Ted Sheehy about filming Samuel Beckett's plays.

Ted Sheehy: Is it just that it's Beckett's work or can you conceive of yourselves otherwise wanting to make short films that are formally experimental?

Anthony Minghella: I think you'd get a different answer from every director but in my case it was entirely connected with a long-held admiration for Beckett. I studied Beckett, I tried to do a doctorate on Beckett's work, *Play* was the first play I ever directed—it was a very particular reason to go into the world of short films and I'm not sure that anyone else would have got me into that arena. Having said that I suspect that Michael Colgan and Alan Moloney can persuade anyone to do anything so the likelihood is that we'll all be back here next year doing some project they have up their sleeves.

Damian O'Donnell: It depends on who initiates it really, if you're talking about inspiring established filmmakers to work in the short medium FilmFour have a website and they did something in association with *Dazed and Confused* where they got a load of artists, including people like Harmony Korine, to make one-minute films on digital for broadcast on the web. I think, if someone has any sort of drive, filmmakers are open to experimenting and the thing about short films is that you don't make a huge investment of time and if someone else is looking after production of it, it's fun really.

AM: Well you're doing a thing with Mike Figgis, aren't you?

DD: Yeah, I'm working on a website for Mike Figgis's film, *Hotel*, because I'm interested in all that kind of thing and he's invited me along to work on it, to develop material. It's five weeks work and what I like about it is I don't have to think, is this a year of my life? It's only a couple of months and I think people should always make room for that kind of work.

Neil Jordan: Any opportunity you can get to do something that makes you think of the form, that's what it made me think about. You've got this strange wonderful piece of work and you've got to think of a way in which to make cinema, cameras and all the cumbersome stuff, express this lovely thing. It was great.

AM: The play that I did was called *Play*, his one excursion into film was called *Film*, and it tells you that he was a formalist long before he was obsessed with content. It's interesting that Neil's done this installation at the Museum of Modern Art [IMMA] with seven versions . . .

NJ: He does force you to rethink the medium because Julianne [Moore] had to do this—it only made sense if it was one long take so every angle we did had to encompass the entire performance. Mostly in a film, if you look at the bits you've got, the tiny bits, the entire film is a composite of those bits. In this case the bits I had were all of the same length, of the entire piece. It was interesting just to say let's put all these bits together and let people look at them at the same time. Beckett makes you think that way.

TS: Is that a paradoxical aspect of the project, that the concerns of the Beckett estate and the precision of Beckett's dialogue and stage directions gives you the opportunity to draw back right into the camera?

NJ: You stick yourself in a tiny confine and you have to work out not only how to photograph it but what the act of photographing it means. For me it was an opportunity to do something you'd never get the opportunity to do, to engage with ideas you'd never get the chance to engage with in commercial cinema, at all.

DD: For me, and I'm obviously a fan of short films, I just find that people move on from that and part of the delight of this project is that people who'd never make a short film have gone back and made a short film and I hope to keep on making short films, it's a beautiful medium.

NJ: And having made a film that's so short it's odd to have to publicize it so much! [Laughter all round.]

Film Ireland: Will the experience inform what you do next?

DD: I think so, absolutely, it has made me think seriously about the kind of films I want to make and the form of films both short and long. I found the whole thing quite revitalizing in a way.

AM: One of the things I think is really good about this project is that one of the most contentious areas of movie-making is the possessory credit—"A Neil Jordan Film," "A Damien O'Donnell Film," "An Anthony Minghella Film." What's interesting here is that it's a Samuel Beckett Season, a cycle of Samuel Beckett films, and our contribution is muted and rightly so. The other odd phenomenon is that it's very strange if you're a filmmaker because you very rarely meet other filmmakers. You meet actors, you meet editors, you meet all kinds of other people, production designers, but directors are very rarely in the same place or working together on the same project so this has been fantastic and really nourishing—to be in Toronto with Damien and Conor McPherson and Kieron J. Walsh—just talking about being a filmmaker. Talking about our reactions to working in this particular world and environment. It reminds us that we're all trying to say something using this form, that everybody loves Beckett, that everybody loves film.

TS: Does the normal industrial way of working militate against what Anthony's just spoken about?

NJ: Yeah, of course. For one thing you work in a medium where the audience just gets younger and younger and as you get older and older [laughter] you don't still want to speak to seventeen-year-old males. What I found liberating about this was the ideas were impenetrable but liberating in a strange way because you never encounter these ideas. I have to go back to watching some of those obscure Bergman movies like *In the Life of the Marionettes*, the weird ones, where the guy was battling with ideas of performance and reality.

AM: One of the things about Beckett is that he was writing very much in a period where people working in literature became terribly conscious about their words whereas if you were working in a different discipline, like music or painting, you were able to create—you were involved—in abstract language. In literature you were having to coopt the stuff of everyday life, people are talking and using language all the time. So he became so sensitized to not getting caught in the trap of idiom that he forced himself to go into another language to work. When he goes into theatre he's like someone who's never been in a theatre before, he reimagines what the theatre could be about, how it might work. I feel that it forces you to, as Neil was saying when you go into the arena of cinema, to reconsider the fact that you've got a camera, you've got an actor, and you're making sound. Everything somehow is refreshed through his eyes and I think that has happened with this entire series. It's not only about being important and impenetrable and difficult, it's also about simply revitalizing everybody.

NJ: It's also about making different kinds of movies.

DD: Nineteen people got to make a Samuel Beckett film, everyone should have a go at it, I think. Every filmmaker should go out and make a Samuel Beckett film.

NJ: I think Joel Schumacher should go out there, and do them all . . .

DD: Definitely . . . [much laughter]

Anthony Minghella: In Conversation (Part 2)

Mario Falsetto / 2003–4

From *The Making of Alternative Cinema Volume 1: Dialogues with Independent Filmmakers*, Mario Falsetto. Copyright © 2008 by Mario Falsetto. Reproduced with permission of ABC-CLIO, Santa Barbara, CA, and the author.

Mario Falsetto: What initially attracted you to Patricia Highsmith's novel *The Talented Mr. Ripley*? What was at the core of it for you, because the character of Ripley is fairly different in the novel. In the novel he seems quite sociopathic, completely amoral and almost asexual. You definitely made him more psychological. In your film, he's more sympathetic and has some sense of morality about his crime.

Anthony Minghella: When I look back, some people think I got Ripley very wrong. People felt that I had larded the character with a conscience. The striking thing about Ripley in the novel for those people is that he has no conscience. And that's probably true, but I think it's a very Catholic film. I think you can tell that the coding of that film is Catholic. When I look at it I think, "This is somebody under the thumb of monks and nuns."

I wrote a song for that film and I tried to work out what I was thinking about when I wrote it. It's about Cain and Abel, original sins, cardinal sins, killing somebody you love and the covetedness that will make you want to destroy somebody because they have what you think they don't deserve. The self-loathing at the center of Ripley really interested me, which maybe is not in the book. The questions I would ask myself when I was working on that film were things like, "What would it take for somebody to extinguish the life of somebody else?" "What really does it require to feel that that's a solution?" "How would I get to a place where I could kill somebody?" The film is incredibly personal for me. It's obsessed with class, with fraudulence, with darkness. I wrote a speech in my play, *Made in Bangkok*, which is so much the primer for Ripley where this character says, "There's a cellar inside me. If you could see it, and how disgusting it is. . . ." And that's where Ripley ends up when he concedes, "You don't want to know me. If you knew me better, who I really was, you would not want me and not love me." The fear people have is that if you were transparent to another human being, they would never accept you. They would never accept you with all your demons. That sort of sewage of the soul, they wouldn't want it. That's why I think it's the most personal film that I've made. I think people felt it wasn't characteristic at all, but I think it's very clearly connected to my sensibility.

I had an experience when I was seventeen which may seem entirely trivial but to me was the loadstone of Ripley. As I've mentioned, my father was an ice cream maker on the Isle of Wight, and when I was growing up I worked for him and in the summers would deliver ice cream around the island. It's a very interesting place insofar as 99 percent of the population is either involved in a mediocre tourist industry or in agricultural activity. The other 1 percent is this incredibly elite aristocracy, or so it seemed to me when I was growing up. Just around the perimeter of the island would be these grand houses and grand society, sort of vestigial remnants of when Queen Victoria lived on the Isle of Wight. There was a time when Dickens and Tolstoy and Turgenev would all come to the Isle of Wight to write. It's the center of the yachting world, it's where all the boats arrive in the summer and there's always been this sort of odd, aristocratic mascara around this otherwise rural environment.

My collar couldn't have been any bluer than it was at that time. I remember driving my delivery van wearing a yellow nylon jacket, which I so objected to when I was seventeen, this yellow jacket with "Minghella's Ice Cream" written on it. Anyway, I'm driving along and these two teenagers were hitchhiking and they were exquisite—I mean, just "kissed" people. I remember the girl had this sort of sweater tied just so and these gorgeous deck shoes and brown skin, and they were hitchhiking. So I stopped because people stopped then and gave people lifts. They got into the truck and I'm driving along and they're sort of giggling. And I said, "Where can I take you?" And they said, "Where are you going?" And I said where I was going. "Well, we'll just come with you because we just wanted to find out what it was like to hitch a ride." Basically they were just experimenting with brushing up against the locals. If you want to know what the fabric of the scenes between Marge and Dickie and Ripley was it's the sense memory of that drive with my equivalent of Marge and Dickie. And my absolute sense of feeling grotesque and that I could never be admitted to that world. It was a world of privilege and a world of beauty. This was the river in which I was fishing and it was a pretty ugly river.

MF: Do you think many people are dissatisfied with themselves as human beings?

AM: I do. I think lots of people have this idea of pressing your face up against the world you can't be part of. I was at this marketing meeting at Paramount and I said, "There's a bit of Ripley in everybody. That's why Ripley is so fascinating as a character because everybody knows what it means to feel like him." And this woman said, "Excuse me. Could you please not say that because I certainly have nothing in common with him. I like my life. I have no desire to kill anybody. Please don't say this in any interview that you think there is a part of Ripley in everybody because there's not." I realize it's a sore point, that moment of shame.

MF: I think Matt Damon is pretty amazing in the film. He really surprised me.

AM: I thought Matt Damon was absolutely superb, a completely unsung hero of that film in terms of what he did as an actor. It's totally extraordinary because it's so honest and it's so achieved in the sense that the moment he turns on Dickie, the moment he kills, you understand the gear changes and the helpless cranking up to the point where he wants to bludgeon everything and anybody in front of him. That's when he gets very cold to me, and he captured something where his humanity disappears. The Cain and Abel story is the primary story of men.

I also felt Ripley was a tourist. I remember having a discussion with my line producer on the film, a great guy named Alessandro von Norman who was the production manager on *La Dolce Vita*—he died unfortunately—but he was one of the great navigators for me in my time making movies in Italy, which I hope is not finished. I wanted to shoot in Piazza di San Marco in Venice and he said, "You can't shoot properly in that square. You just can't do it. You'll be struggling and it won't work. There is a great little square I can take you to. It's beautiful, it's containable, we can control it, we can lock it all off and you'll get everything you want." And I said, "Can you imagine if you're Tom Ripley, and all your life you've wanted to be one of these people who travels to Europe and you say to somebody you're going to meet them and you're not going to meet them in the Piazza di San Marco? Ripley wants to be photographed against every monument. What are you talking about?" He's not going to invite you to some square off-the-off. He'll want to meet you in San Marco because that's where Tom Ripley belongs. Dickie Greenleaf is not going to go to the second best hotel in Rome, he's going to go to the first one. It's the obligation of the film to deliver him to these locations, he has to be in these squares. Whether it's impossible or difficult or makes no sense, the film makes no sense if we take him to some little piazza. I didn't want to make it difficult for myself, but I just knew it was wrong. That, to me, was paramount. He's the ultimate American tourist in Europe and he wants to be that person. He's writing a diary of himself all the time. In fact, they make references to it. I remember saying to Cate Blanchett, "Just imagine that everything you're doing is a diary of a trip." There's this sense of italics for all of these characters. They're all writing their young years in Europe. I think that happened a lot. If you read the journals of Americans in Europe from the 1950s and 1960s, essentially everything they do is for their diary.

I don't know how true and final it is but it feels true to me as we are speaking. If you took off all of the blubber and skin of Ripley, and just peeled off all of its flesh, what you would end up with is the Isle of Wight. You wouldn't end up with Italy, you wouldn't end up with Americans, it really is as personal as that to me. All the rest of it is just "stuff." I remember when Ripley and Dickie go off on the boat on which Dickie eventually gets killed, and thinking "that's San Remo 1959, I was there on that beach. I could be on that beach right now." My parents took me there when I was five. I looked around this beach hoping to find myself. For some reason, those were the things that I was thinking about: my own feelings about being in Italy, my own relationship to Fellini and Italian cinema. What I was delivering in that film was something almost solipsistic. That's the fact of it, and the rest of it is just blubber. It's just stuff.

MF: You were essentially exploring your Italianness?
AM: Yes. I'm not saying Ripley is a biographical film, quite the reverse. I mean, I haven't ever wanted to kill anybody. But there are so many internal compass points and some very explicit external ones. For instance, I was given this prize called the Capri-Hollywood prize. And I was thinking about doing Ripley and how to write it and where I would shoot it. I got a call from this guy saying, "We want to give you this prize on Capri. Do you want to come? It's a weekend, it's a nice hotel." And I said, "Well, I don't know. I don't think so." And he said, "Please, please come,

it will be great." And I thought I probably will end up somewhere in the Bay of Naples and Capri and I'd been there once before and had a great time, so I went. I went to this place and of course, it was just like the previous time when I won a Prix Italia in 1988, which I went to get it in the opera house in Naples. What was hilarious about that evening was I went flushed with having won a prize for a play but the whole event was about dancing girls and was punctuated, as quickly as possible, by handing somebody a little trophy. Here's the Prix Italia and now you have to get off, we've got more girls to get up for the variety show. It was an extraordinary evening.

So I went to get this Capri-Hollywood award and they had Miss Naples happening the same night and there were lots of scantily clad girls in bikinis and I was given this appalling piece of crystal or whatever it was. It was all entirely specious, it was just about having a ride-the-wave evening with girls. I was annoyed with myself for falling into it and annoyed with myself for going. This producer was full of incredibly effervescent producer-talk, "It's great, huh? We're going to get some girls and we're going to go to a club after." And I said, "No, I don't want to go to a club, thanks very much." He said, "No, you've got to come." And then this very charismatic, handsome guy showed up and said, "Minghella! How you doing? Michael Jackson, yeah yeah yeah. . . ." I thought, "Oh God." And he said, "You're going to come with me to this club?" I said "No, no. There is no way I'm going to any clubs." He said, "You come for one drink in this great club and then we'll go home." So I said okay, one drink in this club. So we go to this club and as we walk in there is this huge, rapturous reception and I thought my status in Italy was definitely greater than I'd thought. But no, they weren't interested in me at all. The guy I was with was this television presenter, a household name as it turned out. He runs up on the stage of this club, the band starts playing, he starts singing, they're all so excited about him singing and the whole place is jam-packed. He's singing and he says, "And now, all the way from Hollywood America. Anthony Ming-hel-la!" And I get pulled up on the stage in this little tiny club. Of course I used to be a singer and in a band, and they start to play and I start to sing and I have this great, great night. In the end, they had to drag me off at two in the morning after this incredible night in this club where I'd sung for an hour and a half with this band. I had the time of my life. And of course that's in the movie. Not only that, but the guy is the character in the movie, Fiorello who is also the guy who pulled me up on that stage. There are so many gestures in the film which feed my own sense of exploring some sense of not belonging, some desire to belong, the thrill when you let go which Ripley has. That thrill of opportunity.

MF: The film unfolds in somewhat musical terms. It has something to do with jazz and improvisation defining one character and the classical form defining the other.
AM: More than that because the fact is improvisation was appropriated by jazz but actually belongs to classical music. Bach was apparently the greatest improviser. You listen to the *Goldberg Variations* which are a series, basically, of elaborate improvisations.

MF: Ripley actually ends up being the great improviser.
AM: And Dickie is as square as you could possibly be. At one level it was a very practical decision because in the novel it's about the art world and I just couldn't imagine watching Dickie with a paintbrush and easel. It felt awful to me, rather pretentious. Music binds you into a period so easily. You hear a particular sound and it's so transporting. Sound is the cheapest locating device there is. What we are watching is so modified in a really intense way by what we are hearing. Because my background is sound, and Walter's background is sound, I think both of us are very keen to play on the relationship between what we are looking at and what we are listening to. The whole nature of jazz as a form of music intrigues me anyway. So it's a great device in the film because the scene in New York at that time was so much about the emergence of jazz in America and the license of jazz. Italy was so obsessed with American music in that period, it felt very legitimate. It felt legitimate that Dickie would want to think of the saxophone as an escape route from his father. The father says at the beginning, "Dickie likes jazzzzz . . . jazz is a noise, just a noise."

It also defines that period. I mean, look at the Blue Note covers, which we use in the credit sequence. It's a period in which these striations and fragmentations are so prevalent in all the visual narratives that are happening. The fact is the film is about a guy who is fragmenting, the many personalities of Tom Ripley.

MF: When I think of your work the idea of textures is so important. It's not unlike what painters do in terms of layering different kinds of textures. When you talk about sound and the different aspects of the image and light, it's just a different way of thinking about textures as opposed to this narrative drive that everyone talks about when they talk movies.

AM: That [idea of narrative drive] doesn't interest me in the slightest. I think *Ripley* is the most achieved film. I remember thinking when we were doing it that this was a film that was closer to its intention than *The English Patient*. It's more assured in how it's trying to deliver itself. It may not be as good a film but it's much closer to what I thought it was going to be.

MF: It's harder edged. It's not a question of it being better or worse but there's this complexity about it which I like.

AM: The problem with *Ripley* is it struggles. One of its obligations is to deliver a pleasing plausibility and I don't know if it can really do that. As a book, and as an idea, it's dependent on a series of devices which really strain credibility. It's one of those things that if anybody thought about for ten seconds, the whole film would stop because you can't pretend to be someone else for very long. It's hard. As a device it's hard. But I don't care about that.

MF: You either buy the premise or you don't.

AM: People get very bogged down in film with issues of plausibility in a way that is sometimes defeating to those of us who don't care much about it. I did a lot of work just on a simple dramaturgical level to have it make as much sense as it possibly could. One thing about adaptation is how it exposes books. Adaptation is a horrible flashlight on the narrative and plotting skills of an author. The glare in this film is just so naked and I defy you to really make sense of the novel. It's interesting that when René Clement made his movie [*Plein Soleil*, 1960], he jettisoned half the plot completely. In terms of its thematic ideas and how they work themselves out in my film, I was really satisfied.

MF: Could you just say something about *Play* before we move on to *Cold Mountain*? I was quite taken with it and it seems riskier in form in some ways than your other work. Why did you choose that particular one to do? You had written about Beckett in graduate school, right?

AM: Yes, my doctoral thesis was on Beckett. I was obsessed with Beckett. This is one of the very few jobs I've lobbied for in my life, to do one of the Beckett films. I was in Australia and I read on the plane that somebody was doing a series of all the Beckett plays. When I got to the London airport I called my agent and said, "I want to do one of those Beckett films." And by the time I'd gotten my bag, I'd spoken to the producer and was involved.

One of the first plays I ever directed was *Play* when I was a post-graduate student. I know that play by heart, or I did when I was a student. I think it's a perfect piece of writing, a perfect piece of theater. I remember when I was teaching, in that rather self-congratulatory way that young teachers have of getting excited by their own discoveries, I gave a tutorial and said, "I want you to come back tomorrow and tell me what the most important piece of writing is in this play. One line that you think is the most significant line in the play." They would come back and say, "It's when he says" or "It's when she says." I said, "No, the most important line is *repeat*." That's what tells you categorically and in the most beautiful way that this is a piece of dramatic literature. That it's not about what anybody says to anybody else, it's about form. It's the repetition that speaks to you and not any individual line. When you go to see a play the experience is not about what A says to B or why A says something to B, it's the fact that A says the same thing to B many, many times.

When I was doing my research on Beckett, I went to Reading to the library there where his work is collected. *Play* is a piece of writing in which the stage instructions are "as quick as possible, with as little inflection as possible." Two things which I don't think many directors say to actors. Meaning is not important. And yet, when you go to the library and see the twenty-one versions of that play, which are so meticulously worked up, each line so refined from draft to draft, this constant abrading of the language until it's as crisp and clean and precise as he knew how to make it. Yet, his intention was that half of this would not be heard. This seemed to me such a perfect provocation in the sense that on the one hand it's full of emotion and people struggling with identity and with themselves, and yet the form is so austere and so cool. When people say to me, "Where is the influence of Beckett on you? You talk about Beckett so much but I don't see any Beckett in your work at all." It is that, it is that. It's not romantic and yet it's full of heart, it's full of emotion, yet the vehicle to contain those emotions is rather cold. In the case of Beckett, they're often disembodied. Often the body itself is broken up into its salient parts. But the stuff of it could not be more lyrical and compassionate and funny. *Play* is funny. It's full of wit. But its overall tone is unbelievably dark, terrifying, the idea that purgatory would be this imperative to rehearse the same tawdry bits of our lives again and again and again. It's such a Dante-esque vision.

MF: How much of your aesthetic choices, with light for example, were described in the text?

AM: In fact, there was a bit of controversy about some of my decisions. Beckett famously didn't like too much fiddling around with his work. There is no mention of other pots on stage, for example, except the three that the principle characters are in. There was a photograph of the production of the film in the *New York Sunday Times Magazine* and it aroused such hostility that suddenly the Beckett estate got all these calls from people saying, "There is a tree! A tree! And there are lots of pots. What does he think he is doing? This is a disgrace." And it was only for the fact that this great guy who wrote Beckett's biography, James Knowlson, saw the film and thought it was the definitive production of *Play*, otherwise they would not have shown it. They were so worried about what I'd done.

In the play it says "swiveling light" which interrogates these three characters. But obviously in film, light sources can't be so uniform, otherwise you're just stuck with the camera behind the light. As soon as you start moving you can't work light in that way. You have to find some cinematic equivalent, some correlative, and to me the lens is the correlative.

MF: The editing is also interesting.
AM: Yes, it is interesting. A lot of dropped frames, a lot of accelerated frames. Because he wanted to do this as quickly as possible and you could do that, you can just drop frames out. And I worked the focus gun and the zoom myself on the camera because I knew the piece so well and I was working with Benoît Delhomme who lit the film with me. We were like a little team on the camera. I could rack focus really quickly because I knew who was going to talk next. We worked together so well. It was fun.

I wrote a radio piece on Verdi around the same time which is also completely fractured and fragmented. I think it's just me trying to work the muscle a little. In some ways, *Play* and the Verdi piece, are much closer to my own noise. My own way of wanting to make things. What I'm writing now is going to confound this run of movies because if I do get to the end of it and I can make it, it's going to be completely different.

MF: I used to think you were a very classical director, but both *Ripley* and the Beckett film have confounded that. I think it's a very modern take on how to do Beckett, and it was a surprise to see it.
AM: Well somebody just did an interview with me, and it was funny because I said, "If you think the Beckett piece is odd, listen to this Verdi monologue." This thing kind of dumfounded them. I have no desire and

no ability to step outside my own sensibility and figure out what it's up to now. It's not helpful. I think what's happened is that the little journey that I feel I'm on as a filmmaker doesn't necessarily harness all the things that I care about. So one of the questions that I have very much on my mind is whether the next film I make is going to be another large scale adaptation which harnesses all of the opportunities that are available to me. Or do I make a small film which is more personal, which might disturb an audience as much as the Beckett piece disturbed your sense of what my aesthetic is?

MF: It didn't disturb it. I was happily surprised.

AM: It wasn't a conscious gear change. I just thought it was the way to do that film. I suppose what's changed is that I know a little more about the potential of cinema. Let me use an analogy. One of the reasons I stopped composing, and why I stopped thinking I'd write music for every film I made, was because I realized that I only know how to make one kind of music. My technique is not able to adjust to content. Whereas I think in film I'm learning a slightly wider vocabulary. This is the terrible torture of being a filmmaker. Sydney [Pollack] was making a film every year at one point, and I'm like a tortoise, but it doesn't mean I'm a totally unsophisticated tortoise. I wish I could go a bit faster. One of the things that keeps me getting up in the morning and working eighteen- or twenty-hour days is because I feel like I've got a lot to learn.

MF: You've made it very hard on yourself because your most recent films are such big projects. You have these massive amounts of money and expectation riding on each film, so maybe it would be good to make a small film again.

AM: Well one of the problems is this, Mario. If I were a novelist and decided to write a version of the *Odyssey* or to write about a single person's experience in the course of a day, it would have no impact economically. I could write about Pompeii or about the walk from my office to my house in the morning, the book would cost about the same amount. It would just be content that would be different. In film, the election of subject has an enormous financial consequence. So it's not been so much that I've wanted to make expensive films, it's been that the content of the films I've wanted to make has determined their cost. If I could have made *Cold Mountain* for $3 million, I would have. I would love to have done it because every one of those dollars that I spent comes with a claw attached to it.

MF: These last three films are such daunting projects, I mean just physically. I can't even imagine what you've gone through to make them.

AM: There's nearly twice as much labor in *Cold Mountain* as anything I've done. *Cold Mountain* is five years of my life.

MF: Okay, let's move on to *Cold Mountain*. Did you feel badly treated by some of the film's reception? It's obviously a very ambitious film and quite an achievement but there seemed to be some resistance to it. And certainly Hollywood didn't treat you very well. Well, maybe that's overstating it but not to nominate you for Best Writing or Best Directing Oscars seemed a bit harsh to me. Were you bothered by that?

AM: Well, it's interesting that on the day of the nominations, and we got seven nominations, it was as if somebody had died. I got a couple hundred e-mails of commiseration and I thought, "This is a very weird place to be in my life where a movie gets nominated for seven Academy Awards and people are saying 'Oh my God, I can't believe this. This is a disgrace. What's happened is a conspiracy.'"

MF: It seemed like a personal snub.

AM: It did a bit, didn't it? [laughs]

MF: I felt maybe it was a backlash against Miramax.

AM: There was a lot of stuff going on. I read somewhere something like, "The problem with this film is it knows how good it is." And I thought, "What are you talking about?" It was a very vindictive review which liked the movie but was annoyed with what it perceived was its self-importance. Why would people feel so obliged to go after it? The last thing we should be talking about, in a way, is the boring "it" of *Cold Mountain*, but I do know that people were written to and contacted. I got letters from director friends of mine saying, "What's the big deal about it? People are calling saying not to vote for this movie, because of this and because of that." There was definitely an active campaign against the film. Every member of the Director's Guild got a letter.

Miramax have written the book on getting people's attention for films. They've written the book on how you do it and people have learned from it. Perhaps this was an occasion where there was some bad reaction to that, or some bad reaction to me, or some bad reaction to the content of the film. The film was not supported. Michael Moore said a very interesting thing about *Cold Mountain*. He wrote very beautifully about the film and was a huge supporter of it. He said it's the most political, theatrical film in a long time. I think some people resented the fact that a British filmmaker had come in and said anything at all about either the Civil War or the war in Iraq, extrapolating from it some sense of what was going on in the world then. There was some hostility towards me because of that. On the other hand, at the time of *The English Patient*, I felt that the noise that grew around it was disproportionate to what it was. I couldn't quite see how we went from what we'd done to a kind of rapture that was attendant to it. And I felt the corollary of that with *Cold Mountain*. I felt that the resistance was rather disproportionate to what it was.

One of the things that happened that I knew was problematic was Nicole [Kidman] winning an Oscar in the March of the year it came out. I knew that was a shame at some level because she had been so anointed and in a way Hollywood had given her her presents. "That's enough for a while, Nicole." I felt that very much, that the tide was going out when we arrived. That doesn't explain it all. I have no objectivity about the film, I certainly gave it my best shot.

MF: Did you follow the same method of working as your previous two films?

AM: *Cold Mountain* is the clearest illustration of a particular method of working. And it's probably the last illustration of it. I felt that this process of how to make a film, which started with *The English Patient* and developed in *Ripley*, came to some kind of culmination in *Cold Mountain*. As I was doing it, I was thinking, "I shouldn't do this again. I shouldn't make a film in this way again because I don't want it to become a procedure." It felt to me like it was becoming institutionalized with my group of people, the way I go about making the movie, the way I go about the adaptation, the way I go about bringing the image to the screen. It felt to me like it was hardening into a procedure as I was doing it. I wanted it to be the best one done this way, but I want it to be the last one. I don't want to repeat the shaping of process. Even though I felt every part of it was a better expression of that process than I'd managed before: the research was more detailed; the collection of the research was more structured; the design process was the most rigorous.

MF: Are you saying that your meticulousness could become a limitation in some way in the future if you kept making films in the same way?

AM: I just felt that there was something about it which was in danger of becoming too set. This is what we do. This is how our guys work. Walter gets this. John comes in here. It felt like a pattern and I don't want it to be a pattern. I feel like the next movie I make mustn't have a research element to it, it must be contemporary. It must be original and it must be smaller. Just the scale of *Cold Mountain* knocked me out. It knocked me out in terms of what was required of me. Maybe part of the resistance was a resistance to that sense of entitlement or something, that every frame is going to work so hard. There is something in that and I feel it myself. I feel that there is an egging-on that we do collectively: who is going to leave the cutting room last? How much ADR writing can I do on this film? How many more times can I go back in and get another line from Nicole? On the very last day of the mix I'm calling Jude, in New York I think, to see if I could get one line to turn differently. There is something between Harvey [Weinstein] and me as well, where we just push and push and jostle like these tectonic plates grinding against each other to try and see if there is anything more that we can do. Part of me feels that's great. But I made the Beckett film in one week. It's not that it was thrown together because I know the play. I'd done my work. But it's got a different sort of metabolism and part of what I've been doing is suffocating the metabolism.

MF: Maybe working the clay too much.
AM: Yes. Maybe that's what people felt, that it was slightly overworked. The most important thing I've realized is that my investment cannot be in the result. It can't be in the result of films because you can't live the results. If you came in this morning and said, "Hey! Three hundred million dollars and ten Academy Awards. How do you feel?" I would feel exactly the same as I feel now. "What has that got to do with the scene I can't write at the moment? What's it got to do with my headache?" I have to say that on an emotional level, I'm a bit detached from the result. Maybe not as much as I believe, but I'm largely detached from it. I realize that when you say *Cold Mountain* you mean two hours and thirty-two minutes, and when I say *Cold Mountain* I mean five years, and those were a great five years of my life. A fantastic period of struggle and determination and experience and discovery, fantastic. You could give me nothing to replace that experience. Where I went and what I did and what I saw and what I asked of myself was an amazing thing. I wouldn't give you any of it back for anything. So I'm quite clear about that in my mind, that process has to be honorable, process has to be good, process has to be rigorous. The way that I work with people has to be rewarding to me.

MF: Any film is always judged, to some extent, by the hype at the moment when it's released. And there was a lot of anticipation of the film.
AM: There was, maybe too much. It will be interesting to see if it holds up or not when the dust settles, and frankly, I don't know. I don't know if it's any good or not and nothing I can do now will make it better or worse.

MF: I'm sure it will hold up. But these things all have different meanings, ten, twenty years from now.
AM: A review in that same magazine I spoke to you about earlier said, "I don't need to see *Cold Mountain* to know I will hate it." Which I thought was an interesting place to get to with a movie, "I don't need to see it." Maybe it also had something to do with the way we presented ourselves. You know, "This is a movie that's been five years in the making and they've built every location and this is the most authentic. . . ." Sydney [Pollack] sounded this rather odd note of warning and said, "People are talking too much about this movie and nobody has seen it." I think that was a problem, that we didn't finish it until very late so nobody saw it.

MF: How much of what we finally see was in the original script of *Cold Mountain?*
AM: I would say this, I feel that I made that film in my room in Hampshire, where I go to write, way before I showed up on a set. It doesn't mean that the film wasn't absolutely reimagined when I was shooting, or reimagined in editing. But I saw every moment of that film, and tried to corral it when I was by myself. It doesn't mean that I don't feel entirely enthralled to performance, to the camera, to the location.

I saw a movie and I recorded it in my notebooks. I saw it when I read the book of *Cold Mountain.* I dreamt it and many of the images in the film have not altered from that. I was looking at a notebook from 1998 of *Cold Mountain,* which describes an image that is the first image, in a different form and with different details to how the movie opens now.

As a screenwriter, increasingly as I know I'm directing my own films, I put less and less information in the screenplay because I don't feel it's required. I feel like I'm designing a building when I write a screenplay. I'm just imagining a movie instead of a building. The obligation of the architect is to work in a space, and work within the constraints of planning. When I write, I imagine a movie in the same way that an architect imagines a functioning building.

MF: You've said in interviews that one of the biggest issues for you in *Cold Mountain* was to examine the nature of violence in human beings. That's probably not what a mainstream audience wants to think about. They want the romantic epic but this film isn't interested in doing that.

AM: The lovers are not together for 90 percent of the film. People kept questioning why I did that, but that's the whole point. The *Odyssey* is about an odyssey. You take away the odyssey, there's no *Odyssey* [laughs]. I wanted to make a movie about walking. Before I'd found *Cold Mountain* I had written a bunch of notes about walking for atonement, for redemption.

MF: This is another Catholic movie . . .

AM: It is. If *Ripley* was a purgatory film then this is a redemption film. This is about what happens if you stay true to your course. The tradition of life as a spiritual struggle on a road. Life as a road, and your choices, the straight and narrow of it all. In some ways, Inman is a very conventional hero. He sets off and he's visited along the way by obstacles and confrontations and opportunities, and the rosary of his decisions will determine whether he gets home or not. And home is both geographical and metaphysical. It is both a real place and a place of the heart and spirit. Again, that is rather a cool architecture for an idea. It's not about running back into the arms of a woman. In fact, when they meet, they don't really recognize each other. A studio head told Nicole that the problem with the film when they read the script is that it didn't deliver the return. It seemed to me such a misreading of what the film was trying to say, which is that it's about a man and a woman, what hope is and what reality is.

MF: You and Walter Murch have mentioned that one way to think about the film is as if Inman was already dead. That's an interesting idea and it makes you think about the film differently.

AM: The film is full of ghosts. I thought about Pincher Martin when I was writing. It did occur to me that he falls and the bird throbbing and the heart dying and finally going, that it's his bones that get up. He says it himself, "I always stood toe-to-toe with my enemy. He never killed me and I always killed him. I don't understand it. I don't know why." It's this thing that you're dead already. It's just your will getting home, your spirit returning. I wrote a scene that I cut which says, "She puts a scarecrow in the field just in case his spirit flies over looking out for me." In the original writing there was much more of this idea.

There is a Wilfred Owen poem called "Strange Meeting" which was very instructive to me in terms of mood about a British and a German soldier who meet in some sort of resting place after they've killed each other in battle. It has this notion of the spirit walking, trying to find home, trying to find its destination. "Cold mountain" in Chinese poetry is a spiritual destination. "Men asked the way to cold mountain. Cold mountain, there is no easy route. Would you recognize cold mountain?" I started writing all these cold mountain poems when I was turning it into a screenplay, little aphorisms.

MF: The acting in the film is quite astonishing. Do you think that Jude Law achieves something in the film that he hasn't done before as an actor?

AM: There is enormous gravity in his appearance in *Cold Mountain* and there is almost none in *Ripley*. I've got so much time for Jude as an actor, as a man, as a colleague. There is nobody you would want to be on a set with more than him because there is nothing he won't do, there is nowhere he won't go. He's like a puppy in terms of his appetite to work, his appetite to play, his appetite to explore. You're never in the way of his ego. There is nothing between you and him in terms of work. He'll just go anywhere with you. I feel an enormous love for him and I feel it back from him.

MF: What about Nicole Kidman? I found her character a little precious.

AM: Ada is a thistly character. She is awkward and uncomfortable. I don't think of these people as Nicole and Jude at all. Nicole is a larky Australian girl, she's not Ada Munroe. I think of who she made, and who she made was spiky and uncomfortable, and sometimes self-regarding and coquettish; at other times, incredibly frail. I wouldn't change a beat of what she or Jude did. I thought they were perfect.

MF: What about Renée Zellweger?

AM: If you'd said to me when I made *Ripley*, "Who is going to get attention in this movie?" I would have said Jude Law. If you said to me, "Who is going to get attention in *Cold Mountain*?" I would have said Renée Zellweger before we even began shooting. Those are the two great parts. When you're playing Dickie Greenleaf and the whole film is about you, even though it was called *The Talented Mr. Ripley*, everybody spends the whole time talking about you in the film. "Dickie this," "Dickie that." The word "Dickie" is mentioned more times than any other in *The Tal-*

ented Mr. Ripley. In *Cold Mountain*, in your first scene you come in and rip the head off a chicken. It's one of the great entrances in a movie. And you are in this place where you can be a sort of *Annie Get Your Gun* character, but actually yours is the emotional journey.

I loved her in the film and it was very important because the film was bleak. If you take that character out, it would be one of the bleakest films of recent times. It's full of torture and annihilation and dead lovers and hopelessness. The one relief from that is this spirit that will not lie down and leaps from scene to scene. I felt that was very important. A lot of people saw the opening gestures of the performance as somehow naturalistic, as opposed to somebody who so refuses to own their emotion, which is what my discussions with Renée were always about. This is somebody who will not concede that they feel. She shields her emotions. Ada, who is incapable of hiding, is like jellyfish that changes color with emotion all the time. The other person has this carapace of resistance to emotion. "I'm fine! Hey! I'm great, I'm great! What? No, no. My dad? Who cares about my dad? I hate my dad. That's my DADDY!!" She's paralyzed with emotion and paralyzed with hurt, and very damaged. She's been an abandoned child, so of course she's not going to say to you, "I don't feel good." Sentences beginning with "I" are anathema to her. She doesn't want to have an "I." So the performance is all about where it gets to. It's not where it starts, it's about where it arrives.

When we did previews of this film, the reaction of audiences to her was so extraordinary. There was not a single preview that we did where she didn't go completely off the charts in terms of an audience embracing her character. They just loved her. It sort of stopped the film from collapsing a lot of the time because people were so distressed by the violence in it, and what they clung to was how much they loved Renée's performance.

MF: As in your previous films, there is a distance that you bring to your work. For example, I don't find *Cold Mountain* romantic in the least. It doesn't let you in easily.
AM: It's not romantic. One of the problems may be that I'm not romantic. I think one of the reasons people sometimes get disappointed is because it doesn't deliver, and I don't know how to deliver the romance that is required, or I resist it. Whether those two things are the same or different, I don't know, but I think you're absolutely right. I'm writing at the moment and it's interesting for me to be in a place where I'm writing and I'm not hostage to anybody else's design. My writing is not misan-

thropic but it's not altogether compassionate, it's not altogether kind. It's quite bilious.

People didn't cry in the movie and maybe they should have. Maybe I should have let them or found a way to deliver their tears a bit. I can tell you that it was as rigorous a piece of filmmaking as I know how to do. I worked as hard as I know how, the crew did, the cast did. It was made with enormous devotion and you couldn't wish for a triumvirate of more committed, generous, and good people than Nicole, Renée, and Jude. I felt that John [Seale] did great work, Walter [Murch] did great work, everybody did their best work. Either the alchemy is present or it's not. I suppose down the road the film will find its own feet. I mean, it was a nominated film and made a lot of money. It made $98 million in North America alone. It's done good business and people respected it. People did not fall in love with it. Is that a fair assessment? I don't think people were in love with it. And that's a shame. It's a shame when something takes five years of your life.

MF: I suppose ultimately it not only has to do with your sensibility but a more basic question of why you make movies in the first place.
AM: The question below the question of intention is the question of function, and the one thing that doesn't get asked sufficiently often is, "Why do you make movies in the first place? What is the movie for?" That question is so rarely asked by anybody. Okay, so we agree that there is this deluge of cultural documents, but nobody seems to know what they're supposed to do. If you were flooding a store with yellow plastic objects, at a certain point somebody would ask, "What are we supposed to buy these yellow objects for? What do you do with them? You just stack them up?" But we make these yellow objects called films and we stack them up in DVD collections and we go to cinemas, but nobody seems to ever say, "What am I doing this for? Is it simply so I've got a way of using up some time in my life?" And the odd thing now, and it's such an interesting commentary on our time, is that now our expectation of the yellow object is that it doesn't preoccupy us too much. It shouldn't take too much of our time. We don't mind what we pay for it but it mustn't outstay its welcome. A yellow object is only worth having for ninety-five or a hundred minutes. If it starts to say it's going to be a three-hour yellow object then we get furious with it.

MF: For me, films are very meaningful and I'm sure as an artist you find your meaning in making art. You need to make it, don't you? You need to do it for yourself.

AM: I think about it more often than I should and for longer than I should. Specifically right now, I'm thinking about it all day, every day. What is the purpose of this in my life? Why am I inflicting this on other people? What do I want? What am I imagining?

MF: You are a filmmaker who values the imagination, who believes in the power of art and the imagination to transform the world. That's an important thing.

AM: The thing that I cling to is that the nature of dramatic fiction— and it's the most simple thing to say about it, but finally it's the most fundamental and powerful thing to say—is that it shifts perspective. It allows a multiplicity of perspective. If you get to the truth of that then the world is a better place. It's not about the truth of the opinion, it's simply about the variety of the opinion, the variety of the perspective and the acknowledgment of the point-of-view. Somehow, if you can for one second look from a different angle at an experience, it changes the world slightly and it changes us slightly. I kept thinking after 9/11, why hasn't somebody asked the question "Why?" not the question, "Who?" or the questions "What are we going to do to those people and how are we going to punish them? How are we going to find them?" but the questions "Why did they do it? What have we done that might provoke that kind of reaction in somebody else? What does it require of somebody to want to do that?" Fiction is the vehicle that, for a second, allows us to remove ourselves from the arena and say there are circumstances in which I can imagine myself going to a place that is extreme. It allows for an opportunity to inhabit, for one second, an opposing point-of-view, freely and without shame and without real cost. It's so important. I think this dialectic, which is at the heart of dramatic fiction, is the thing that we grapple with.

As I mentioned earlier, I worked on this television series called *Inspector Morse*. And I remember this great moment where I had written a story—and it was nothing, it was a very thin thing—about a woman who'd killed her husband. What transpired finally was she had killed him. By the time the thing had finished, I think you understood why she might have done it and there was a great compassion for this character. The core of what I'm saying is that compassion has to be at the root of everything. If you can't embrace and understand and feel compassion towards the people you're writing then how can you expect anybody else to feel anything? Compassion is the petrol tank that we fill up as writers and as filmmakers. So I wrote this woman as compassionately as I knew how and tried to inhabit every beat and moment of this woman. The actress who played this part was momentarily rather famous in Britain and the show was very successful. So the next day they had a phone-in where the leading characters were on a breakfast show and you could call in and talk to them about what had happened. This woman was interviewed and callers said, "You're so nice and it was terrible when it turned out that you had killed your husband." And she said, "Well, you know, I don't think I did it. With all due respect to the writer, I don't think I did." I'm sitting watching and thinking, "What is she talking about?" Of course I realized that the actor so wants the vindication of motive, so wants not to be guilty, which seems to me to be at the heart of all of us. Somehow film, at its best, shows that. It lets you into that secret that none of us want to be guilty. We all want to be saved and we all want to be right. It's like Macbeth denying that he killed anyone! "I didn't do it, God, honest" [laughs]. That seemed such an epiphany to me. Ray Winstone in *Cold Mountain*, who I love, was always saying to me, "Well you've got to understand from Teague's point-of-view. . . ." And he's right, it's his place and they've stolen it. He was so into the fact that the world was misjudging him. If only Ada would look at him properly, she'd realize he was a much better bet than Inman.

MF: There is so much more to say about this amazing film. We probably should wrap up with a few final thoughts about your relationship to the industry and directing. Do you prefer one phase of production to another: preproduction, shooting, postproduction?
AM: No. I think that I'm most like myself when I'm writing. That's the truth of it. But I love the process of filmmaking. I love the fact that I'm going to sit down with ten people, then fifty people, then one hundred people, then two people, that there is going to be this sort of rhythm of public-private-public-private, big-small. I wouldn't give any of it up. The writing has become delicious because I know what is to come. If I thought that they wouldn't let me carry on to continue that process through its public processes and struggles then I don't think I'd enjoy the writing process as much as I do. Part of it is defined by the quietness, knowing that there is a lot of noise to follow.

MF: The shooting phase is very intense. No part of it bothers you?
AM: I don't mind. It has its own delights. Part of the problem with being a filmmaker is that it's just banal. There is a banal element to making films in that it requires an enormous amount of energy to physically realize a film. I shot for five-and-a-half months in Romania and I probably

had five-and-a-half minutes to myself. At the end of it, I could barely stand up in terms of what was required of me on a physical level. So I think there is the endurance element in directing a film.

MF: So that's the most difficult part of being a director for you?

AM: It's the most challenging part but I wouldn't give it up. I'm sure every director you've ever met has said, "Filmmaking is like a drug." There is a sort of opiate quality, which is that however much you despise any particular moment of it, if somebody said, "Well, we're not going to give you any more," there would be a terrible sense of agony of loss.

MF: What's your relationship to Hollywood? Do you see yourself as an independent filmmaker, an international filmmaker, an English filmmaker? None of the above?

AM: None of the above. I neither feel the need to have a relationship nor to try and define what it is. This is the world I live in here. You're right in the middle of it. It's a building in London and a little house where I go to write.

MF: Do you think you're part of any tradition of British filmmaking?

AM: What is that? It's a tradition of non-tradition. Most people in Britain think I live in America, even my crew. I remember on *Cold Mountain*, my Italian grip Tomaso said to me, "I bet you can't wait to go home and get some good California sun." And I said, "I've never lived in California, what are you talking about? I live in London, there's no sun in London." I've made my films away from Britain but not in America. Even though I tried to make *Cold Mountain* in America, I wound up in Romania.

MF: But doesn't the money come from America?

AM: Yeah. I'm not denying the industrial element of this. I'm just saying my day-to-day experience is not connected to Hollywood.

MF: How do you think the industry has changed in the last few years? Is it harder to get riskier material made now than ten years ago?

AM: I would say that whenever you conduct these interviews, whatever year it is, it's a bad year and the great years are just over the horizon. Five years ago people seemed to be able to make whatever film they wanted and now it's so hard. I think every year I've been a film director people talk about how bad it's got, the decline of filmmaking, the decline of opportunity. But somehow films do get made, new talent emerges, and great filmmakers make great films. I've been excited by films I've seen in the last couple of years which seem to be extraordinary.

MF: What's the best part of being a director?

AM: That I'm allowed and paid to explore my hobbies, and also the obligation to learn, which I think is a great privilege. I mean, I'm fifty years old and I'm allowed to be a student every day of my life. I love being a student. Even though I'm writing an original screenplay right now, it's got so many elements of things that I have to discover. Because of the writing, you can't write a word unless it's got some real locus. It has to sit on something. Every character is a research project, every idea requires such a degree of excavation. And the fact that I'm allowed to do that, even encouraged and required to do that is a fantastic blessing.

Down from Cold Mountain

Andrew Pulver / 2003

Strange as it may seem, Anthony Minghella regards himself as something of an outsider, cinematically speaking. "I live in London," he says in his rich, sonorous voice, "but I've never made a film here since *Truly, Madly, Deeply*. I don't know anybody. I'm so detached from what's happening."

It's hard to take this entirely at face value. At forty-nine, Minghella is arguably this country's most blue-chip film director. He is an Oscar winner, double BAFTA winner and, with *The English Patient*, the maker of a landmark in the British film renaissance. Recently he was appointed chairman of the British Film Institute, the government-funded body charged with monitoring and protecting our film culture. Someone closer to the heart of the film establishment it would be hard to imagine.

On the other hand, there's some truth in what he says. Minghella is, if nothing else, a working filmmaker and, since his debut in 1991 with *Truly, Madly, Deeply*, his high-powered intellect and expansive imagination have taken him away from our shores, towards the bigger budgets and willingness to take risks of the US independent sector. *The English Patient* catapulted him into the front rank of global filmmaking. Its follow-up, *The Talented Mr. Ripley*, showed his ability to manipulate cinematic style as well as to bring out the best in A-list acting talent. And his latest, *Cold Mountain*, is conceived on an epic scale, its cost—$83m (£48m)—over double the investment of his previous film. All three started out as Hollywood projects, and all three were eventually financed by Miramax, the Disney-owned powerhouse of whose Anglophilia Minghella has been a major beneficiary.

"The truth is," he says, "I've never set out to make a film with Miramax. *The English Patient* was with Fox, *Ripley* was with Paramount and *Cold Mountain* was with MGM. Miramax was the one company, when these others abandoned the projects, that said: we'll do it. No studio in Hollywood wanted *Cold Mountain*. None. No one wanted *Ripley*, no one wanted *The English Patient*. That tells you there isn't really an appetite for ambitious movie-making out there.

"You meet extraordinary anxiety about the negative cost. Look at it this way: if you write the novel of *Cold Mountain*, it costs exactly the same to produce and market as a novel set in a room. If you make the film, the disparity of costs is huge. Miramax have been one of the very few companies prepared to gamble on this kind of film. Without them I would have no career."

Minghella's presidential detachment from the general run of British filmmaking is further reinforced by his own carefully nurtured production set-up. Though he is established in offices in a converted chapel in north-west London, Minghella's business partner is Sydney Pollack, director of *The Firm*, *Tootsie*, and *The Way We Were*—as Hollywood as they come. And over the years he has worked regularly with such industry legends as editor Walter Murch, cinematographer John Seale, and costume designer Ann Roth. In front of the camera, he has earned the loyalty of Jude Law and, less noticeably, the likes of Philip Seymour Hoffman, who returns for a small part in *Cold Mountain* after a signature tour de force in *The Talented Mr. Ripley*.

"It's been a preoccupation of mine," Minghella says, "to put together a film crew that will travel with me and help me. Being a writer-director can sometimes make you incredibly blinkered. You need to have a group around you sufficiently muscular and curmudgeonly to take issue with you, to teach you. I love the internationalism of it too—Australians, Italians, Americans, British . . . the film set is a passport-free zone.

"And if you work with the same actors you can progress from film to film, rather than constantly having to start again in describing your film language, or describing the way you work best. I love working with Phil Hoffman—why wouldn't you? He has made me better, and that's all I'm trying to do. It's self-serving in that way. But it's also an issue of loyalty—they've helped me, and I owe them."

Cold Mountain, adapted from the novel by Charles Frazier and by far Minghella's most expensive project, is a case in point. His usual team is augmented by major star wattage in the shape of Nicole Kidman and Renée Zellweger. The shoot may have received a large dose of publicity with tabloid tittle-tattle over Law's unraveling marriage and rumors of an affair with Kidman, but for Minghella, such concerns are an irrelevance. Instead, he waxes with practiced eloquence on what, in the end, is his favorite subject: books.

"I don't hold with the notion that only bad books make good movies. That's the advertised idea of Hollywood. Why would something like that be true? I think what is behind this is the disavowal of narrative in twentieth-century literature—that most modern literature is an argument with fiction. The novel in its heyday, in the nineteenth century, was all about story and entertaining an audience with a tale, then using the structure of a tale to convey thematic notions and political notions, or theoretical notions. I love that idea. Film tends to work best when it's in the safe hands of a storyteller. I suppose I felt I could coopt a story like *Cold Mountain*, have my say, rehearse my own preoccupations—knowing that, at the very least, I'm presenting the audience with a pretty muscular piece of narrative as well.

"The book appealed to me mainly because it's a palimpsest: it's written over many other texts. The *Odyssey*, very consciously; a lot of documentation of the Civil War; the real story of a relative of the author's who deserted the Civil War and went back to the actual Cold Mountain. It also evokes some Chinese Buddhist poetry about a spiritual journey to a place also called Cold Mountain."

Few filmmakers would be happy to appear so unashamedly bookish; those that do tend to be silver-tongued pseuds. But Minghella is the real thing: a superb, if scholarly, prose writer, an obsessive medievalist (who else would cite the sixteenth-century morality play *Everyman* as a major influence on his scriptwriting?), and a fearless experimenter prepared to dabble in any available medium. Minghella's non-feature film work has encompassed puppetry via the Jim Henson–produced *The Storyteller*, avant-garde theatre-film (he adapted Samuel Beckett's *Play* as part of the recent RTE/Channel 4 Beckett cycle), and radio plays, such as his recent Verdi monologue. "I have the freedom to be much more experimental because it's a medium that's inexpensive," he says of his multi-perspective radio work. "I came into film as a writer, dependent on language and actors—and gradually I found that the thing I like to do best is to open up the canvas. I feel more at home with this scale of filmmaking than I ever expected."

Cold Mountain is certainly large-scale. An epic opening battle scene sets the tone ("I'd never shot an action sequence in my life!"), while the main action switches between Law's trek back from the front and Kidman's turmoil at home. Though there's an element of socio-political myopia in the narrative—not since *Notting Hill* have black people been so comprehensively erased from a movie in which by rights they should loom large—Minghella is emphatic that his film should be read in symbolic, fabular terms, not as a comment on the American Civil War.

"To be honest, I could care less about Union soldiers and Confederate soldiers. I kept thinking about the Cultural Revolution in China. What was interesting to me about this material was the war away from the battlefield, and the abuses that accrue when there's chaos in the land and people are empowered to police when the men are gone. The home guard interested me as much as the armies."

So what does Minghella care about? Cinema in its purest form, and literary matters too. These days, however, his post as chairman of the BFI means he also is an advocate for the kind of subsidized culture that, he is proud to assert, nourished him as a child on the Isle of Wight and later as a student in Hull. He was personally recruited by Film Council chairman Alan Parker, who turned up on the *Cold Mountain* set in Romania (although, says Minghella, they barely knew each other at the time), and he laughingly dismisses any idea that the relationship between the Film Council and the BFI is at all fractious. "Since I've been there I've encountered only enormous support and conviction that the BFI has a significant role. I think there's a bit of fiction that accrues about Alan's supposed anti-arthouse bias, but he is a great film man and a great film lover."

At the moment, Minghella seems to be in an unrivalled position: able to command top-dollar respect as a filmmaker, yet also to indulge his own predilections. Whether he is bemoaning the paucity of historical imagination in our homegrown cinema ("America has a tiny history and is constantly patrolling it; we have a huge history and are constantly ignoring it") or meditating on the dangers of cultural over-enrichment ("We educate ourselves to the point of uselessness"), he is clearly a creative artist fully at ease with himself.

Now, he says, he's looking forward to not having another project to go to. "It's the first time in my life that I don't have a job. I'm keeping my distance from deciding what to do next until I'm desperate. By the same token, I feel that old urgency to make another film because I want to get better at it. That one will probably take over." So he'll definitely get a script going soon? He chuckles. "I'm not *definitely* doing anything."

The Man with the Epic in His Eyes

David Gritten / 2003

From the *Daily Telegraph*, March 1, 2003. © David Gritten/Telegraph Media Group Limited 2003. Reprinted by permission.

It's a trim Anthony Minghella who greets me at his office, an exquisitely converted Victorian chapel near Hampstead Heath, all sliding doors, hardwood floors, and open-plan work spaces. He's lost forty-eight pounds in the last year, a fact I didn't register when we met in Transylvania last October on the set of *Cold Mountain*, the new film he has written and directed; back then Minghella wore layers of bulky clothes to keep the chilly weather at bay. On learning he was putting on weight due to a thyroid condition prevalent in his family, he embarked on a radical new diet; lots of protein but no carbohydrates (and thus no pasta, a grievous loss for a man with Italian bloodlines).

It's tempting to call the new Minghella lean and mean, but it doesn't truly fit; he's known as gracious, charming, and nice in the film industry, a world where such qualities are rare. Yet beneath his affable exterior, he's tough and stubborn. "I've had visions of films that have seemed overambitious or difficult to achieve," he says. "I've often been advised they would never be realized. So many people in my career have put an arm around me and said: 'Please give up on this, it can't be done.'"

It happened with his Oscar-winning hit *The English Patient*, which was abandoned by Fox before Miramax finally backed it. Minghella argued strenuously to convince Paramount about the virtues of *The Talented Mr. Ripley*, with its amoral, closet-gay hero. And he now concedes, "*Cold Mountain*, at some level, is a folly."

An American Civil War epic starring Nicole Kidman and Jude Law, the film required a massive $80-million budget and a grueling six-month shoot in rural Romania; the crew suffered blistering summer temperatures of 105 degrees, twenty-one consecutive days of torrential rain, then snowstorms at twenty-five below zero.

"All this has trained me to believe films are willed into being, often in unlikely circumstances," says Minghella, forty-nine, in deceptively mild tones. "So I'm used to fighting hard for what I believe in."

He will need all his stubbornness for his newest task. Last month he succeeded Joan Bakewell as chairman of the British Film Institute, an appointment raising suspicions that he had drawn the shortest of straws. The BFI is an unloved body, resembling an octopus without a central nervous system; its several arms flail around independently of each other.

Its library and archive are in serious decline, its Museum of the Moving Image on the South Bank closed three years ago and may never reopen, and the adjacent National Film Theatre needs replacing. Its monthly magazine for film buffs, *Sight & Sound*, manages to be provocative and thoughtful despite a dauntingly small budget. The BFI's production arm is now defunct, and currently it has neither a director nor a finance officer.

Shaven-headed, with an enthusiastic manner and a beaming smile, Minghella turns grim when he assesses the prospects: "It's hard to talk about the BFI without sounding pious," he admits. "People may think it might be like spinach—good for them, but not any fun.

"It's a tough thing to sell. Take the National Film Theatre. What goes on inside that building, the films they show, it's extraordinary. But the building is awful—dilapidated, apologetic, squeezed under a bridge." He also feels that the BFI is too London-oriented ("it should be called the LFI") and frets that its core membership is ageing and dwindling.

You wonder why he is so bothered about British film culture, when much of the population cares so little. He is, after all, one of our most successful practitioners in the industry. And besides, isn't cinema attendance rather buoyant at the moment?

Ah, he says, but it's the films people go to see: overwhelmingly American, off some Hollywood conveyor-belt, viewed in multiplexes with medium-sized screens. "It's like imagining Waterstone's or Books Etc only stocked books written in the last year. What about world cinema, or cinema from the past? If I were to draw up a list of films that have had an impact on me as a person, I don't think any of them have come out of Hollywood."

This is ironic, given that Hollywood studios have provided his livelihood for the last decade. "I'm a British filmmaker who doesn't work in Britain and has no connections in the British film industry except through friendships," Minghella admits.

The same is true of the other British filmmaker holding public office in this country: Alan Parker, chairman of the Film Council, who flew to the *Cold Mountain* set in Romania and urged him to take the BFI job.

"Alan was alert to that neurosis and pointed it out to me," Minghella says. "We're in a strong position to make a contribution. He certainly scratched at my conscience about being involved."

Even colleagues have long assumed Minghella to be in virtually permanent exile. "When I was shooting in Romania, one of my regular crew said to me as we were shivering on some bleak mountain, 'Bet you can't wait to get home and warm up.' I said, 'I don't suppose it's much warmer at home.' And he said, 'But it's always warm in Los Angeles.'"

Yet Minghella had already reclaimed his British roots before taking the BFI post. The renovation of the Hampstead chapel was a protracted affair, but now he has an office within walking distance of home, where he lives with his wife, the film producer Carolyn Choa, a daughter who graduated from university last year and a seventeen-year-old son in sixth form. "I stroll back for lunch, or spend an hour at home in the afternoon," he says. "I can't tell you how sane and grounded it makes me feel."

Finally, work has effectively come to him. Instead of spending most of this year in Los Angeles, supervising postproduction of *Cold Mountain*, he has installed the great Walter Murch (Francis Ford Coppola's editor in his 1970s *Godfather Part II* and *Apocalypse Now* heyday) in the custom-built editing suite upstairs in the chapel. From his ground-floor work space, Minghella hits a switch on a flat screen to see which scene from *Cold Mountain* is currently receiving the Murch treatment.

On the screen is a dense forest carpeted with snow. The camera tracks behind trees for the prelude to a tense shootout between Law and another man, both on horseback. Kidman, her strawberry blonde hair cascading over her shoulders, watches the standoff tensely. The scene has all the hallmarks of a Minghella movie—fluid, handsome, dramatic, and big in every sense.

"I've found nothing so fulfilling as working and creating images on a large scale," Minghella admits. "*Cold Mountain* will take up five years of my life. But I don't mind because it corrals a certain appetite I have for disappearing into a film, working and working, and making that your life."

His taste for epics was not always apparent. He was born and raised on the Isle of Wight, where his parents were ice cream makers. He read drama at Hull University, where he got to know Philip Larkin and learned stage writing under Alan Plater's tutelage. After a stint writing scripts for television's *Grange Hill*, he became known as a dramatist in the 1980s with works such as *Cigarettes and Coffee* and *Made in Bangkok*. His film debut as a writer-director was *Truly, Madly, Deeply*, shot on a modest budget for the BBC; then after the agreeable American romantic comedy *Mr. Wonderful*, his first big film, *The English Patient*, opened in 1997.

His taste for big, complex pictures feeds his work ethic. Apart from finishing *Cold Mountain*, he is also (with the veteran American director Sydney Pollack) a partner in Mirage, the production company behind *Iris*, *Heaven*, and *The Quiet American*.

"All labors of love," he notes, "but not immediately attractive to the industry." Mirage is working on several films, including a script from Allison Pearson's best-seller *I Don't Know How She Does It*. Oh, and Minghella has started writing "an original British film."

"I've discovered the more you do, the more you can do," he muses. "At first glance, it doesn't seem there's room in my life to steer the BFI. But I just have to be efficient with my time. There's no distinction in my life between working and living, and I don't particularly want to make one, because I'm enjoying myself." And no one can complain that he's an exile any more, ensconced as he is in his chapel in NW3.

Mastering the Mountain

Bob McCabe / 2004

From *Empire Magazine*, January 2004. Copyright © Empire Magazine. Reprinted by permission.

Anthony Minghella, the Isle of Wight's most famous son, heir to his parents' famous ice cream empire and, lest we forget, Academy Award–winning director, would like to set the record straight on what he describes as "one of the great myths of my life." He never wrote for *Grange Hill*. He was a story editor on the program for four years, his first post-university job in television. But still, as he laughs, "It doesn't go away. Somehow I've acquired it as a great writing credit."

When *Empire* meets up with the delightful, softly spoken filmmaker, it is late on a rainy November night in Soho. He is only two days away from the 100 percent–finished cut of *Cold Mountain*, but tonight he has just seen a cut of around 99.9 percent of it for the first time—and *Empire* has had the privilege of watching with him. Needless to say, he is rather pleased and has every good reason to be. The movie, all 150 minutes of it, is both epic and intimate. "Today is the first day I feel I've surfaced with the film," he says. "Soon it'll be in front of people and they're going to have to decide what they think about it."

Minghella's travelled a long way from Tucker and his mates to the power trio of Nicole Kidman, Renée Zellweger, and his leading man, Jude Law. Law and Minghella are reprising the relationship that proved so effective on *The Talented Mr. Ripley* with another literary adaptation, this time of Charles Frazier's sweeping, lyrical tale that revolves around a love story and an odyssey through the turbulent days of the American Civil War. *Cold Mountain* is a book—and now a film—that is both epic in scale and intimate in feel. It tells of Southern deserter Inman's (Law) long walk home, returning to the love of his life, Ada (Kidman). In his absence, Ada sees her home in the shadow of Cold Mountain fall apart, only to find herself saved, redeemed, and ultimately changed by her friendship with a young, wild mountain girl, Ruby (Zellweger).

Cold Mountain is a haunting book and one that seems to have haunted its filmmaker, too. "It was really quite bizarre because I'd decided not to do another literary adaptation. Then I went to Toronto to visit Michael Ondaatje (author of *The English Patient*), and he gave me this book which his publisher had given him to give to me. So I rather reluctantly put it in my bag, and when I got back to London there were two more copies waiting for me, and subsequently I discovered that, four months before, they'd sent me the galleys of the book. So within days this book kept flying at me, and when I read it, it was very clear why people thought that I might be interested in it."

Minghella, a former university lecturer, had regularly taught on the subject of medieval theatre and was, at the time, discussing the idea of a story based on pilgrimage. "I was thinking about all these stories of spiritual journeys and walking as atonement," he says. "So reading this book, which is so much about earning your return in some way, having to overcome a series of obstacles to merit redemption, it intrigued me. It felt like this was a fictional nod to a lot of things I was dealing with. It was just chiming so loudly."

As a screenwriter, Minghella avoids the slavish page-by-page, line-by-line notion of adapting a novel for the screen. He educated himself about North and South Carolina, the battles and the people, reading countless letters from soldiers and brushing up on things about which he "was profoundly ignorant."

"I'd read the book many, many times," he continues, "so, in the end, I thought the best thing to do was to leave the book to one side and just go off and create the film and the narrative, with as strong a recollection as I could muster, in the ways that stories get passed on. That's how storytelling originated, it was a vernacular. On a practical level that's the only way I knew how to do it. I was too superstitious to sneak a peek at the book to check things. If I needed something, if there was some half-remembered detail that I liked, I'd call someone in my office and ask him to look in the book and tell me what it was."

One thing Minghella knew he wanted to add right from the outset was the Battle of Gettysburg. "My first note," he says, "was, 'The film should begin with nature in collision. You should see an animal or something and then see that men are reduced to animals. . . .' So it starts with this rabbit, and that's like *Watership Down*, and then it collides with this madness."

And madness it is. The Battle of Gettysburg saw forty thousand men die, many of them in a pit they had dug themselves, which was intended to take the enemy by surprise. As one character says in the opening salvo, it was "a turkey shoot," and one that Minghella captures in a spectacular visceral form, showing both the nightmare and intimacy of combat in a way that gives *Saving Private Ryan* a run for its money.

"That I'm not an action director was the most interesting thing for me, because I don't know how to do it in the way it's supposed to be done," he explains of this brutal, epic scene. "But I wanted to create something more mythic. Something like Dante, in a way. I'm interesting in what effect the battle might have had on somebody. I wanted it to be possible for the audience to say, 'I know why this man has lost faith, I know why this man doesn't want to stay.' It's only five minutes of the film, but I wanted it to resonate throughout the rest of the movie."

One, or indeed several, of the movie's stars are the stunning locations through which Inman travels on his journey, and that Ada and Ruby fight to protect. The movie is set in North Carolina and is about the people and the history of North Carolina. So, North Carolina would have seemed the obvious place to go. But not. "I went to do some helicopter shots in North Carolina and South Carolina," explains Minghella, "and as you fly over you realize that the tattoos of industry can be seen on the ground—it's been written on by the twentieth and twenty-first centuries. Even in Gettysburg—we went to the battle site and in the intervening years, someone's built a golf course nearby!"

And there were other problems, too. The climax of the movie required snow, and the Carolinas have been pitifully short of it in recent years. In addition, the budget came back, and given the expense of filming on location in the US, there was no way this movie was going to be made, leaving its then backers, UA and Miramax, to shudder as if they themselves were standing naked on the top of Cold Mountain itself. But, in such budgetary and logistical concerns, fortuitous solutions may be found. Minghella and his designer, the multi-award-winning Dante Ferretti, went to scout Romania—and found the South of the 1800s.

"There were two significant elements—one was that the landscape has not been subjected to an industrial revolution, while the other was that the way people build there is still nineteenth century, it's all wooden structures. So when we came to build the set, and we built everything—every farm, every house—we had Romanian craftsmen who knew how to do those buildings."

With the background "star" in place, it was time to fill the foreground. Three leads dominate, all of whom interact in different ways, in different relationships, and even in different sections of the film. So how did Minghella get the right combination? "That's exactly the right question, because you don't cast individual actors in a film, you end up with a community. I didn't cast anybody until I felt I knew who the main population of the film would be. So one day there was nobody cast, the next day I cast fourteen. Certainly I offered it to Jude, Nicole, and Renée on the same day, because if any one of them couldn't have done the movie, I felt the whole triumvirate would have to be different."

Ms. Zellweger was certainly pleased. Back when the book was in galley form she had tried to option it for herself, with the hope of playing Ada, the part that would shortly go to Kidman. "I didn't know her particularly," the director continues. "And when we met, all the time I thought, 'This is the woman who was born to play Ruby.' Also, it's very hard to know what Renée looks like. She's a chameleon, she's always reinventing herself in movies, and I just thought she could play this feral mountain child."

Although Minghella quietly thought he was a third of the way there, he was still keeping his cards—or rather, his Polaroids—close to his chest. It was a gig writing a film review for the *New York Times*, no less, that persuaded him that, with Nicole Kidman on board as Ada, he might be most of the way home. "I saw *The Others*," he explains. "I watched it a number of times and kept thinking, 'She's amazing in this film.' I'd never really understood how good she was. That was hot on the heels of *Moulin Rouge*, then I saw *Birthday Girl*, and I thought, 'She's on incredible form, and she's really a magnificent woman.' Because I saw the two ladies together, then it was a question of who would play Inman."

Although Jude Law may be one of the UK's biggest tabloid superstars, and a pretty decent actor to boot, Minghella—and more importantly, those who were supplying the $80 million budget—still worried that he could be too big a risk to land the lead in a movie of this size. "I think Jude was a very big gamble for Miramax, potentially. It would have been easy to cast a more substantial star. But it was very important for me to find, for an American audience, an actor who could be anonymous. Although I don't think he'll be anonymous in three or four months' time!

"Still, I needed somebody I knew would be as passionately committed in front of the camera as I was behind it. I felt if I did my job correctly, it would be the opportunity he needed to make the transition from being this big somebody who shows up and dazzles in a film, to somebody who takes hold of a film and leads it. And he's grown up. I think I caught him just at the moment when he was ready to do that part."

With the journey Inman undertakes inviting comparisons to Homer's *Odyssey*, the supporting cast needed to be equally strong. As Inman travels he has a chamber scene with each of the other characters, and they become central characters while they're in the film. Think Ray Winstone, Brendan Gleeson, Natalie Portman, Philip Seymour Hoffman—the list goes on.

Given Minghella's previous track record, not to mention Miramax's notoriously aggressive marketing campaigns for its "late winter season releases" (*Cold Mountain* opens on Christmas Day in the States), the filmmaker could be digging out the tux come Oscar night. But, Anthony Minghella has just seen his film for the first time. So tonight, at least, he's not playing that game. "I would like to have released the movie four or five months ago, I just wasn't ready. I shot so much on this film, my first cut was five hours. So it's taken me that time to get it to where it is now. It's joining the tide of end-of-the-year releases, when I tried very hard not to. The competitive nature of films is very bizarre. I don't think directors feel competitive with each other. I just feel very competitive with myself."

He Shoots, He Scores

Nick Taylor / 2005

From the *Guardian*, March 11, 2005. Copyright Guardian News & Media Ltd 2005. Reprinted by permission.

The offices of Mirage, the production company Anthony Minghella owns with the producer Sydney Pollack, are in a former chapel in north London. The walls are decorated with huge prints of Kristin Scott Thomas and Juliet Stevenson, Jude Law and Nicole Kidman—images shot on the sets of Minghella's films.

But in a previous life the building was the studio of photographer Gered Mankowitz, whose pictures of the Rolling Stones and Jimi Hendrix have become some of the most iconic rock images of the 1960s.

Minghella is a writer and director with a giant passion for music, and the ghosts that haunt this building clearly thrill him. "The last person Mankowitz photographed here was Leonard Cohen," he says, "which is especially meaningful for me. Without Cohen, I don't think I'd have started writing."

It was Leonard Cohen's lyrics that first awoke a passion for words in a teenage Minghella. Ever since, he admits, music has remained a major influence on all his work. "Every other serious writer I know works in silence. But I can't. When I write, I lock myself in a room and put on very, very loud music. If the music's right, I can work for eighteen hours straight. I only stop to change the CD."

Minghella sees himself more as a writer than a director—a writer who directs is how he describes it. But even before he starts working on a script he has to work out what the film sounds like.

"My idea of a great day is one spent making lists of music," he says. "I love having reasons to buy more albums, to accumulate more CDs, and spend hours poring over obscure tracks. On *Cold Mountain* there were four hundred pieces of music at one point that I had assembled from various libraries and musicologists. The same was true for *The Talented Mr. Ripley*. In a way that film only started to exist for me when I found out that it could be about music—about jazz and classical and their relationship."

Truly, Madly, Deeply, the first film Minghella made, didn't have a story until he found the right music. "All I had was the idea of two people meeting once a week to play classical music. Then I found what they were playing—a collection of Bach's sonatas—and the story came from there. Everything grew out of the music."

For Minghella's latest film, *Breaking and Entering*, P. J. Harvey was his muse. "I listened to nothing else for months," he says. "I'm not entirely sure why—it's not the music the characters in the story would listen to. But hearing a woman's voice, especially one as raw as Polly Harvey's, was crucial to the writing process."

As you might expect from someone who draws so much creative fuel from music, Minghella gets deeply involved in the process of scoring his films. On every project he works with the composer Gabriel Yared, often in collaboration with other artists in a plethora of styles and from different backgrounds.

On *The English Patient*, Yared worked with Hungarian folk singer Marta Sebestyen. Jazz artist Guy Barker sung on the Ripley score, and for Minghella's last film, *Cold Mountain*, Yared collaborated with Alison Krauss, T-Bone Burnett, and Jack White of the White Stripes.

"Gabriel is very generous with me," Minghella says. "He lets me invade his process in a way I'm sure no other composer would dream of. I suggest artists and he's versatile enough to create a score around what I give him."

Minghella and Yared start sketching out ideas for their scores very early in the production process of the film—sometimes at the same time Minghella is writing the first drafts of the script. "On *Cold Mountain*, Gabriel wrote some of the principal themes in my writing room—he was working on one side of the room writing the music and I was on the other writing the script. It's a very codependent relationship. It feels like we're making the movie together. In the same way that I'll write ten or twenty drafts of the script, I expect Gabriel to keep changing and redrafting the score."

The way Minghella and Yared work, the score is built up in tandem with the script, evolving and growing as the words firm up on the page. But this working method isn't typical. Most films are written and shot before much attention is paid to the score. Then a composer comes in to write a soundtrack to accompany the scenes. It's a process Minghella is critical of.

"The music is an integral part of the look and feel of the film. It's not something you can throw on afterwards. But that's the way the industry often tries to do it. Directors will get almost to the end of the process of making the movie and then a composer is asked to come in, under enormous time pressure, and decorate the film. Often directors are bewildered by the sounds that subsequently appear over their scenes. It's like adding a new character into the story at the last minute."

Minghella says the score can also become the punching bag of the film—the place where the producer, the studio, and the director squabble about how they want the movie to play. "It's the one thing that you can keep changing very late on in the process, so if someone's unhappy with the way a movie has turned out, they start messing with the score. The music becomes a battleground rather than what it should be, which is one of the elements that is present and organic in the process of creating a film."

On a critical level at least, Minghella's method works. Yared won an Oscar for the first score he did with Minghella, *The English Patient*, and has received nominations for every one since then.

"None of this is foolproof," says Minghella. "None of it's fixed. But if you give the music the time and space it deserves, you get startling results. That's obvious to me."

As part of the events Abbey Road is putting on this month, Minghella and Yared will be giving a master class on their way of working, accompanied by a live instrumental ensemble to illustrate the way they build up ideas for a score. Minghella has worked many times at the studio, but says he still thrives off its atmosphere.

"Like every other music fan in the world, I'm in awe of that building and its history. It's very hard to become casual about the studio, and I've never been there without getting a buzz. It's a fantastic church of music and it will never lose that magic for me."

The idea of the film festival receives his backing too. "It will remind people of the unsung role of the recording studio in the movies. That's an often-overlooked part of filmmaking, but certainly a crucial one. Perhaps it will remind audiences when they go to see a film that they're also listening to it and the extent to which the listening affects the seeing."

Actors

Anthony Minghella / 2005

I don't have any special pleading about my relationship with actors. I like actors. A lot of directors don't like actors and think that they get in the way of the mechanics of filmmaking, of the pyrotechnics of film-making. But I'm not attracted to the kind of movies where the actor takes second place.

I know as an absolute fact that the best moments in movies are acting moments. They're not shots, and they're not locations, and they're not effects. When I think about the moments in movies that I have loved, it's always about an actor revealing himself or herself. I'm absolutely secure about that. I know that, finally, that is the thing that's always astonished me. It doesn't matter what you've spent on a film, it doesn't matter how much you've prepared a shot, none of it matters in the end. You end up with a lens and somebody doing something. It's all about that. It can be the lens on a little video-camera recorder or on the most expensive Pan-avision camera. It's all about somebody revealing themselves and letting you in to something. That's all I'm ever trying to do: to make those moments, or to allow those moments to happen, and to make an actor feel sufficiently comfortable so that they can be emotionally unadorned.

I've lost much of my attachment to rehearsal because I've learned that film is a nastier medium than we like to believe, in the sense that film is cruelly indifferent to how an effect is achieved. So much so that you can steal a reaction from another moment in a film and it feels totally organic and real. It doesn't matter, in the end, that the actor had no understanding at the time that that's what they were working toward.

John Seale and I have a process where sometimes he doesn't turn the camera off, or sometimes it's running for a long time before I call "Action," and often Walter Murch and I have chosen those areas on the take in the cutting room.

That said, however, I think rehearsal is vital. You might get an actor who wants to find the performance in the first or second take without a rehearsal, and that's their skill and that's their metabolism as actors, that they're on immediately. They don't want to go through an exploration. They want to be on film and they want to be delivering. And there may be exactly the same scene with an actor who needs to rehearse fifty times, who needs fourteen takes to refine a performance, who can't go to the first idea quickly.

Rehearsal is useful as an unencumbered forum in which you can talk out some things about the film and share them: share the research, show things, watch movies together, and do anything which makes you into a collective team. However, I don't think rehearsal is a place to come to trap a performance, because you want to trap that on film. What I've come to understand is that you're not looking to repeat anything. In the theatre, you're looking for ways of organizing a performance for repetition. On film, you don't need ever to have the same moment twice: you just need it once, in focus, without any scratches on the film. Then you're all right.

I was lucky enough, for ten years or so, to be a writer who wasn't directing. I worked with a lot of different directors, and I remember one particular incident. I'd written a play that was on in the West End, directed by a wonderful Australian director called Michael Blakemore. He had a technique with me: he allowed me into all the rehearsals, all of the time, but asked me not to speak. But at the end of each day, we'd go for dinner across the street from the rehearsal room, and he'd say, "Well, what do you think?" And this torrent would pour out of what I thought about the day. There was one particular performance which was very distressing to me because it seemed to be completely missing the point, and I would say at the end of my menu of anxieties, "And as for So-and-So, I just don't think he understands this part." And Michael would say, "Um . . ." and write it down. And the next day we'd rehearse, and nothing would happen.

Finally, we had a first run-through of the play, and all the actors were on-stage in the Aldwych theatre, and I was very excited. Suddenly, this incredible performance emerged from this actor. And so we went for our dinner at the end of the day, and I said, "Well, what did you say to So-and-So?" He said, "'Nothing. He doesn't like being interfered with when he's preparing his role. Then he gets to a point where he's put it all together, and it tends to emerge when he gets up on his feet." And I suddenly realized that you can't have a technique with which, like a paintbrush, you paint all actors in exactly the same way. You can't afford to bring too much technique to an actor because it presupposes that every actor can be dealt with in the same way. The thing I noticed about Michael Blakemore was that he seemed to have a technique which altered to suit each actor. Some actors require an enormous amount of invasion of their process: they want to be directed. Other actors require much more space. If you invade their space, they feel it's impossible for them to work.

You have to work out, as a director, what an actor wants from you. There are some actors who want you to hold them very, very tightly throughout the entire filming process. They want to know everything, and that's what you've got to do—you've got to hug those people. But, with other people, if you go and hug them, they are so alarmed they can't function. Your job is to diagnose the amount of emotional space in which people can work. And you have to determine how much of that space feels comfortable. If it's too tight, some people can feel claustrophobic. Your activity is to try and work out how present you need to be in their process. But that sounds more analytic than I believe it to be. First of all, I think it's very hard in film for an actor to be wrong. If you're playing Count Almásy in *The English Patient*, who is to say what you're doing is wrong? Nobody else is going to play that role. So, in a way, you're definitely correct in every moment in the film. All I can do is to say, of those possible correct choices, which one is more preferable or more in service to where we are in the film. And sometimes I'm not even sure if I know that any better than the actor does.

When we did the scene in *The English Patient* where Hana is swung up into the air in the cathedral to look at the frescoes, I talked to the actors about the intention of the scene. I had talked about the fact that it was a way of making love without there being sexual content. There's some kind of absolute exhilaration, freedom, and tenderness; Hana felt like somebody was taking her somewhere to show her something as a gift, and she was liberated by it. I talked a lot with the two actors and suggested this was a way for two rather shy and not particularly sexually inclined people to commune. In a film where there was a great deal of carnal interaction, their love for each other was much more like sibling love. It wasn't about lust, particularly. I was trying to think of gestures of giving. And so there is a sense, in a most prosaic way, of soaring, but mostly of freedom.

Juliette was so alert. By that point our communication had become monosyllabic, because we simply understood where we were in the filming process and we were so comfortable with each other. There are people whose frequency you feel you're instantly on. She made me feel like I could really direct an actor.

One thing that I've tried to do with actors is remind them of the needs and restrictions of the film in relation to their performance. I remember when Ralph Fiennes and I were shooting in a monastery for *The English Patient*. Willem Dafoe had leant over and made some accusations, and Ralph's line was: "You think I killed the Cliftons." Ralph is the most brilliant actor, the most hard-working, and a good man. And it took two minutes and twelve seconds for him to say that line. Every second of it was intense, and real, and true, and accurate, and felt, and painful for him. But it was two minutes and twelve seconds, and it just couldn't be in the film. There was no way the world's audience was going to sit and wait for this line. It was absurd in the context of the whole movie, but absolutely accurate in the context of what he was doing in his performance. My job there is simply to say, "That is absolutely right, and is of no value whatsoever to the film." I had to take the actor away from the place. It was very discombobulating to Ralph because he felt that I was undervaluing his performance. But I wasn't. I just wanted it to be in the film. I wanted that beautiful thing to occur in the movie and not in some out-take where we'd said, "Gosh, if only it was a different kind of movie, that could have been there."

So part of my job is to find ways of saying, "Just think: it's a cut from here to here. This has got to happen. Try and imagine that music and that dynamic." I have to reset the metronome sometimes, which is a rather objective thing in a mostly subjective activity. Just imagine the metronome. It cannot be. That is why film is a director's medium, not a writer's medium, not an actor's medium. The director, finally, can cut the performance. The director has the means of making the metronome pulse activate a scene.

Of course, the film is changed radically by who is in the movie and how they are. It is being made in front of you when you're shooting and there's only so much you can interfere with in the cutting room. You often see movies where they've tried to accelerate performances, and the performances seem terribly abbreviated. And that wasn't what I was interested in doing. I loved what Ralph was doing. And he knew that I believed in his choices. I just wanted his choices to fit into the structure of the film.

It's almost always, unfortunately, to do with pacing. What feels true as a generated moment for an actor often doesn't feel true inside the context of the film sentence. If nothing else, what you're trying to do with an actor is remind them that a particular moment is an adjective in a long sentence, or it's the whole sentence, or it's a noun and it's going to be decorated by that adjective, which is a different shot. I try and make actors into filmmakers with me so they are not just batting their particular corner.

Inman is a verb: it's a doing part, he is an action. You could write down all the things that Jude Law says in *Cold Mountain* and it wouldn't take up more than a few pages. It's a silent character; you could create his whole performance simply by looking at a sequence of images, of action. Things are done to him; he does things to people.

Jude's preparation was almost entirely physical. There were days when I remember looking out a window of the hotel when we were rehearsing and seeing him running with his trainer on his back, or digging in the ground, preparing himself for the stamina the role would demand of him. And I think that what Jude discovered was that he could simply *behave* in film, which is not something that British actors get an opportunity to do so much because their training is always through language, and British film is still generally language dependent. Behavior is something that has been appropriated by the American actor because American film always looks more towards action than it does to language. Similarly, very few American actors can manage the intricacies of a line with the flair that many British actors have. And because the camera is most magical when it's collecting the thought of an actor, most exciting when the inner life is teased out by the camera, all the time Jude's focus was on trying to find ways of externalizing an inner moment. He spent a lot of time reading the *Pilgrim's Progress* or the Book of Job, reading a lot of meditational texts about the attritions of the spirit. Consequently, there's a gravitas in the performance that seems to age him. In postproduction, when we did our first ADR session with Jude, he was standing in the booth looking up at his performance on the screen, and I looked at him and it was as if Inman's kid brother had turned up to impersonate him: there was no relationship between the face on the screen and his; there seemed to be fifteen or twenty years' difference in age. The heaviness of the spirit that was weighing on Inman has very little to do with the lightness of spirit that weighs on Jude naturally. I think he put many pounds of spiritual weight on in the film. His skin seems pulled so tightly around his features, and that's entirely a generated understanding that Jude developed of the psychomachia, the spiritual odyssey that the character is on. It's the film in which—if you can make such a glib assessment—a promising actor becomes a man, becomes a star. That was fantastic to witness and contribute to.

I sent Nicole Kidman a poem called "The Glass Essay" by Anne Carson, which had been as big a compass in writing Ada as anything that I'd read elsewhere. "The Glass Essay" is both a meditation on the Brontës and the writing of *Wuthering Heights*, but also on the loss of a relationship with, funnily enough, a man called Law. It's also about a relationship with a father who's dying. This convergence of themes in a bleak landscape of snowy Canada seemed to have so many clues, and is also a most beautifully written poem. It seemed to be a real secret text for Nicole, which she immediately understood when I sent it. I even borrowed from it directly, in a scene where Ruby and Ada are lying on the bed reading from *Wuthering Heights*. The quotation "Little visible delight, but necessary" is the piece of *Wuthering Heights* that Anne Carson dwells on in the poem. The other model for Ada, as I have mentioned, was myself. A certain development of the inner being and a perilous starvation of the outer being, an inability to function in the world and make sense of practical challenges.

Renée Zellweger had lived with *Cold Mountain* for longer than any other person involved with the film. She had tried to buy the rights before we did and had been in love with the book before we'd heard of it. She came with a southern mentality for the material and a very, very firm notion of who Ruby was. In discussing Ruby, what I did was suggest some kind of equivalency with a fruit with a very, very hard skin, just to remind Renée that Ruby was a feeling character whose whole presentation was to resist feeling. There's a constant tension in her performance between the demonstration of personality and this resistance to feeling; there's a sense of a dialectic between what she was feeling and what she acknowledged that she was feeling. So when she reveals to Ada that she had been abandoned by her father for several weeks as a child, and Ada responds in horror, she closes down as soon as any sympathy is offered. We tried to use that moment as a fastener for the rest of her performance.

The only theory that I have about acting is that there's a space to work in, and the more of that space I occupy, the less space there is for the actor. And so one of the things I try to do is reduce the amount of space that I take up when I'm working with them, so that they feel that they can move into it. At the same time, there has to be a perimeter around that space which is entirely safe so that they feel they can jump into the space without falling over. Melanie Klein talked about this in terms of her approach to therapy—that predominantly by listening you might create space in which people can feel safe to explore, to drop their defenses. I think that's a very good way of looking at the relationship between a director and an actor. It's certainly true that the best actors I've worked with have functioned with the same alchemy of searching and relaxation.

When we were shooting *Truly, Madly, Deeply*, I always imagined myself as a tailor with a tape measure running around Juliet Stevenson's skills. I felt so confident in her technique and the range of delicious characteristics I could dress. I remember one critic, who was not a fan of the film, saying that the whole movie felt as if I were Juliet's doting maiden aunt following her around with a camera. It was meant as a criticism but I quite liked that idea of dutifully following her talent around through a movie. I don't think it is a fair comment about the film's intentions, achieved or otherwise, which were to examine the nature of loss as best I could, but I accept the insult.

The director's not there to do anything. The director's there to catch somebody, which means that they feel that they can fall without hurting themselves. I don't always know quite how that operates in a filmic circumstance because it's so contingent—often the amount of focus that you can give to an individual actor is predetermined by how many actors are working, how many cameras are being used, how much light there's left. It's never a clean room, it's never a laboratory environment. When you're working, you're always working in a mess. Chaos is the air you're breathing; it's never a pristine place where all you can do is think about that moment of work. One of the things that you're doing when you're filming is trying to silence the ten feet around the actor so that you can both concentrate on whatever it is you're trying to achieve.

Filming the killing of Dickie in *Ripley*, we were plagued by wasps. There's one shot where you can see one around Matt's head; he was extremely disturbed by these wasps. Jude and he both were. There were hundreds of them because the blood make-up had some syrup in it, and it was the wasp season. I said to Matt that, rather than fight it, he should actually use it. So that when he kills Dickie, he shouldn't imagine a human being there but a huge wasp. This wasp should be a threat to him and, just as with a real wasp, he would have to really kill it because, if it's not killed, it's going to sting him very badly.

It was also important to establish that Dickie was capable of more violence than Ripley, that there was some sense that Dickie lashes out.

That's what he does—he lashes out. And you discover later in the film that he's almost killed a man before.

Ripley's killing of Dickie was a defensive action. He felt that this own life was in danger. That's where the wasp metaphor came in useful. Ripley was so terrified of being stung that he lost all sense of the fact that he was battering another human being. He was battering a big sting.

It is moments like that where you realize that half a page of writing in the screenplay can be enormous. I understood that for the first time on *The English Patient,* where I had a collection of actors who were thoroughbreds and who were excavators of the material, who weren't skimming the surface of the parts in any way, shape, or form and who burrowed deeply into the behavior of the characters. Ralph Fiennes and Kristin Scott Thomas were so committed to their characters and so committed to their characters' journeys that a glance could speak volumes. Their evocation of character was rewriting the screenplay without changing any of the lines, in the sense that there was so much gravity in the performances that often the dialogue was the second thing they needed in the scene, not the first. As I found in the rich prose of the novel, where Michael's lines were like those paper worms expanding, so the dialogue, when performed, became that too. There was a concentration in the dialogue by the time I'd reduced the screenplay. The two hundred pages of my first draft were still contained somehow within the 120 pages of the final shooting script. Once we started work, the weight went back on. It happened on *Cold Mountain* as well. Irrespective of how long the shooting script is, it contains within it the ideas and the flesh of the much longer pieces of material that I had begun with. I feel like I have a rigorously achieved film in the screenplay, but something happens with me because I'm the director of the film. I continue to reimagine and discover the movie when I'm shooting. I think if somebody else directed my screenplays they would emerge very differently. I realize that they're full of shorthands, or rather that I don't write everything down that I'm imagining—I think I do, but I don't—and so what seems absolutely apparent to me on the page often surprises people when I shoot because it was always in my mind that a scene would be this way or have this characteristic. It's just that I don't communicate it perfectly on the page. I get very intrigued by performance and what happens when performers get together, and I invest totally in that process as much as I do in the writing process. And so, inevitably, what happens is a huge expansion. That's the reason why I've walked into a cutting room with Walter Murch, three times in a row, with a truckload of film that has always presented us with a huge challenge. Unfortunately, it's how I work, and one of the things I've learnt to my cost is that you can't fight yourself as a filmmaker. You can be exasperated with your method and exasperated with the problems you create, but you can't deliberately trip yourself up because it's counter-productive.

One of the consequences of dealing with the expansion of the material and the long editing process we, therefore, always go through is that I do a lot of ADR in postproduction. I love this process and see it as an extension of the writing process.

Actors deal with ADR in exactly the same way as they deal with their parts. There are very few actors who are different creatures in the ADR room than they are on the set, so any easygoing, obliging, intelligent actor will relish the opportunities of ADR. Some actors see the ADR room as the opportunity to do exactly for themselves what you're trying to do for the film. They've seen the performance; they start to try to balance things out; they wish they'd come into the scene more strongly; they wish they hadn't landed so hard on this line; they can reassess their performance and try and repair it as they see fit. They relish the opportunity to grow parts of the performance using new lines. Other actors who work out of struggle and who work out of a more negative place will bring the baggage into the ADR room and quarrel with why we're replacing this line: "I can hear it perfectly. Why are we adding this line? I liked what we had before." There'll be an argument with the process; it doesn't mean they'll be bad at it, it doesn't mean that they won't finally understand why it's been helpful to them, but they are the same creatures wherever they are—in rehearsals, in shooting, in the ADR room or in promoting the film. It's all part of the job and some of them are good at it and some of them wrestle with it. Actors are extremely concerned with truth so they can be alarmed by replacing dialogue. Likewise, they can be alarmed when you've suddenly employed a close-up from scene twenty-six to attend to a missing moment in scene twelve. "Well, I wasn't in that place in that moment, so how can you use that look?" You can use it because the construction of a performance in a film unfortunately is scavenging, roguish, indifferent activity, and *The English Patient*, for instance, is full of appropriation of reactions and lines and events from other scenes that we used to upholster some scenes that we maintained. It's full of the artifice of the editing room. The actor gives you a performance, and the filmmaker's job is to respect its intention. Beyond that are all the realities of the editing room, where the performance has to be worked into the fabric of the film and where the performance can also be refined. It's rare that a director is trying to damage an actor's work in the cutting room. However, it's understandable if an actor feels aggrieved if what he or she perceived as a vital moment has been attenuated or cut or repositioned. There is a constant tension between the truth of the work and the fiction of it. You're making everything up and you're manipulating everything.

An actor has to believe that he or she is in command of their particular strut of the manipulation, when, in reality, they're not. Crudely, film is about editing and marketing. It's about what we do with what we shot and what the company does with what we deliver. Those are the only two unequivocal things: how the film is assembled and then how the film is presented to an audience. And no matter how much good goes into the preceding elements, it is all dispiritingly determined by those two things. It doesn't matter how good a speech was during shooting: a performance suffers if the director adds a reaction shot at an insensitive moment. If we keep returning to the reaction shot, that character will be amplified in their significance whether their performance was or not. So actors are very vulnerable in the cutting room, and many of them get aggrieved by what happens to their work; they see it as a series of lies because it was never meant for that. But, of course, the whole thing is a lie in the sense that none of it is real, nobody dies. Our soldiers in *Cold Mountain* were Romanian soldiers in American costumes, grey in the morning and blue in the afternoon. It doesn't mean that their run into the pit is dishonest because earlier that day they were Confederates shooting into the pit; it just means that, at the moment of looking, the film's truth is always going to overwhelm any particular actor's integrity. I say this as a director who has been blessed by actors, dignified by them, rescued by them. It's a conundrum and an important one to acknowledge because there has to be a profound respect on either side of the camera. Surrender to the actor during shooting; surrender from the actor in the editing room.

Breaking and Entering: Screenplay by Anthony Minghella

Jason Davis / 2006

From *Creative Screenwriting* 13, no. 6 (November 2006). Reprinted by permission.

"I'd never intended to divert into the role of an adapter of novels," begins writer/director Anthony Minghella. "It happened because I had a great adventure with *The English Patient*, and, while that film took its time to find financing, I took a job adapting *The Talented Mr. Ripley* not intending ever to direct it. After I made *The English Patient*, I didn't want to let go of *Ripley*, so I directed it and then found *Cold Mountain* almost as soon as I'd begun *Ripley*. There was a kind of queue of adaptations," explains Minghella, who scored Academy Award nominations for his first two adaptations and a Best Picture statuette for *The English Patient*. While contemplating the scale of *Cold Mountain* on location in Romania, the filmmaker vowed to scale back his next project and do something original. Now, Minghella has turned his attention to *Breaking and Entering*, a story that had a lengthy period of gestation.

"Many years ago, when I was writing plays, I had an idea for a play called *Breaking and Entering*. The idea was, essentially, that a couple came home from some kind of social event and discovered their house has been ransacked. When they did an inventory of what had been stolen, they discovered that things had been added. And what had been added were, in some ways, emblems of what was missing in their marriage."

Minghella struggled with the initial concept, but had difficulty developing a dramatic venue to contain the idea. "When I was in Romania [shooting *Cold Mountain*], the building that we worked from in London had some break-ins. It reminded me of the idea I'd had. It seemed to me that perhaps there was some way of using the notion of burglary to talk about all kinds of issues to do with London, citizenship, rights, and responsibilities."

The same story also lent itself to "this idea of things getting broken to fix them, which is at the heart of the original idea—that somehow, not all breaking is bad in the long term." The filmmaker clarifies his dichotomous conceit: "It's a riff on the implications of damage to a relationship which might finally be the cause of its more permanent and robust repair."

"There's a danger in the world that we work in, a sort of expectancy of what kind of film you're going to make and that you're locked into it. Like every filmmaker, I want to feel like I could do a comedy next, or do a thriller." After three adaptations, Minghella found the writing of *Breaking and Entering* quite liberating. "You're not enthralled to the obligations of the novel in the sense that the novel has created a map," he explains, "Whatever you do [in an adaptation] is in a dialectical relationship to that map."

Calling the process a "delicate and precarious activity," Minghella notes the difficulty in hewing close to the source material while still telling a filmic story, but says that the perk of adaptation is that "you know there's been a big support in the past for the concerns of the story you're telling. Whereas, if you're creating a new narrative, you're going to discover only after you've made the film whether anyone else is interested in what you have to say. There's no security. There are blessings and curses both to original material and to adaptation."

Minghella explains that *Breaking and Entering* came from the idea of writing "a morality play with a strange point of entry," from "the notion of a moral fable and then trying to find some way to animate it." The film, which follows architect Will Francis's (Jude Law) interactions with a young thief (Rafi Gavron) who burgles his office, takes its title from both the literal crime being committed as well as the emotional intrusions of the characters into one another's lives.

"The thrust of it, for me, was imagining a courtroom scene in which really no one was innocent. Perhaps the most innocent person was the person who was on trial," says Minghella. "Often, the context of crime is unknown to us," adds the filmmaker, who has his protagonist follow the young thief back to his home where he meets the boy's mother (Juliette Binoche), a Bosnian expatriate living in the bad side of London. "When we collide with people who've committed crimes, they're never what one would imagine. The circumstances are always more complex, and partial, and just more redeemable then we'd like to think."

Eschewing the easy view that the world is black and white rather than varying shades of gray, Minghella explains that he sees the world as "comprised of people who make mistakes and, largely, are all aspiring to be decent and failing to be. If a fiction could achieve one thing, which is to make us an ounce more compassionate, that would be a good result."

I Wanted to Make a Film about Home

Tom Charity / 2006

From the *Daily Telegraph*, November 3, 2006. © Telegraph Media Group Limited 2006. Reprinted by permission.

Over the course of his fifteen-year career as a film director, Anthony Minghella has travelled far and wide. *The English Patient* (1996) took him to Italy and to North Africa. The *Talented Mr. Ripley* (1999) criss-crossed Sicily, Naples, Rome, Tuscany, and Venice. And, though it was set in and around South Carolina, *Cold Mountain* (2003) was largely shot in the Carpathians, Romania.

All three films were lavish period movies adapted from bestselling novels. Now, for the first time since *Truly, Madly, Deeply* in 1991, Minghella has written an original screenplay and returned home to Britain. It is, as the film's star Juliette Binoche puts it, "closer to his bones."

Breaking and Entering centers on Will (Jude Law), a landscape architect working on a regeneration plan for King's Cross. Successful, and in a long-term relationship with the beautiful Liv (Robin Wright Penn), Will would seem to have all a man could ask for, but his domestic life is fraught—Liv's daughter Bea has autism—and he devotes more and more time to his job. When the firm's office is repeatedly broken into, Will stakes out the place at night, eventually following the teenage culprit back to his home . . . which is how he meets Amira (Binoche), the boy's mother.

"Even before I started *Cold Mountain*, I knew I wanted to make a smaller film at home," Minghella says. "I thought, if I don't write an original film now, it will never happen. Everybody else has already forgotten I was a playwright and I will too. I'll get too frightened.

"I had an equation in my mind that was a false equation," he goes on, thoughtful and erudite as always. "Filmmaking meant packing my suitcase, leaving my family and holing up in some remote place to do my job. I thought that wasn't healthy and I should try to find a way to make films about where I lived. I thought I'll go back to something I know about and start there."

He's quick to add that he soon discovered how much he didn't know—about King's Cross, about architecture, and about Bosnia, which is where Amira and her son come from. "That was a surprise, when Bosnia came into it," he says. "So I went to Sarajevo and spent some time there."

Watching the movie, you begin to see how this supposedly small-scale, intimate project keeps peeling off in unexpected directions as Minghella allows himself to be seduced by, for example, Rafi Gavron's free-running teenage burglar, Miro; or Vera Farmiga's east European prostitute, Oana, who takes to sheltering in Will's Land Rover for a coffee during his nightly watch.

For all that it takes place within "two pages of the *A-Z*," as Minghella puts it, it's every bit as cosmopolitan as his other movies.

He quotes his producing partner, Sydney Pollack, who observed that the problem with Will is "he doesn't know what he doesn't know." That's what the film is about, Minghella reasons. In order to make it, he cut himself off from the close-knit production team who had worked on his previous three movies, including director of photography John Seale and editor Walter Murch.

"By the time we did *Cold Mountain*, this team had a way of working that all just falls into place . . . the dynamic was preordained. I needed to find out whether I was too dependent. On this movie, we didn't know how we were going to do anything."

He hadn't realized—or had forgotten—the "confinements and prescriptions" of period adaptations; "how imprisoned I had been."

He tells me about an incident during *The English Patient*, when he tied himself up in knots shooting a market scene in which the production designer had ingeniously doubled the size of the set with mirrors—only the actors wanted to walk the other way. In contrast, there is an improvised sequence in the new movie in which, instead of cutting from one scene to the next, as he had written in the script, he had the inspiration to hail a passing taxi, piling in with Jude, Juliette, and the camera and shooting en route.

"There was nothing we could do that was wrong," he says. "Those moments where you see them not knowing what's going to happen, not knowing the script—because there wasn't one—they were so extraordinary and liberating to me. These are the blessings of being in your own world.

"I want to get better," he adds. "I am absolutely determined that I'll keep trying to learn and not know too much and just see what happens."

Breaking and Entering is a curious film, alternately light and heavy. On one level it's another urban nexus movie, like *Magnolia* or *Amores perros*, in which half a dozen characters from different social strata interconnect—or don't. On another level, it's a middle-class midlife-crisis movie, with Will shuttling between his job, his partner, their relationship counselor, and somehow getting lost in the shuffle. It's a love story, too, but not what you would call a romance.

It is also, I remark, a rather unhappy film. He shoots me a look, asks if I saw the movie with an audience? (I did.) And did they laugh? (Yes, at first. Not so much later on.)

"Walter Murch told me a very brilliant thing one time," he says. "He said: 'Don't keep talking about the movie you thought you were making, look at the movie you have made.' For a long time I thought it was a comedy idea. I guess my pen doesn't feel the weight of the comedy. I am quite surprised by the melancholy. I didn't feel melancholy when I was writing it, but now I see it very clearly."

Final Thoughts: Theories, Poetry, and Morality

Anthony Minghella / 2005

From *Minghella on Minghella*, edited by Tim Bricknell, Copyright © 2005 by Anthony Minghella. Reprinted by permission of Farrar, Straus and Giroux, LLC, and Faber and Faber Ltd.

I haven't watched many movies, but I've watched some movies many, many, many times. There are some movies I go back to like food—*The Tree of the Wooden Clogs, I Vitelloni, Three Colors: Blue* and the Taviani brothers' movies I watch repeatedly. Each time I go back to great films, I see something I feel I've never seen before. Obviously, all you can do as a filmmaker is aspire to make the kind of movies which you've been excited by as an audience member. What you want is to be part of that process of making pieces that work, which repay analysis and revisiting, and which have their own poetry.

Poetry and film share a realm of mystery and secrets, an intimate purpose. In that regard film is different to theatre in the way that poetry is different to the novel. There's a suggestion in both film and poetry that the audience is gaining direct access to the author's inner life, despite the fact that film is the product of several people's work—sometimes three or four hundred people's work. They also both share a sense of being close to dream states, creating from a condition which conjures the working of the unconscious.

Film, as a descriptive medium, can be extremely inefficient and prosaic. It's oddly banal in some ways. For instance, imagine the difficulty of representing a straightforward idea that could be a line in a bad novel: "Every morning he left home at the same time; it was nearly always raining." These kinds of ideas torment filmmakers. How do you get "He left home every morning"? How do you get "at the same time"? How do you get "It was nearly always raining"? All of this you can write in one sentence of a novel.

Equally, verse is uncomfortable with the overt. For instance, the news is rarely read in verse because we find transparency and poetry to be unhappy bedfellows. Poetry is much better at secrets than it is at news. This door to the "inner-being" quality of film and poetry is achieved in the same two ways: distillation and ellipsis. Robert Bresson said that one doesn't create by adding but by taking away. By contrast, ellipsis is not the chief weapon of the theatre or the novel because language, particularly in the theatre, has become a kind of action. The language of theatre is a much more chewable, active, rhetorical event and depends on a kind of completeness, whereas both film and poetry are marvelous at speaking through image and the relationship of images. There is a kind of phosphorescence that is released in images, particularly when they are stuck up against each other, and this juxtaposition, this aggregation, is one of the other things that poetry and cinema share.

Poetry saved my bacon at school because I was a pretty inadequate pupil and, like many fourteen- or fifteen-year-olds, I thought that literature was something to be avoided like a car crash. But I was very interested in music. A supply teacher in English came into school and produced a Dansette record player, which we all suddenly paid attention to, and he put on a record. It was "Suzanne" by Leonard Cohen: "Suzanne takes you down to her place by the river . . . ," which certainly piqued my interest. The next day I bought a collection of Leonard Cohen poems and that began a whole process of archaeology for me: investigating poetry away from the school curriculum. "School curriculum bad, everything else good" was my philosophy. And I also found a collection of Penguin Modern Poets—I think somebody someday should write a hymn to whoever came up with that idea because I collected every single one—and ever since I've read poetry on a daily basis. It's the rigor of poetry that I most love and am most affected by.

The poet writes in relative freedom and relative obscurity, and the filmmaker works in chains, albeit often golden ones. I think it's noteworthy that when you come across poetry written out of obligation—which is generally the condition of filmmaking—when you come across poems written for the Queen's birthday or for funerals, you often glimpse some of the conditions that make bad films. Films, unfortunately, cost too much and have an industrial imperative. Poetry costs nothing and is often read by nobody.

The only cinema worth talking about is the cinema which aspires to poetry. The poetic cinema of Kieślowski, Tarkovsky, Cocteau, Buñuel, Olmi, Fellini is often seen by very few, and I think it's an indictment that it rarely happens in the English language. While the American cinema is far too concerned with transparency—because transparency is exportable—poetic cinema celebrates the opaque, it doesn't genuflect in front of clarity. Transparency really obsesses most American and British filmmakers, and with good reason, because we're storytellers and we need to tell stories; it's just that there are so many different ways to tell a story, and we've confined ourselves to the very middle of the road. If you're always trying to raise money in America for filmmaking, as I am, the worst thing that anyone can say about your film is that it's an art film. "Are you talking about an art film?" people will say, using the word "art" pejoratively.

In film, you start by writing the film on the page, then you write the film with the camera, then you end up writing the film all over again, reimagining it in the cutting room. That's not dissimilar to the business of writing poetry; a great deal of important work in poetry is done beforehand, before you start writing, and a great deal is done after you've written. The first cut of *The English Patient* was four hours and thirty-five minutes long, *The Talented Mr. Ripley* was four hours and forty-five minutes, *Cold Mountain* was five hours and ten minutes; subsequently you see how much you can take out before the whole thing implodes on itself. I'm sure that's a process all poets know. You also, once the initial collection of the material is complete, try and find out where there are rhymes. Obviously, rhyme in film is different to rhyme in poetry, but they work in the same architectural way: they become hinges or supports for how you construct the whole film, the phrasing of the whole event. A great deal of what is pleasurable and poetic about film language is transition. While film is not particularly adroit at saying, "Every morning he left home and it was nearly always raining," it is brilliant at pushing you forwards in time and making poetic transitions. You can use these as visual rhyme.

One of the disturbing aspects of contemporary cinema is that it does all the work for you and you feel passive in relation to it. Whereas with, let's say, Kieślowski there's an obligation to involve yourself in the making, filling in the dot, dot, dot of ellipsis. In film, each sequence of individual shots and the relationship between each scene is constructed by ellipsis; the verbs at the very heart of making a film are cutting and juxtaposing. Films made ten years ago increasingly look very slow because we, as an audience, require less and less information, whereas the poet working today is not so removed in terms of what he or she is doing from Chaucer or Dante.

What's often most startling about a poem or a film is the *idea* of the poem or film. We are overinfatuated with language in film, with dialogue, as if meaning is carried in dialogue, whereas meaning is nearly always carried in context. The example which springs to my mind are the words "I love you," because if I write in a screenplay "I love you" we think we know what that means. But actually it is constantly modified by context. If I say "I love you" to a large group of people, that means one thing. If I pass a mirror and say "I love you" to the reflection, that means something else. And if I sit in the men's toilet and every time someone comes in I say "I love you," it would probably get me arrested. There are no beautiful lines in a film and no beautiful actions except where context and necessity make them so.

Film, of course, is a moving picture, twenty-four still frames going past the shutter in a second, which means by definition that a part of that second is taken up by blackness. Somebody, probably Walter Murch, has calculated how much of the time you're watching black when you're watching a film. The *not* seen is one of the factors which make it hypnotic. Film, like dreaming, has the ability to flex in shape, in size, in speed. Continuous shots are rare in the cinema and strangely disturbing. Cutting became a convention created to accommodate limitations on how much negative could be fed into the camera. And so the camera stops and starts again, and in the process people work out what's happening. Images follow each other, and we connect. We are guided by an unseen hand that controls what we see and hear and makes it natural for us to see an elephant and a Christmas tree in the same room with a Puccini opera as a soundtrack. It's exactly like a dream, except it is always someone else's dream. The greatest weapon that film has is the relationship between image and sound. That is the thing that most preoccupies me when I'm making a film.

Poetry has borrowed some of the techniques of cutting and juxtaposing from film. If you think of Thom Gunn's "On the Move," which begins: "On motorcycles, up the road they come / Small, black as flies hanging in heat, the boys." That's a classic developing shot in a movie. It's like the long-lens shot of Omar Sharif in *Lawrence of Arabia*. Or the beginning of Larkin's "Mr Bleaney": "Bed, upright chair, sixty-watt bulb, no hook behind the door, no room for books or bags. I'll take it!" which is somehow Michael Caine in a British movie of the era. Look at the beginning of Ted Hughes's "Thrushes": "Terrifying the attendant sleek thrushes on the lawn," which is obviously a close-up, drawing the attention of the reader to something which is particularly significant by abandoning usual syntax and beginning with the word "terrifying." That's also what you do in film: you alter syntax so that information is understood in the way the director wants it to be. The film sentence is constructed with the size and length of shots.

The dream state that cinema creates is exemplified by the sensation you have when you leave a cinema in the late afternoon and walk out into the street: you feel so disorientated because reality seems so much less vivid than the world in which you had just participated. But somehow, through purpose (which the poet and filmmaker share)—when you point the camera with purpose, when you write a line with purpose, however opaque, however transparent the line—then somehow the audience and readers understand something. It's that strange mysteriousness of purpose that I think film and poetry most have in common and that we should most celebrate and preserve.

There's a shot in *The English Patient* where Juliette Binoche is swung up in the air in a cathedral to look at some murals. I've been in various countries and I've seen people react in the same way to that moment. It is clear to me that if there is a very focused intention in a shot, if there's purpose in a shot, it is absolutely catholic. Everybody will understand it. When you achieve that transparency of purpose, it's the most marvelous thing. People just know what it's about. They know to be moved. They know to laugh.

I love the intimate playing out against the public. It is more interesting, more unusual, and more dynamic.

It's absolutely natural to me to think of a larger canvas. An example of that is one of the first collections of plays I had published, which was called *Interior Room, Exterior City*, a title my publisher loathed so much that it got very quickly thrown to one side. But there was one printing before these plays were collected, which was called, *Interior Room, Exterior City*. It was called that because I was interested in behavior, but only insofar as it was impacted by what was going on outside the window. Or rather, I was interested in what was going on outside, but only as it was mediated through what was happening in rooms. Film is so adroit at flexing between situating people in a public landscape and situating them in a private world. The theatre is always confounded by that grammar. However, in movies, when you cut from a woman's neck to a desert landscape, the syntax is perfectly agreeable. In that respect, it seems a natural way of using and exploiting film, in terms of my own thematic interests and preoccupations.

When the periscope comes up, we've got to understand exactly where we are in history and what's going on in the world, so that, when we go down again, the situation is informed by that periscope's look at the exterior world. That's a sort of film manifesto in a way: make sure that, when you go out into the public space, there's a narrative function, that it's not decorative, but feeds back into those private moments.

If you put two boxers in the ring, you know one of them will fall down eventually. There are certain routines that have to take place once you narrow down the parameters of the game. If you put five fighters in a ring the outcome is unknown. This is why the games of the gladiators became more and more complex. More types of weapons and creatures provided some variety in the possible outcome of the contest. On a very mundane level, that is what my instincts are as a dramatist: never let the thing you want to happen, happen.

For example, I am allergic to sex scenes in films. Not because I am a prude or I don't think a film should have an erotic landscape; it is just that once you get to a man and a woman naked in a room it becomes impossible to achieve variety. Suddenly you walk into the realms of ritualized behavior and the constraints of what can be done on film. You collide with convention. I am always trying to find different ways of handling intimacy. *Cold Mountain* presents its own challenges in terms of the required romantic encounters between Inman and Ada. One of the most remarkable scenes from the novel is the scene in which Inman sleeps with Sara but they don't make love. That is the kind of scene I really like writing: where what we expect to happen doesn't and where the tension is about people trying to stay with what they feel to be the right course of action.

I think that I try to create operas using prose, that I'm looking for an unabashed scrutiny of the heart, not apologizing for it but yielding to it. *Cold Mountain,* when all is said and done, is about a man desperate to get home to the woman he loves and a woman desperate for the man to return, both of them clinging to their hope while believing in the hopelessness. The tension in the film comes from both of them wanting something and neither of them really believing it can happen, and so you've got one person who stumbles forward wondering what he's stumbling towards, terrified that he's stumbling towards nothing, assuming that it will all end in tears but, as in Tennyson, "His own thoughts drove him like a goad." I keep thinking of those lines, in "Morte d'Arthur," when I think about Inman, the warrior returning home to ashes: "Dry clash'd his harness in the icy caves and barren chasms, and all to left and right the bare black cliff clang'd round him, as he based his feet on juts of slippery crag."

I prefer to infer rather than imply in my writing, and I am suspicious of what I would describe as primary colors. The American industrial film deals pretty exclusively in primary colors for a reason: primary colors travel better than more complex palettes. If you look at my writing from a dramaturgical perspective, what carries from film to film is that I can't deliver a scene that is exactly what it's supposed to be. I would like to think this is a quality, but often it is a failing. I remember having an argument with Walter Murch about *The English Patient*'s dramaturgy: he said to me, "There's never a scene in which you give us an undiluted chunk of one tone or another." For example, there's a moment where Katharine comes over to Almásy's apartment and they have this odd skirmish where she hits him, he tears her clothes off, and they end up in bed. Then it gets very sweet in the bath scene, only for it to immediately go tart when they're talking about what they love and what they hate, and Almásy says exactly the thing he's frightened of, which is exactly what's happening: possession, ownership—"I don't like that"—and the whole scene sours. I do that all the time. This is why finally it's not opera, it's not primary colors, because whenever I get close to that there's a wicked or, I think, true spirit that says that isn't what happens, that isn't true. In *Cold Mountain*, Ada and Inman finally get themselves into a place where they can speak. They're sitting around a campfire and they start to tell the truth to each other: "If you could see my inside, my spirit or whatever you want to call it, you would hate me, and you wouldn't accept me. I'm ruined, I think I'm ruined." And she's saying basically you're not ruined and I love you, and I remember everything just as you remember everything, it's all fine. But then out comes the demon— Ruby—who says, "If you want to get three feet up a bull's ass then listen to what sweethearts whisper to each other." There's no version of that in the book; it's a comic device, but it's also my feeling that that's how things go. There's always a jester scoffing at the court. It happens in the next scene: Ada comes into the cabin, Inman follows her, and she says, "There's some religion where you say I marry you three times and you're man and wife." "I marry you, I marry you, I marry you," replies Inman, and she says, "No, I actually think it's divorce, isn't it? I divorce you three times and you're not married any more." That's the antic in me.

An ongoing characteristic of my writing is that there's never a free ride in a scene; the scene always has a tripwire in it and the characters inevitably trip over. Ada and Inman are typical: even though they began, like Almásy and Katharine, as someone else's characters, they finally *are* my characters and they graze against each other rather than rush into each other's arms.

Relationships are finally never very successful, don't really work, and are always full of disappointment. All human exchanges are colored by animal instinct. We're all struggling against ourselves. The more I want to believe in the potential goodness in people and the potential of people to love and be decent, the more I'm also conscious of my own shortcomings and of my own warring appetites and desires, and they reflect themselves into my work. Again that's a Catholic thing, I realize, full of guilt. And as always with most writers and people who make things, you learn a lot about yourself from what you've made.

However romantic I might be, I am also full of contradictions about the real possibilities of romance. There seems to be no evidence that romance as a panacea really is obtainable—or, perhaps, I don't think I'm worthy of it. It's an argument that is repeated in scene after scene of my plays, right through to *Cold Mountain*—this failure of nerve or, rather, the belief that what's true is not simple.

I have this theory, which probably doesn't bear any scrutiny whatsoever, which is that you should try and understand the terms of the film in the first few minutes. This is true of *Truly, Madly, Deeply*, where you understand the terms of the character's dilemma in the first minute and a half. It starts off with a woman walking home and a voice-over rehearsing the details of going home, letting herself into her room and brushing her teeth, and all the things she does when she gets home. You realize that she is telling this to an analyst; she goes on to tell her analyst about her lover and what he says to her and what advice he gives her and that he speaks Spanish, which is strange because he couldn't speak Spanish but now he can. You discover at the end of the first speech that her lover is dead. That is the end of the first loop of the film. I remember my brother, who is also a writer, read it and said that I had given the whole film away by the end of the first speech. I realized that that is what you should do. You should, at least, state the terms of the film as quickly as possible. *The English Patient*, *The Talented Mr. Ripley*, and *Cold Mountain* do exactly the same thing.

Telling stories can often be like teaching. I don't mean that it should be didactic or pedagogic, but that the famous structure of teaching where you say, for example, "Today I'm going to tell you why democracy is a great thing, but it has implicit within it a form of tyranny because democracy relies in a way on a consensus that has to be enforced, that freedom for everybody often means disempowering individuals." You might begin with some statement that had an oppositional idea in it and then illustrate that through a series of facts or observations. I think that when you begin a film story there's an obligation to tell the audience what the theme of discussion is or what the story is going to be about: on one level, in *Truly, Madly, Deeply*, that it's important for your spiritual health to let go of pain and to make peace with it; on another, simpler level, that it's a story about a woman who thinks her dead husband is still with her. Or, in *Ripley*, this is a story about a man who is ashamed of who he is, pretends to be somebody else and suffers the consequences. The opening shots of *The English Patient* should suggest that this will be a story about an event that happened in a desert, where no identity and no boundary can be trusted. The beginning of *Cold Mountain* tells you that this will be a story about war, longing, and return—you'll see a man staring at a picture of his sweetheart and, despite the battlefield setting, you'll know that this will also be a love story. The opening of a film can also make a statement of tone: you're going to be able to laugh in this film even though it's serious. So, in *Truly, Madly, Deeply*, you laugh in the first monologue because the story she tells the psychiatrist ends with a joke about this ghost trying to learn Spanish, which allows the audience to know that during the telling of this story they'll be able to laugh as well as cry.

In *Ripley*, if you think the central character is getting away with murder, you're not watching it. It's the most radical departure from the book. A legitimate gripe that fans of the novel might voice is that I entirely missed the point of the book, because the book celebrates an amoral central character who gets away with murder and doesn't seem to suffer for it. And part of the fun of the novel is that he doesn't seem to care. He plans to kill Dickie. He plans to kill Freddie. You know that he'll have no remorse about killing other people to get what he wants. And there's a kind of glee in seeing him do it. But it's not a glee that I wanted to transform into the film, partly because of the nature of the way you experience film. But, if that's my technical position, it's also my moral position: I don't want to tell a story about a man who gets away with murder and doesn't care. It doesn't interest me. I don't want to make films in which there's a sort of delight in malice, a delight in the dog-eats-dog kind of world.

Violence is often so simple in films. People take a gun and fire around, and other people fall over. It's done on the run. You don't stay with the consequences of violence and you don't acknowledge the fact that killing people is an extremely difficult activity. When I was a child, probably in my early teens, a friend and I were driving up the High Street in Ryde and, as the car's headlights hit the top of the hill, we saw a man kicking another man in the head. We watched this man stamping on another man's head until the car reached him. Even when we got out of the car, he just kept stomping on this man's head. It made me feel nauseous. I'd never seen that kind of violence. We went to the police station. The ambulance came. The police came. This man was completely unconscious and there was a river of blood round his head. I assumed he'd died. About three days later, this man came into our shop to have a cup of tea—the same man who'd been lying on the pavement dying. He had a very bruised face, his ear was all swollen up, his lip was like a balloon—but he was going about his business. That was very much in my mind when filming *Ripley*: you can't simply dramatize an act of violence and assume that it's somehow clean. There should be something about killing in the film which is primal and taboo-like, as if the character were crossing some divide. Once he has the mark of blood on him, he can never go back.

It seemed to me that the more human and the more indelible an experience it was, the more valid the film would be. But it's not a film in which life is cheap in any sense, because I don't want it to be. I remember getting to the end of George Sluizer's *The Vanishing* and wanting to throw something at the screen. I hate the idea of a universe which has no mercy and no morality.

The attraction of *Cold Mountain* was that it is a war film without very much war in it—or rather, mostly only its impact. It seemed that the real spurs to conflict were issues of prejudice, suspicion, fear, and the wrestle between the past and the future; the past as demonstrated by a great deal of land ownership and human labor as opposed to less land ownership and more employment of industrial might: machines making money as opposed to labor making money. What gets tugged along in the wake of these theoretical conflicts are simple human vices: fear of the unknown, excuses to fight, the need to be on a side, the sense of having a cause to fight for. You see it in the film that the bloodshed and cruelty extend way beyond any battlefield of men with guns firing at each other, that the real damage is done hundreds of miles away.

I made sure, when we were shooting, that there were no generals in *Cold Mountain*, no officers, no strategists. Robert E. Lee doesn't ride by, Ulysses Grant doesn't ride by, you never see the tents of the dignitaries, the people looking at the war through a telescope. I've tried not to objectify anything and that's a very deliberate perspective in the film. I'm much more interested in what it's like to be a woman with a child who says, "It's pretty much what you'll find if you knock on any door in this war—man gone, woman left." Those stories interest me, stories of what it's like in the "away" as opposed to what it's like in the "it" of it. You couldn't get a more simplistic denial of the value of violence: "If I had my way I'd have metal taken altogether out of this world, every blade, every gun." It's not in the book; it's me wondering why we feel obliged to do that to each other just to make a point. I'm not sure if America was in the market for a bit of ambivalence about the value of war. Did it want a hymn to patriotism, a hymn to American spirit, or did it want a lament to the time when the American spirit was most fractured, most warring with itself, most uncertain of itself, most cruel to itself?

Another thing that provoked me to take on *Cold Mountain* was an interest I've had for many years in psychomachia, the tradition of medieval literature where life is laid out as a journey in which you elect to deviate from the straight and narrow road. You are tempted by vice, and your job is to elect to continue down the straight road or to be tempted off it by various appeals to your lower instincts. The film is quite Catholic in that way: people live with and are haunted by the consequences of their actions. Inman is ashamed of the person he's become by the time he makes it to his destination. The spiritual elements surfaced in the finished film in a way that they hadn't in the longer, less focused incarnations of the film. The movie constantly plays with ideas about the natural order in the animal kingdom. There's a sense that at times human beings are much closer to the animal world than they are to any higher form of life. In the battle, you see men reduced to creatures, lashing out. There's a sort of bestiality in the behavior of Teague; after the Swangers have been killed there's a look he has which has an absolutely dehumanized glee—cold, in the way that you see a cat studying a creature it's about to kill. The film attempts to go on to say that what dignifies humans is their capacity to love and have compassion, and when compassion is removed we retreat into just being another species of the animal kingdom.

There's something about the camera as a window into other people's souls and other people's experiences. As an audience we want to watch other people engage in activities that we do ourselves and in activities we are afraid or unable to do ourselves. Why do societies all over the world make up stories of people doing things we do ourselves in one form or another? Why is it that we need to reenact those things? At some level, it's a requirement for us to be able to experience without danger. We need to be able to stare at death and stare at love and stare at sadness and stare at violence and stare at fear—with a safety belt on.

The camera is not a neutral observer. The camera has nothing neutral about it whatsoever. Where you put somebody in the frame is as critical as what they're doing. You have to acknowledge that as a filmmaker you are orchestrating the way that their action is being perceived. It's not just a neutral action which you are giving to somebody else. You are making a hundred decisions: how you will see it, how you will hear it, how long you'll see and hear it for. It's my job to manipulate every single one of those images so that it has the impact I think it requires. I think there's a moral way of doing that. There's a truthful way of doing it and there's a lying way of doing it.

In the end, directing movies is entirely about stamina. It's got nothing to do with anything else. It's about making sure that you can stand up at the end of every day. One of the main things going through my mind on set is, how can I sneak off and lie down for five minutes? That, to me, is the only activity going on. Directing is survival and stamina, because, I believe, once you're on set, your creative work should mostly be done. Everybody's there and you've narrowed down the avenue to such a tight course, that you can just run down it.

I have never seen my movies again since delivering them. I have no interest. I have no interest whatsoever. I think that in purgatory we'll be required to watch our films repeatedly. I'm happy to wait until then.

Additional Resources

Blinko, Phillip. "Naked in Highgate." *What's On*, August 14, 1991.

Brooks, Richard. "Truly Madly Domestically." *The Observer*, October 10, 1993.

Bygrave, Mike. "*Truly, Madly, Deeply* Missing Crouch End." *The Independent*, March 19, 1992.

Cliff, Nigel. "An Englishman Abroad." *The Times*, February 14, 2000.

Cochrane, Emma. "One on One: Anthony Minghella Interview." *Empire*, no. 129, March 2000.

Collard, James. "The Main Man." *The Times*, October 15, 2005.

Falsetto, Mario. *The Making of Alternative Cinema, Volume 1: Dialogues with Independent Filmmakers*. Westport, Connecticut: Praeger Publishers, 2008.

Frazier, Charles. *Cold Mountain*. New York, NY: Atlantic Monthly Press, 1997.

George, Sandy. "Botswana Production Number One." *Screen International*, December 21, 2007.

Gibbons, Fiachra, and Demetrios Matheou. "Bard's Descendants 'Cannot Write for the Screen.'" *The Guardian*, December 15, 2001.

Glaister, Dan. "Speaking on His Oscar Wins." *The Guardian*, March 26, 1997.

Glass, Charles. "Casualties of Amour." *Premiere*, December 1996.

Gurewitsch, Matthew. "Madama Butterfly Is Ready for Her Close-Up." *New York Times*, September 24, 2006.

Hardesty, Mary. "How To Direct a DGA-Nominated Feature: Jeremy Kagan Interviews Four Who Did." *DGA Magazine*, May–June 1997.

Highsmith, Patricia. *The Talented Mr. Ripley*. New York: Coward-McCann, 1955.

Hoyle, Ben. "Minghella's Democratic Vision of Cinema, But Not As We Know It." *The Times*, October 28, 2006.

Johnston, Trevor. "Romantic Leads." *Time Out*. December 20, 1993.

Katz, Susan Bullington. "A Conversation with Anthony Minghella." *Conversations with Screenwriters*. Portsmouth, NH: Heinemann, 2000.

Koppelman, Charles. *Behind the Seen: How Walter Murch Edited "Cold Mountain" Using Apple's Final Cut Pro and What This Means for Cinema*. Berkeley, CA: New Riders, 2005.

Lowenstein, Stephen. "Anthony Minghella: Truly, Madly, Deeply." In *My First*

Movie: Twenty Celebrated Directors Talk About Their First Film. London: Faber and Faber, 2000.

Lyall, Sarah. "In the Spotlight, Two Sides of London." *New York Times*, December 24, 2006.

Lyttle, John. "Ex in the Head." *City Limits*, July 10, 1986.

Minghella, Anthony. *Breaking and Entering.* London: Faber and Faber, 2006.

———. *Cold Mountain: Screenplay.* London: Faber and Faber, 2004.

———. *The English Patient: A Screenplay.* London: Methuen, 1997.

———. *Jim Henson's The Storyteller.* New York: Random House Children's Books, 1998.

———. *Plays: "Whale Music"; "A Little Like Drowning"; "Two Planks and a Passion"; "Made in Bangkok".* London: Methuen, 1992.

———. *Plays Two: "Cigarettes and Chocolate"; "Hang-Up"; "What If It's Raining"; "Truly, Madly, Deeply"; "Days Like These".* London: Methuen, 1997.

Minghella, Anthony, and Bricknell, Tim, ed. *Minghella on Minghella.* London: Faber and Faber, 2005.

Olson, Mark. "The World Was at His Feet." *Los Angeles Times*, March 21, 2008.

Ondaatje, Michael. *The Conversations: Walter Murch and the Art of Editing.* New York: Knopf Publishers, 2004.

———. *The English Patient.* New York: Vintage Books, 1993.

Preston, John. "Yuppie Love." *Time Out*, July 2 1986.

Simon, Alex. "The Talented Mr. Minghella." *Venice Magazine*, February 2000.

Sischy, Ingrid. "*Cold Mountain.*" *Interview Magazine.* December–January 2004.

Summers, Sue. "The Patient English Director." *Daily Telegraph Weekend Magazine*, February 22, 1997.

Thomson, David. "Film; Without Them, Mr. Ripley Would Be a Nobody." *New York Times*, December 19, 1999.

Weinraub, Bernard. "The Heart of Mr. Ripley." *New York Times*, December 31, 1999.

Wolf, Matt. "Film; *Truly, Madly* Favors Ghosts Without Gimmicks." *New York Times*, April 28, 1991.

Index